Fortunes of War
The Adventures of a German Confederate

Fortunes of War
The Adventures of a German Confederate

A Translation of *Shadows and Bright Spots in American Life during the War of Secession* By August Conrad

Translated by Robert M. Peters

Edited by Karen Stokes

Fortunes of War: The Adventures of a German Confederate

Copyright© 2022 by Karen Stokes

ALL RIGHTS RESERVED. No part of this publication may be reproduced, distributed, or transmitted in any form or by any means, including photocopying, recording, or other electronic or mechanical methods, or by any information storage and retrieval system without the prior written permission of the publisher, except in the case of very brief quotations embodied in critical reviews and certain other noncommercial uses permitted by copyright law.

Produced in the Republic of South Carolina by

SHOTWELL PUBLISHING LLC

Post Office Box 2592

Columbia, So. Carolina 29202

www.ShotwellPublishing.com

Cover Image: Tintype photograph of an unidentified South Carolina soldier. Library of Congress.

ISBN: 978-1-947660-72-4

FIRST EDITION

10 9 8 7 6 5 4 3 2

Contents

Introduction i

Foreword xxi

Chapter 1 1
A Kernel of Politics from a Non-Politician

Chapter 2 5
The American Blackman

Chapter 3 15
Charleston, the Cradle of Rebellion

Chapter 4 25
American Lifestyle and Customs

Chapter 5 35
The Die is Cast

Chapter 6 41
Playing Soldier

Chapter 7 47
The Bombardment of Fort Sumter

Chapter 8 59
Sullivan's Island

Chapter 9 63
Peace in War

CHAPTER 10 91
PROMOTION

CHAPTER 11 97
THE BLOCKADE BUSINESS

CHAPTER 12 103
AN ANXIOUS TRIP

CHAPTER 13 107
THE DEVELOPMENT OF DOOM

CHAPTER 14 111
THE BOMBARDMENT OF CHARLESTON

CHAPTER 15 117
WILMINGTON, NORTH CAROLINA

CHAPTER 16 127
COLUMBIA, SOUTH CAROLINA

CHAPTER 17 137
ON POST IN THE WOODS

CHAPTER 18 141
THE THREATENING DANGER

CHAPTER 19 145
THE OCCUPATION OF COLUMBIA

CHAPTER 20 151
THE NIGHT OF TERROR

CHAPTER 21 161
THE RESULTS OF THE DESTRUCTION

CHAPTER 22 169
A STILL-LIFE UNDER CONSTRAINT

CHAPTER 23 177
AN EXPEDITION

CHAPTER 24 187
HARD HEARTEDNESS AND HUMAN KINDNESS

CHAPTER 25 193
TRAVEL PLANS

CHAPTER 26 197
HOMEWARD

CHAPTER 27 203
RICHMOND IN VIRGINIA

CHAPTER 28 207
DESPERATE SITUATION

CHAPTER 29 223
HELP IN DISTRESS

CHAPTER 30 229
ON THE POTOMAC AND THROUGH THE BLOCKADE

CHAPTER 31 237
IMPRISONMENT

Chapter 32 245
Point Lookout

Chapter 33 249
Glimpses of the Sun

Chapter 34 257
New York

Bibliography 271

Introduction

The Book

IN 1859, WHEN A HOPEFUL, earnest young man named August Conrad immigrated to South Carolina from Germany, he could hardly have known that he was entering a country which would soon be in the throes of a cataclysmic war—a war which would plunge him into hardships, extreme dangers, and horrific experiences that would change him forever.

In Conrad's later years, after he had returned to his homeland, his friends and family urged him to write a memoir of his "sojourn in America," and he obliged them with a book which he entitled *Schatten und Lichtblicke aus dem Amerikanischen Leben wahrend des Secessions-Krieges* (*Shadows and Bright Spots in American Life During the War of Secession*). Published in Germany in 1879, it apparently received little attention, and was virtually unknown in the United States until about 1902, when a Virginia scholar, Dr. William Henry Pleasants, translated several chapters from the German and published them as a pamphlet entitled *The Destruction of Columbia, S.C.*[1] August Conrad was in Columbia when General William T. Sherman's army sacked and burned the city in February 1865, and Dr. Pleasants, a college professor and later dean of Hollins College (now Hollins University) in Virginia, believed that Conrad's eyewitness account of this event was an important part of history that should be made known to all Americans.

---

1   Conrad's memoir was published by Th. Schulze Buchhandlung in Hanover (Hannover). Pleasants' translation, which was somewhat abbreviated, numbered 31 pages, and was published in Roanoke, Virginia, by The Stone Printing and Manufacturing Company.

In a preface to his translation, Pleasants explained his reasons for presenting Conrad's account:

> The destruction of the City of Columbia, S.C., in February 1865, by the United States troops under command of General Sherman was an act of barbarity which surpasses all similar acts which are to be found in the long annals of the world's warfare. Columbia, entirely unfortified and undefended, its population consisting entirely of old men, women and children, was surrendered without a blow, under the promise given by the Commanding General of protection to persons and property.
>
> The following description of the destruction of Columbia was written by an eye-witness of that deplorable event—a German gentleman of intelligence and culture. This gentleman had been residing for some years in Charleston, in the capacity of a cotton buyer, and after the outbreak of the Civil War and closing of the ports by blockade, was employed as the secretary and treasurer of the largest company engaged in the business of blockade-running. If the question is asked: "Why, by publishing a detailed description of these horrors, do you revive memories of scenes we would gladly forget?"—the first answer is, that it is due to the truth of history. The Southern writers who have undertaken to write the history of our Civil conflict have not the ear of the world; the Northern writers of history, not only for general reading, but especially of school-books, are notoriously unfair. They write with a strong partisan and political bias—they misrepresent the motives and principles of action of the South, and they err, not simply by the *suppressio veri* [suppressing the truth], but by the *suggestio falsi* [suggesting falsehoods].
>
> A second reason why this description of the obliteration of Columbia is published is that very few, except the inhabitants of that ill-fated city, have any just conception of the horrors of that night of incendiarism and

robbery; of unchecked license, of insult and every crime mentionable and unmentionable. In the histories above alluded to I doubt whether the destruction of Columbia is mentioned at all; but if noticed, it is lauded as one of the heroic actions of their most admired general. But if heroic and splendid deeds deserve to be painted in glowing words for the admiration and improvement of mankind, surely shameful deeds should not be covered up, but displayed in their naked deformity to the candid judgment of an enlightened world. [2]

Just a year before Dr. William H. Pleasant's book was published, another college professor had undertaken to translate a portion of Conrad's chapters that dealt with the burning of Columbia. Herman L. Spahr, an instructor in modern languages at the University of South Carolina, and later the U. S. consul at Breslau, Germany, learned about August Conrad's book from a colleague, Professor R. Means Davis. Professor Davis had been sent a copy by Erich Felix Rath, who was August Conrad's nephew. [3] Rath had immigrated to the United States from Germany and became a music professor at Hollins University in Virginia in 1891. In 1900, Rath visited South Carolina as a faculty member of the state summer school, where he met Professor Davis. At Davis's suggestion, Herman L Spahr translated part of Conrad's book, which was published in the Charleston newspaper *The Sunday News* on February 24, 1901, under the title "The Burning of Columbia."

---

2   Further in the preface, Pleasants deplored that the fact that "atrocities of our Civil War" were "pleaded as justification of what is now going on in the Philippines and South Africa." Cruelties and atrocities in those conflicts, he wrote, "have been defended upon the floor of the American Congress by citing similar examples in American warfare, and in the English Parliament a member of the government has justified by the treatment of the hapless and helpless Boer women and children by the example of the illustrious American, General Sherman."

3   Erich Felix Rath was the son of Conrad's sister Henriette Karoline Luise Clacius Rath (1840-1915), the wife of Adolf Rath (1832-1897). Erich Felix Rath died in 1949. Rath and Pleasants are buried in the same cemetery in Hollins, Va. It was probably through Rath, his fellow professor at Hollins, that Dr. William Henry Pleasants (1831-1915) also learned of August Conrad's 1879 memoir.

Spahr's article explained how he learned about Conrad's book, and more importantly, revealed that it had been written under a pseudonym. "August Conrad" was in fact the pen name of Conrad August Wilhelm Felix Clacius.[4]

In 1926, the Wade Hampton Chapter of the United Daughters of the Confederacy in Columbia reprinted Dr. Pleasants' partial translation, but the whole of August Conrad's 1879 book, which consists of thirty-four chapters covering all the events of his life in America from 1859 to 1865, has never been published in English until now. It is offered as a valuable and interesting addition to the literature of the war, and a fresh resource for historians and all students of history.

August Conrad, alias Felix Clacius

Conrad August Wilhelm Felix Clacius, who usually called himself Felix A. Clacius, was the son of Georg Wilhelm Clacius (1798-1857) and Charlotte Stephan Clacius (1808-1896) of the Kingdom of Hanover, one of many sovereign states in the German Confederation. Records of the Lutheran church document that he was born on January 3, 1842. Felix Clacius chose to write his memoir under the name August Conrad, and this introduction will also refer to him by that name.

Conrad was seventeen years old when he arrived in Charleston, South Carolina, in November 1859. [5] At that time, Charleston was a bustling, thriving port city, rich both culturally and materially, and noted for much architectural beauty. In 1865, a writer for *Harper's New Monthly Magazine* described the city as it was before the war:

---

4 In his book *Who Burnt Columbia?* (1902), James G. Gibbes quoted a portion of August Conrad's book, noting that the author's real name was Felix Clacius, a fact he may have learned from Spahr's newspaper article.

5 By the time Conrad (Felix Clacius) decided to emigrate, at least two of his siblings were already settled in the United States. His brother Charles F. W. E. Clacius, who was naturalized in 1860, was a druggist in Rock Island, Illinois, and later in Chicago. Another brother, Clemens W. Clacius, lived in Charleston.

Introduction

Not many years ago, Charleston sat like a queen upon the waters, her broad and beautiful bay covered with the sails of every nation, and her great export, cotton, affording employment to thousands of looms. There was no city in the South whose present was more prosperous or whose future seemed brighter. Added to its commercial advantages were those of a highly cultivated society. There was no city in the United States that enjoyed a higher reputation for intellectual culture than Charleston, and with it a refinement of taste, an elegance of manner, and a respect for high and noble lineage which made Charleston appear more like some aristocratic European city than the metropolis of an American state.

The general appearance of the city was in keeping with the historical precedents of the people. Its churches were of the old English style of building, grand and spacious, but devoid of tinsel and useless ornament. Its libraries, orphanages, and halls of public gathering were solidly constructed, well finished, and unique as specimens of architecture. Its dwellings combined elegance with comfort, simplicity with taste. The antique appearance of the city and its European character was the remark of almost everyone who visited it.

Upon his arrival in South Carolina, through the help of his brother Clemens Clacius, a Charleston merchant, Conrad found employment with a company he described as "an export business run by a German." His salary was at first nominal, but he worked diligently to improve his commercial skills, taking courses in penmanship and accounting, and, as time went on, his career prospects began to look bright. While improving his command of the English language, he honed his social skills with dance lessons. By the beginning of 1861, Conrad had advanced to a higher, better paying position. His employer, G. C. Baurmeister, who was the "consul of the Kingdom of Hanover," as well as a merchant, also appointed the young man as his consular secretary.

Conrad resided at a boarding establishment on Broad Street. He called it the Carolina House, but it was better known as the Carolina Hotel. [6] His brother, Clemens Clacius, also lived there. Its proprietress was Mrs. Rebecca C. Finney, whom Conrad praised as an "active, amiable and caring lady."[7] The Clacius brothers enjoyed the food and the fellowship of the Carolina Hotel and all its entertainments, which included dances.

In his memoir, Conrad described Charleston and its people extensively, and mostly in complimentary terms. He made many observations about the religious life of Charlestonians and noted their strict observance of the Sabbath, which came as a surprise to the young German. On Sundays, all businesses and modes of transportation were closed, and every activity "other than to busy oneself with God's Word" was considered irreligious. Rosalie Roos, a young Swedish woman who spent several years in South Carolina in the 1850s, was also struck by the "very religious" Charlestonians, reporting in her letters home:

> Sundays here are held to be very holy; church services are never neglected; no pastime or work is to disturb the day of rest ... Many go so far as to think it a sin to take a walk in God's glorious creation, that they will not pick a flower or fruit on Sundays, that they will not even prepare food; and to read anything other than a Sunday book is thought to be extremely wrong. [8]

---

6   The building, which still stands, was originally constructed around 1800, and beginning in 1834, operated as the Carolina Hotel. The 1860 Charleston city directory refers to it as the Carolina Hotel, naming Mrs. Finney as proprietress. Conrad called it the Carolina House, and it may have been known by both names. In 1867, it became a charitable institution offering shelter to the widows, mothers, and orphans of Confederate soldiers, later adding a college for young women.

7   Rebecca C. Finney (1815-1895), a native of Beaufort, S.C., was the widow of Walter Finney (1810-1852). Her maiden name was Slosson, or Slawson. Her daughter Kate married Conrad's brother Clemens W. Clacius (1829-1886) in 1868. The Carolina Hotel closed in 1867, and in the 1869-70 Charleston city directory, Mrs. Finney is listed as the proprietress of the Mansion House at 69 Broad Street.

8   Roos, *Travels in America,* 28, 118.

INTRODUCTION

Conrad frequently attended church, but he allowed himself Sunday walks to the Battery and outlying areas such as Magnolia Cemetery, a tranquil and beautiful place along the Cooper River.

His memoir opens with two chapters dealing first with the politics of American slavery, and then slavery in South Carolina, which he observed firsthand. As his book was published for a German readership, it seems likely that he opened with these subjects to offer some explanation and justification for his Southern sympathies and support. Unlike Great Britain and France, there had been little support for the Confederacy among the German states. In fact, tens of thousands of Germans were recruited into the Union army during the war, and the majority of the war bonds issued by the United States government were sold in the German states, generating some 300 million dollars in investments for the North's war effort. [9] Ambrose Dudley Mann, who served as a Confederate diplomat in Europe, strongly believed that the Confederacy would have won its independence but for the assistance provided by Germans. Writing to his friend Jefferson Davis on August 24, 1870, Mann declared, "Our poor fallen country would have maintained triumphantly its independence but for German arms and German money."[10]

Writing about the political tensions in America prior to the war, Conrad noted the crucial significance and consequences of Abraham Lincoln's election to the presidency as well as the rise of the Republican Party. Despite the fact that the Republican Party platform of 1860 did not call for the abolition of slavery, but only opposed its extension into the U. S. territories, Conrad explained that, because of the radical elements in that party, the South felt threatened and unsafe, fearing that "the abolition of slavery would be made law." Personally, Conrad thought it best to do away with the institution, but opined that an immediate and complete emancipation of the slaves was not the way to go about it. He maintained that although the South would have

---

9   A contemporary London newspaper, *The Economist,* reported that "up to 1864 as many as 100,000 Germans had entered the northern army." Owsley, *King Cotton Diplomacy,* 497.

10   Davis, *The Papers of Jefferson Davis,* 12: 490.

supported a gradual program of emancipation, it could not "accept the demand of the abolitionist that all slaves should be freed at once."[11] Wishing to govern themselves, to throw off the yoke of Northern political and economic dominance and oppression (including shipping monopolies and protective tariffs), and to deal with the problem of slavery on their own terms, Southern states began to secede from the Union, beginning with South Carolina. The fact that the South valued its own independence more than the institution of slavery is borne out by support for the enlistment of black Confederate troops during the war, and most notably by the Confederacy's promise to emancipate the slaves in return for official recognition by Great Britain and France. [12]

Conrad displayed a keen, sympathetic interest in the people of the "colored race" and devoted his second chapter to a description of their work, customs, and characteristics. Although, along with the vast majority of 19th century white Americans (North and South), he viewed them as social and intellectual inferiors, he did not believe that they should be enslaved, even if the system of slavery he witnessed in the South was comparatively mild and benevolent. "Based on my years of experience and observation," Conrad wrote, "I assert that the lot of the negro slaves in the Southern states was in no way hard." His observations about their lives and treatment are comparable to those of the aforementioned Swede, Rosalie Roos, who reported in a letter home that "I have not yet seen any Negro looking downcast or oppressed; on the contrary." Like her, Conrad saw nothing of the cruel treatment described by Harriet Beecher Stowe and other abolitionist writers. When Roos's father wrote to her to inquire as to whether Stowe's Uncle Tom's Cabin was an accurate portrayal of slavery, she replied:

---

11   When Great Britain abolished slavery in most of its empire in the 1830s, the government paid millions of pounds in compensation to British slaveholders. No such proposition was offered to the Southern states before the war.

12   In late 1864, President Jefferson Davis sent Duncan F. Kenner on an urgent mission to Europe to make this offer of emancipation to Great Britain and France. After a meeting in Paris, Kenner went to London to meet with the prime minister on March 14, 1865. A bill had just passed in the Confederate Congress authorizing the arming and emancipation of 300,000 slaves, but this measure, as well as Kenner's mission, came too late, as the war ended disastrously for the South the following month.

Introduction

> I like much of what I have read of Uncle Tom's Cabin; the manners and the speech of the Negroes and also of the planters are faithfully depicted ... However, I have, thank God, not seen any such planters like a couple of them described there nor witnessed the least mistreatment; on the contrary, they are treated more humanely and are more outspoken than white servants at home. [13]

In his descriptions of Charleston, which begin in the third chapter, Conrad noted how the city had figured significantly "in the fight for American freedom and independence" during the previous century, and that in 1860, as "a pillar of the Union of pure democratic hue," she rejected the unconstitutional policies of the federal government, now controlled by northern interests, thus becoming the "cradle of secession." The Secession Convention, composed of delegates from every part of the state, voted unanimously to secede from the union, signing the Ordinance of Secession in Charleston on December 20, 1860. At this time there was a small federal garrison at Fort Moultrie, which was located near Charleston on Sullivan's Island. About a week after the state seceded, Major Robert Anderson, the garrison commander, unexpectedly moved his men by boats from Fort Moultrie to Fort Sumter in Charleston harbor. The garrison completed its move stealthily at night, after spiking and setting fire to the cannons at Fort Moultrie. The South Carolinians regarded Anderson's actions as warlike, and in response, took possession of the federal arsenal in Charleston and harbor forts. One of those forts was Castle Pinckney, where August Conrad would serve as a member of the Charleston Zouave Cadets.

Located on a little island at the mouth of the Cooper River known as Shute's Folly, the earliest fortification here, an earth and timber battery known as Fort Pinckney, was completed in 1804. A hurricane destroyed the fort that same year, and a few years later it was replaced by a brick and mortar structure known as Castle Pinckney. Later still, a sea wall was added. Castle Pinckney was garrisoned during the War of 1812

---

13 Roos, *Travels in America*, 80.

and the Nullification Crisis of the 1830s, but otherwise mostly went unused as an active fort until 1860. It did serve as a powder storehouse of the city arsenal, and in 1855, a lighthouse was established there. In 1858, general repairs were made to Castle Pinckney, so that by the time South Carolina troops took over in December 1860, the buildings and mounted cannonry were in good condition. Detachments from artillery regiments manned the fort beginning in the spring of 1861, following the bombardment of Fort Sumter and the commencement of the war, and in the summer of that year, Captain C. E. Chichester brought a detachment of his Zouave Cadets, a local militia company, to Castle Pinckney as its garrison. [14] Conrad had known Chichester for some months before the war began, he and his wife being fellow boarders at the Carolina Hotel, and with some encouragement from the newly commissioned captain, he enlisted in his company of Zouaves. [15]

Writing in the late 1870s, Conrad was inaccurate in his memories of a few events, and in describing how the bombardment of Fort Sumter came about in April 1861, he misattributed its cause to the incident involving the ship Star of the West, which actually took place in January 1861. The real cause of the bombardment of Fort Sumter was the approach of several federal warships making their way to Charleston harbor. The governments of South Carolina and the Confederate States had repeatedly made attempts to have Major Anderson's garrison removed, and to effect a peaceful transfer of the property, offering monetary compensation to the federal government for Fort Sumter. Southern commissioners also tried to establish friendly relations with the government in Washington, D. C., but President Lincoln refused to deal with them. He chose instead to send warships to Charleston to provision Fort Sumter, by force if necessary, even though the garrison was allowed to purchase fresh food from the city markets. The Confederate president, Jefferson Davis, could not

---

14 The Chichester Zoauves, also called the Charleston Zoauve Cadets, were part of the 1st Regiment of Rifles, South Carolina Militia. Their first commander was Peter Fayssoux Stevens, who resigned in November 1861 to take command of the Holcombe Legion.

15 Anthony W. Riecke, a member of the Charleston Zouave Cadets, published a brief history of the unit in a Charleston newspaper in 1898. He included a roll of the officers and privates in which the name Felix Clacius appears. Riecke, "Scrapbook," 213.

Introduction

allow this incursion, and he ordered that Fort Sumter be reduced (that is, neutralized), since the fort might join forces with the warships to attack Charleston.

In an unusual arrangement, Captain Chichester's wife also resided at Castle Pinckney. The following extracts from a memoir she published in 1895 offer a useful introduction to the fort and events there in 1861:

> After the First Battle of Manassas in Virginia, in July, 1861, a number of Federal prisoners captured on that occasion, were sent to different places in the South for safe keeping. The detachment sent to Charleston, consisting of about 30 officers and 100 privates, was confined in Castle Pinckney which had been hastily fitted up for their reception, by putting floors and bunks in the casemates with heavy doors to close and lock at night, for the privates, and up the eastern half of the quarters for the officers.
>
> The castle is built in a semi-circular form, with a curtain or straight wall on the North side, in the centre of which is the sally-port or entrance to the parade ground, around which the casemates are built. In the centre of the parade a hot-shot furnace stood. Around this building, grates were built for the different messes to cook their food. My husband's company, "The Charleston Zouave Cadets," was detailed by orders of Gen. Ripley to garrison the castle and guard the prisoners.
>
> The latter made themselves as comfortable as possible; each [casemate] was occupied by a certain number, who gave fancy names to them, thus for instance, one was called, "No 1 Hotel de Zouave," as it contained a number of men belonging to a New York Zouave Regiment. Another was called, "No 7 Music Hall, 444 Broadway."

Conrad wrote in detail about Castle Pinckney and the activities of its soldiers and prisoners of war. George S. Cook, a notable Charleston photographer, set up his camera at the fort in the summer of 1861 and took photographs of both groups. Cook's biographer wrote of this:

> Union prisoners were jailed at Castle Pinckney. Cook went to the prison, pictured the inmates and the cell blocks. One view showed soldiers standing outside a casement, men from Cameron's 79th New York Regiment. Members of Michael Corcoran's Irish Regiment were the subjects of another. A small sign was visible above a cell entryway that read "Music Hall, 444 Broadway," the address of the theatre in which Christy's Minstrels performed. [16]

Eventually, the prisoners of war were transferred to quarters in the city of Charleston, and the fort was fitted up again for its original purpose. Later still, the Zouave Cadets were ordered away from garrison duty, and the company dissolved. Unlike most if not all of his comrades, Conrad did not re-enlist in another military organization. As a foreign national, he was not required—nor did he feel duty bound—to do so. "I had no desire to be shot to death," he admitted, "even though I was committed to the cause of the South." He would soon find, however, that he could offer another kind of service to the Confederacy.

In the summer of 1862 he moved back to the Carolina Hotel, and before long found employment as a bookkeeper for W. C. Bee & Company. Conrad came to have great admiration for William C. Bee and his partner Theodore D. Jervey, describing them as "noble" and "gentlemen through and through." William C. Bee's obituary of 1881 stated the following of him:

> Universally respected and admired for his purity, his diligence and his ability in commercial affairs, he was ardently loved by those who had the happiness to know how affectionate was his nature and how generous his soul ... In business affairs he was deservedly successful,

---

16 Ramsay, *Photographer Under Fire*, 59.

a high type of the irreproachable merchant who feels a stain like a wound. And large was his charity. [17]

In 1862, when Mr. Bee decided to go into the blockade running business, he established the Exporting and Exporting Company of South Carolina, in which Conrad was also involved. In the winter of 1863, Theodore D. Jervey volunteered for military service, and Conrad stepped into his position as secretary and treasurer of the blockade running firm.

The Importing and Exporting Company of South Carolina was first established as an unincorporated stock company, which, despite the loss of two ships in its first year of operation, proved to be very profitable, but in order to raise funds for purchasing new vessels, the company was incorporated so that it could increase the shares of stock that could be sold. [18] William C. Bee was the company president, and on its board of directors were Theodore D. Jervey, William P. Ravenel, C. T. Mitchell, and Benjamin Mordecai. The company purchased six blockade running vessels, and employed nine senior captains.

Working for a blockade running enterprise, Conrad was part of a valuable contribution to the war effort. The ships took away cargoes of cotton and transported them to Nassau or Bermuda, and from those places the cotton was shipped to Liverpool on neutral vessels and sold there. On their return trips through the blockade, the blockade runners brought in needed military supplies, hardware, dry goods, foods, and medical supplies and equipment. In her article about William C. Bee's company, Lynda W. Skelton stressed the importance of the blockade running industry during the war:

> The existence of companies such as the Importing and Exporting Company of South Carolina made military operations possible for the Confederacy. Furthermore

---

17 Obituary published in the Charleston *News and Courier* on 16 February 1881. Bee Family Vertical File, SCHS.

18 "On or about June 20, 1862, the Company declared its first dividend of $99,025 or $850 per share, and began payment on the second dividend on July 26 of $202,168. 52, or $1735. 36 per share." Skelton, "The Importing and Exporting Company," 26-27.

blockade running companies kept inflation from being even greater than it was by importing manufactured goods into a region which could manufacture almost nothing for itself. Profits made by the blockade running companies, far from being the terrible evil that Southerners often claimed them to be, were actually basic to the Southern ability to withstand Federal armies for four years. With no profits there would have been little or no blockade running activities and the lifetime of the Confederacy would have been decidedly shorter than it was. [19]

In the spring of 1864, William C. Bee transferred the capital and financial records of the Importing and Exporting Company to Columbia, South Carolina, which, being away from the coast, was thought to be "a more secure place." Conrad moved to Columbia to maintain the company headquarters there, while Bee remained in Charleston.

Columbia, like Charleston, was noted for its beauty, particularly its many splendid trees and gardens. A novel of 1860 characterized it as "the paradise city of the South."[20] Conrad admired its "romantic setting" in hilly terrain, its "pleasant and healthy" climate, and its congenial inhabitants. He was happy in Columbia and made many good friends there, most notably among two families named McCully and Groning.[21] He resided at the boarding house of Madame Rutjes, the daughter of a French aristocrat. She formerly lived in Charleston, where she and her husband, a native of Prussia, had owned a confectionery business and restaurant.

Like many others residing in South Carolina in the winter of 1865, August Conrad had reckoned that the capital city of Columbia, located

---

19 *Ibid.,* 31-32.

20 Ingraham, *The Sunny South,* 517.

21 Conrad formed such a friendship with the McCully family that he was still corresponding with them at the time his memoir was written in 1879. It also appears that he kept up a correspondence with Mr. William C. Bee after the war.

in the heart of the state, was not likely to be in the path of General William T. Sherman's army, but he was wrong. Part of this massive force of over 60,000 troops began an invasion into the lower part of the state in January 1865, and by the first of February, the main advance was underway. Later that month, it became clear that the invading army was on a course for Columbia, looting and burning towns, villages, farms and plantations along its march. As Sherman's army approached the capital in mid-February, a small force of Confederate cavalry under the command of generals Wade Hampton, Joseph Wheeler, and Matthew C. Butler attempted to check its progress, but the Confederates were vastly outnumbered and were soon forced to retreat and abandon the city. [22]

Conrad devoted several chapters of his memoir to a detailed account of the occupation, sack, and burning of Columbia, which one Northern journalist described as "the most monstrous barbarity of the barbarous march."[23] During the terrible night of February 17th, he was robbed and threatened, and was forced to flee to the home of some friends for safety, only to find that Sherman's men were setting fire to that residence, where he happened upon one soldier who was about to fire to the bed of an infirm, elderly woman. Conrad stopped him, saving the old lady, and was shocked and mortified to find that this murderous soldier was a fellow German who could barely speak English.

Among the items stolen from Conrad in Columbia were bills of exchange belonging to his company which were worth a fortune in dividends, and which would have to be annulled before the thieves could cash them in. [24] In the aftermath of the city's destruction, Conrad decided that he must at all costs find Mr. Bee to inform him of the robbery, and get the information to the company's representatives in England so that the bills of exchange would not be paid out. Some of

---

22 At about the same time, the Confederate troops in Charleston evacuated that city, which was immediately occupied by the besieging enemy forces.

23 Reid, *Ohio in the War,* 475.

24 A bill of exchange is a written order for the payment of a certain sum to another party on demand (similar to a check or promissory note).

his most harrowing experiences occurred as he searched the state for Mr. Bee's whereabouts, and also during his later difficult and perilous journey to the North, where he hoped to obtain passage to England.

As Conrad made his way through South Carolina looking for his employer, he observed some of the results of Sherman's infamous "march" through the state:

> In those places where the woods opened into cultivated land, I found everywhere the devastation of the enemy. The few houses which I passed in the first two days were for the most part destroyed. Wherever I met human beings and requested a drink of water, I heard the sad reports of the plundering and destruction by the enemy. Cadavers of horses, cows and pigs which the gruesome enemy could not take with him, killed and sometimes burned rather than leave them for the hapless people, lay in heaps along the way and on the fields, effusing an awful stench which was as terrible as the sight of the them which attended my way for miles.

After a long search, Conrad finally found his employer in Spartanburg. "Mr. Bee," he reported, "fully concurred with my plan to travel to England to cancel the payment of stocks to illegitimate holders and to personally put the affairs of the business in order while there, since correspondence was not possible for a long time." Conrad returned to Columbia, and from there, on March 20, he set out on horseback on an arduous journey north, during which he frequently feared for his life. In April 1865, he finally reached New York, where he was able to obtain enough financial assistance to book passage on a ship.

The day before his ship was to set sail, Conrad learned that President Abraham Lincoln had been shot. He confessed that he had entertained an "aversion" to Lincoln because of the sufferings he had inflicted upon the South, but that while in the North, his sentiments had changed because of the "descriptions of his good character traits" he heard there. In New York, after the shooting, Conrad noted numerous indications of mourning such as black flags and ladies

INTRODUCTION

dressed in black, and he believed that the grief thus demonstrated was sincere. Much of it may have been sincere, but in New York and other parts of the country, many such expressions of sorrow were certainly not genuine. During his presidency, Abraham Lincoln had been hated and reviled by hundreds of thousands of people, North and South, for a number of reasons—one being that thousands of northerners had been persecuted and imprisoned for merely expressing any opinions against his policies. [25] As he lay dying, and especially after his death, any public unwillingness to manifest sorrow over his shooting proved dangerous. In his book *The Unpopular Mr. Lincoln*, Larry Tagg noted, "As the news of the assassination spread across the country, violence was widespread against anyone who spoke lightly of the tragedy ... The Democratic newspapers quickly realized that if they didn't repent of their opposition to Lincoln, they risked ruin by mobs."[26] A man in Chicago was killed for saying that it served Lincoln right to be shot, and a newspaper editor in Maryland was murdered by a mob for publishing criticism of the president on the day of his death. In the occupied South, it was also perilous not to display mourning, even if it was only a pretense. "Ministers delivered the mandatory sermons, and Southern newspapers issued the compulsory regrets. Where the Union army was strongest, Southern protestations of sorrow for Lincoln's death were loudest."[27]

Lincoln did not die immediately after the shooting at Ford's Theater, and the captain of the *Etna*, the ship that was to take Conrad to England,

---

25 In his book *American Bastille*, published in 1883, John A. Marshall recorded the stories of numerous persons, mostly northerners, who were thrown into various prisons as political prisoners without due process. "Citizens were arrested by the thousands, and incarcerated without warrant ... The writ of *Habeas Corpus* was a blank, and all our inheritable rights, 'poor, poor, dumb mouths.'" Marshall, *American Bastille*, xv.

26 Tagg, *The Unpopular Mr. Lincoln,* 465-66. As part of the political weaponization of his death, Abraham Lincoln was suddenly transformed into a saint, even by former enemies, who used it to solidify their power. The famous preacher and abolitionist Henry Ward Beecher, who had criticized and attacked Lincoln throughout his presidency, now glorified him from the pulpit (while demonizing the South). Lincoln's "Radical enemies saw that his death was a propaganda windfall—Lincoln could be made to stand for the North, for freedom, and his murderer for the South, for slavery." Tagg, 463.

27 *Ibid.,* 469.

delayed its departure for hours awaiting the official announcement of his death "for the honor of bringing the news thereof to Europe." The ship had been scheduled to depart at 1 o'clock in the afternoon, but it was not until about 6 p. m. that "the telegraph brought the news out of Washington that Lincoln was dead." After that, Conrad recalled, "The machine was set in motion, and the important trip got underway." As the *Etna* sailed away from the port of New York, Conrad reflected on his life in America, a country he had come to treasure, although he had regrettably come to know it during its "darkest days."

His memoir ends at this point and gives no further record of his experiences. [28]

---

[28] According to some genealogical information found online, Felix Clacius married Theda Catharina Edzards in Germany in 1873, and he died in 1911 in Wunstorf, a town in Lower Saxony located near the city of Hanover (Hannover). An 1873 handbook about industry in Germany lists "Felix A. Clacius" as a partner in the C. G. Mueller Company, which was founded in 1871. Sandler, *Handbuch,* 133.

Introduction

TRANSLATOR'S NOTES

Mrs. Karen Stokes, an archivist at the South Carolina Historical Society, commissioned the translation of the memoirs of August Conrad which were published in Hannover in 1879 and republished by the British Library, Historical Print Editions. The title of the German edition is *Schatten und Lichtblicke aus dem Aamerikanischen Leben wärhend des Secessions - Krieges*.

A portion of the text entitled *The Destruction of Columbia, S.C.* was translated into English by W. H. Pleasants in 1902, but that translation was not referenced or used in the current translation. This is the first translation of the entire text into English.

The challenge was to capture the sentiments of Conrad as he rendered them in 19th century German but to present those sentiments in a style of English which successfully transmits to the modern reader what Conrad thought and experienced.

While modern German syntax and idioms provide the translator with unique opportunities to demonstrate his skill and craft, nineteenth century German syntax and idioms demand even more concentration and attention to detail to render the essence which they embody into understandable and enjoyable English. The intent has therefore been to make the essence of Conrad's work understandable to the English reader and to convey his joy and hope through hardships which he endured.

Dr. Robert M. Peters holds a Ph. D. in German from the University of Southern California and has experience as a translator and interpreter for various agencies in numerous venues.

Foreword

THIS PRESENT WORK, small in format, was begun in part with the intent to awaken memories of both happy and sad events from my long sojourn in America and to retain them for myself and in part to leave, as a legacy to my relatives and friends, a collection of my fortunes and misfortunes from those times, something which has been requested of me on numerous occasions.

Although the following narration, based on the original purpose, primarily concerns the person of the author and is, therefore, particularly ordained for readers nearest to him, it is nevertheless possible that the diverse and extraordinary experiences, the observations of the country, the people and the circumstances in the large American republic and from unique episodes from the War of Secession, among others, will create an interest in wider circles since that part of the world has close ties to the German fatherland. Here there is hardly a family which does not have a branch stretching across the Atlantic Ocean.

Even though I dare to hope that my modest work will find such interest, I must emphasize that I do not intend to provide either a history of the American war or a detailed description of the country, its inhabitants and relations. For that, I possess neither the ability nor the requisite experience. I am not a writer and do not have the least intent of ever becoming one. I have only described that which I have experienced myself, those occurrences, scenes and impressions which moved through my life while I was there.

I must, however, give absolute assurance that everything is based on truth; that I consistently avoid every exaggeration and every embellishment, even if it is a disadvantage for the work before me; and that I have kept myself to the facts which I myself have experienced and observed.

I will leave it to the esteemed reader to determine whether or not he shares or embraces the opinions which I have attempted to make known and my reverence for the country and its people. I have acquired these pronounced opinions and dispositions through my own observations and experiences, and I therefore assert their correctness.

As I appeal to the valued reader that he not judge this lay-work too harshly and that he not have expectations which are too high, I, however, hope to engender conversation worthy of his time and attention.

For the honor evident in this endeavor, I want to express my gratitude to the reader and the wish that he never encounter similar strokes of fate which befell this obedient story teller.

Hannover, in March 1879.

The Author

Chapter 1

A Kernel of Politics from a Non-Politician

The far-reaching and most important campaign since the beginning of the Republic, namely the campaign of 1860, was decided and thereby confirmed the victory of the Republican Party, in that its candidate, Abraham Lincoln, was elected to be the President of the United States of America and received this high office in the spring of 1861 from the hands of President James Buchanan. This election result, by which the abolitionists (radical opponents of slavery) would soon take command of the ship of state, could leave no doubt about the future of the Southern States over which a thunderstorm had been brewing in the last few years and which were now looking at the inevitable discharge of that storm. By means of the rapidly growing population in the North, likely because of climate and other considerations, as compared to that of the South, the Republican Party, the party with an animus to slavery, was able to gradually gain a hold and ultimately outflank the Democratic Party which tended to support slavery. [29]

---

[29] The Republican Party's "animus to slavery" was less a moral stance than a pragmatic and political one, although there was a small number of sincere abolitionists in the party. Thomas J. DiLorenzo wrote that a "more prominent concern was that slaves would compete with white labor in the territories, which the Republican Party wanted to keep as the exclusive preserve of whites ... This idea ... defined the Republican Party's position on slavery in 1860. As Lincoln confidante and Secretary of State William Seward explained, 'The motive of those who protested against the extension of slavery had always really been concern for the welfare of the white man, and not an *unnatural* sympathy for the Negro.'" DiLorenzo, *The Real Lincoln*, 21-22.

It was completely clear to Southerners that with the newly elected head of state's ascension to office, whose politics were well enough known, and with a Congress made up of a majority which shared his policies, the abolition of slavery would be made law.

The likelihood of such a law, which indeed afterward became fact, had to raise alarm for slaveholders as well as for those closely associated with them, namely those citizens engaged in commerce and business.

What must a country be facing if suddenly robbed of its national wealth or its lifestyle without the ability to garner other sustaining resources? Impoverishment, demoralization and ruin would be the inevitable results which, according to the nature of things and experience, would come to pass.

Think what one will, and far be it from me to support slavery, but from the philanthropical perspective everyone must recognize the necessity to guarantee to every human being the freedom to pursue his own destiny as long as the pursuit is founded in law and custom, even if a man is of a lower cultural level. Precisely on this point, however, the baby should not have been thrown out with the wash! With concern for the national welfare and for the poor creatures themselves, one should have avoided providing an advantage which was neither understood nor known and which robbed them of the tutelage which was quite necessary.

Considering that slavery has existed for hundreds of years and that it continues to exist in many countries, it would have been absolutely justified to have enacted its abolition; however, the appointed time for the effective date of such a law should be deferred as long as possible, so that the slave could prepare himself for the pending freedom and independence which would be imminent or so that his complete freedom could be vouchsafed to him after a certain number of years or so that all current slaves would carry their yoke while those thereafter born to them would be declared free. The owners of the mothers would be obliged to care for said freed offspring up to a certain age and to provide for their education.

The South, although it would have sustained some loss, would have supported this or a similar emancipation of slaves for humanitarian reasons and for the progress of civilization. The South neither could have nor wanted to accept the demand of the abolitionists that all slaves should be freed at once.

The climate and the composition of the soil which stretched from Maryland, Virginia and Kentucky to the slave states which lay to the south determined the source of their commerce, in that such was not in the least suited for industry but was best suited for agriculture. With the exception of some grains (namely corn) and tobacco, the extent of cultivation was mainly that of cotton and of sugar cane as well as rice in the river bottoms. The Negro is precisely predisposed for working this soil and for the cultivation of produce; only his constitution can bear the conditions and drawbacks of the climate to which the Caucasian would immediately succumb.

As long as he is under the strict discipline and has to work, he is a diligent and able worker. As soon as he is not under the eye of his master – I roundly challenge the need for the whip and other physical means of punishment, the use of which did not take place save in the rarest of cases and then were certainly also necessary, although this horrendous treatment is assumed – he lapses into loafing which is uniquely more congenial to him. If he cannot be compelled to work due to the freedom granted to him, then he does not take it up until it is absolutely necessary and executes it sluggishly and poorly. He prefers, however, to procure for himself the most temporary subsistence by the easier means of stealing from his fellow men, from nature and from public property respectively. [30] It is quite easy to understand that a country whose natural resources have been so egregiously exploited must endure substantial suffering.

---

30   J. M. Johnston, a Freedmen's Bureau agent, filed a report in 1866 asserting that there was "much idleness and vagrance" among the freed people on James Island near Charleston, adding that they were "gaining a livelihood by theft and robbery." In June 1866, General R. K. Scott, a Freedmen's Bureau commissioner, issued an order noting "the increasing amount of theft, drunkenness and vagrancy" among the freed people in South Carolina, and directing that those who left agricultural employment be arrested and put to work on public roads. Stokes, *Incidents in the Life of Cecilia Lawton,* xxxii.

It is not only that the previous slave owners suddenly lost enormous capital through Emancipation, and thus since they were unable to gain capital out of their property, they were unable to count on a voluntary work force; but it is also that these freed, indolent and ignorant men feel no inclination to make themselves useful and thereby become a burden on the states just impoverished.

Chapter 2

The American Blackman

The Negroes or rather the colored race, according to the laws of the slave states, was not allowed any intellectual education, neither reading nor writing. In spite of these laws, many of them acquired these competencies, something which was tacitly tolerated. The exceptions were those who had bought their freedom or who had gained it from their masters, the latter being subordinate to whites with only some restrictions. They had to allow whites to pass on the sidewalks. They could only use the road embankment. They were not allowed to visit the theater. They could carry no weapons. They could not be on the street before 6:00 a. m. or after 9:00 p. m. without a pass from their master or their employer. It was forbidden to sell them spirits, which were nevertheless widely enjoyed – I want to gladly admit though to some exceptions which are not well known – a right easy and satisfied life which many of our workers would have envied. [31]

---

[31] Rosalie Roos, a Swedish governess, made a similar assertion about workers in her homeland in an 1853 letter to her father. She wrote this from a plantation owned by the Charleston family for whom she worked: "It cannot be denied that slavery can give rise to misfortunes and appalling behavior, but in general it is far, far better than we are able to conceive. They also seem satisfied and happy, are especially devoted to their master and mistress, and often lead a more carefree life than they. If any of them become sick, they immediately receive medication and sympathetic care until they have completely recovered. The tenant farmers on many estates in Sweden are far unhappier than slaves on many plantations and are more likely to be mistreated, indeed to be more enslaved than the former. I have not seen the slightest mistreatment of a Negro." Roos, *Travels in America*, 81.

In the cities, they lived in their own dwellings, most of the time connected to the houses of their master; and here they led a life which corresponded to their conditions and which was congenial to their inclinations. I have failed to find in the intercourse of our lower classes such humor or such satisfying laughter which always accompanied their vacuous amusement which I often heard with particular interest. Once the master was finished with supper, then the servants gathered themselves in their rooms; they were therein free. What should they then lack? They had ample food, clothing, their bed and their rest and a certain degree also of love which might be said to arise even if such also often comes from self-interest on the part of the master in order to keep his property healthy and fruitful.

The Negroes of the plantations and farms, whom their city cousins called "country niggers" and whom their counterparts viewed with contempt, had defined working hours during which they were not in the least overstrained. The rest of the time, they were left to themselves. Their huts were aggregated into small or large colonies, usually ringed with the remainder of a primeval forest of pines or live oaks. They often imparted an idyllic picture: here they rested in sweet idleness in the shade of the giant trees. They bred chickens for their own use. They made many things for which many of them had acquired the skill. They indulged themselves with the joy of dancing with the monotone music of the banjo or tambourine. Their master provided them with substantial victuals, uniform dress and all that they needed for their livelihood. Were they befallen with illness, they received the greatest care and the attention of a doctor. The charity which a Negro no longer capable of working received would be the envy of very free white man.

The horrible murder stories associated with whiplashing, without which those who do not know the situation must imagine slavery, stories which the popular writings of Beecher-Stowe and our own renowned writers through such fiction have engendered in people so inclined, are for the most part not justified. It may indeed be that a cruel overseer overstepped the bounds set by his employer, the law, and human decency and employed such methods of discipline against which neither the victim nor his fellow slaves may rebel. Such violations occur, however, everywhere. One has heard of similar stories about German non-commissioned officers and about German teachers. [32]

Based on my years of experience and observation, I assert that the lot of the Negro slaves in the Southern states was in no way hard and that life without a care for food and without an understanding of the felicity of freedom was quite pleasant and enjoyable.

In the courtyard of my hotel I observed with particular pleasure the peculiar Negro parties hosted by their masters – they were proud when they were observed in their activities by whites – to which numerous black friends were invited. The black hosts greeted their guests, male and female, who were clothed in the most flamboyant colors, in selected forms of hospitality of the white race which they effortlessly and skillfully mimicked, with no little exaggeration by means of the most facetious movements and expressions. After the preliminaries of the reception, the fairer sex was led by the hosts or by young black gentlemen to the seating arranged in a circle where she was offered the prepared refreshments. These consisted of pastries: corn cakes, small pies, namely the favorite delicatessen of the Negro, a little tart made with syrup and roasted peanuts as well as a sweet-potato pudding (potato poon) as well as a drink, a sweet, sparkling beer (ginger pop). In addition to the sumptuous indulgences, the heart of the black man refreshed itself on mutual laughter, conversation, handshaking and caressing of the younger generation. Here each colored gentleman had, in addition to common first names such as Jim or John used among whites or even officially, high-toned names: Mr. Washington, Mr. Lafayette, the Black Beauty, otherwise plainly known as Susan or Sarah, or the title Mistress Calhoun, Miss Irving and so forth.

---

32 Frederick A. Porcher, a South Carolina planter and historian, made the same argument in an 1868 essay, contending that crimes and cruelties were not peculiar to the institution of slavery, writing "when these crimes are found among slave holders, they are charged directly against the system; when they are found elsewhere they are ascribed to the inherent sinfulness of humanity." He argued that slaves were subject to the same evils as any other class of humans, not because they were slaves, but because they were human beings in a world where the strong can abuse the weak. Porcher, "A Newly Discovered Chapter," 239-40.

The main entertainment at such festivities climaxed in the dance after music of monotone sounds and quick tempo was produced by one of the members on a banjo, a tambourine, a castanet or at best a violin with two or three strings. This dance, which without a doubt was imported to us by the ancestors of our friends and which was handed down, unadulterated, to posterity, is a type of "contra," but without all of the rules and which is performed by each individual for himself. The entire body, driven by extreme ecstasy, shifts into the most boisterous of moves so that one is not able to follow the diverse twists of the legs and arms. The untamed leaps, the unfettered exuberance and wild jubilation dominate and transform the participants, understandable only to the observer, into a state of the highest bliss.

At this opportunity, there is another, possibly greater, happiness that is to be mentioned in which the Negro can take part: namely participation in a funeral. He who can obtain by any means a reason or permission for attending a funeral will not allow this pleasure to pass. Far from a sad event but rather in a sensibility of delight, both sexes of black society gather in the quarters of the deceased acquaintance. A congeneric preacher, who by his character is a common worker, would give a congenial sermon full of parables and rich phrases which spoke to the religious mind of the Negroes, a sermon which was accompanied by the gathered crowd with a divine enthusiasm of annunciating sighs and groans. Afterward, those there gathered intoned a dirge and then set out on a funeral cortege or better said a parade. Many interested parties followed the hearse: two by two, man and woman, arm in arm, in fanciful suits and dresses. The men would be clothed with black or colorful tails with the longest possible peplums, black cylinder hats, which quite independent of the fashion, might have been discarded by a white gentleman a hundred years before, which might have acquired a dent with the yearly wear, and which perhaps had lost the brim or the crown. The scarves, always colorful, were bound around the white chokers in which black cheeks were cramped. Both hands were covered with white gloves on which the finger lengths had to be quite long. Accompanying that, in one of the hands, was the inevitable red umbrella, even with clear skies, since such constituted the main component of "full dress."The black lady at his arm distinguished herself by greater straightforwardness in grooming, particularly with regards to colors. She was clothed with a simple black garment and a similar kerchief which covered the nappy head and out of which garish earrings, quite cheap but quite pronounced, protruded.

The long parade of joyous pallbearers and attendants moved through the streets and gave the corpse over to the earth, the corpse merely a means to an end for this pleasant event. This opportunity of togetherness was used for a delightful party in the woods in some spot near the cemetery, where, of course, the dance constituted the focal point of the entertainment.

After this digression, limited but truthful, into the habits and customs of the Negro with which I intend to establish that the colored slaves led a thoroughly pleasant and satisfactory life, whereby, of course, their nature and level of education have to be taken into account, I return to the purpose of this narration.

The dark point in the relationship of the slave to his master, who, as has been shown, with few exceptions, was concerned for the welfare and wellbeing of the slave, remained nevertheless the legally regulated use of force which the master could use against the slave, the privation of freedom and the sale of the slave, with this last possibility alone being degrading. There prevail some very perverse opinions by the correction of which the shocking aspects of such conditions are greatly reduced. First of all, the master cannot use force against the life of the slave. He cannot mistreat him, save for incremental corporal punishment whose limit, the number of rod or whip strikes, was set by law. Without cause, this punishment was applied in the rarest of cases.[33] The master could, however, sell his property; and admittedly this occurred often enough,

---

33 In his 1848 pamphlet *The Negro Law of South Carolina*, John Belton O'Neall cited many laws enacted for the protection of the slaves, including the following: "Although slaves, by the Act of 1740, are declared to be chattels personal, yet they are also, in our law, considered as persons with many rights and liabilities, civil and criminal," and, "By the Act of 1821, the murder of a slave is declared to be a felony, without the benefit of clergy." In 1854, two white men, one of them from a wealthy Charleston family, were executed in Walterboro for the murder of a slave. Emerson, *Sons of Privilege*, 6-7.

sometimes out of pecuniary interests as well as when a slave could not be controlled by his master if he refused to obey his master, if he repeatedly caused trouble, or otherwise through theft, by misleading other slaves or by insurgency caused his master to suffer damage. He then ridded himself of such culprits by handing him over to the agent who sold him out of hand or at the market. Just as little as the Negro himself knew the blessings of freedom and did without them, so too was he in general little moved by a change in owner as long as his circumstances did not get worse. As often as I was present at the public auction of one or more blacks, I never got a sense of sadness or dissatisfaction due to this process on the part of the object of purchase. To the contrary, his own physical and mental virtues or capabilities were asserted or portrayed. The slave was filled with pride when his person generated a high bid.

The often conditional separation from spouse, parents and children caused by such a sale is according to our notions an appalling misfortune; here one must again consider in this context the nature and the character of the colored race for which an intimate family life and relationships are alien. In such cases, the marriage could be annulled and a new one entered into. [34] I became aware of one case in which the wife of a driver made a permanent move with her mistress to another state. The husband by his own reflection felt no pain over the separation but rather, after a short period of time, found the appropriate substitute and was indeed happy at the thought that his new beauty was a degree lighter than this previous one. Actually, the colored man put a great deal of weight on skin color and with that the degree of crossing with white blood. While this nuanced difference made little difference to whites, giving not even minor consideration to those who were less black, quadroons looked with contempt on mestizos and mulattos, as they in turn did on the Negroes.

---

34 "During the 1850s, Southern clergymen and laity responded to abolitionist attacks on slavery by urging reforms for the institution that would bring it more in line with Christian principles. At the annual convention of the Protestant Episcopal Church in South Carolina in 1859 and 1860, for example, prominent laymen proposed resolutions concerning marriage, stating that 'the marriage relation between slaves has the same divine obligation as that between masters and mistresses.'" Emerson, *Days of Destruction*, 10.

Although up to this point I have attempted to show that the slave certainly had every reason to feel comfortable and although I have based the proof of my assertions on those who know the relationships by personal observation and not on those who judge the matter according to feelings, principles or descriptions by poorly informed poets and idealists, I must still comment on some aspects concerning the nature and the character of blacks.

I say in advance that I have never met an educated Negro or one of mixed blood, and I am not in a position to judge whether he is capable of a degree of civilization which, in education, in savoir faire, and manners, would place him on a completely equal footing with the white man, be that because of his skull structure and constitution, because of the bad smell which he gives off through his black skin, because of the always coarse unappealing facial features, or because of the apparent inability to speak a language fluently.

I stipulate the possibility; but I adhere to the conviction reached by my own observation, pending countervailing experiences, that the white race is superior to the black race in intellect, in capacity for learning, will power, disposition, manners and above all a sense of the higher and the nobler. I consider it to be unthinkable that there can be a profound relationship between an educated white man and a black man.

The Negro is in his stultification, in which he was kept before his emancipation, sly and shrewd so that he attempts to procure every possible advantage for himself. His progenitor Ham appears to have bequeathed this characteristic to his descendants, a characteristic which he shared with his brother Shem.

Up to a certain point, he possesses the talent for handicraft and has therein easily and quickly acquired for himself a certain competence.

He is good-natured and not impetuous and is compliant and industrious when he knows that he must complete a certain task. He is, however, indolent if he is not watched and monitored, even if his livelihood depends on it. He definitely prefers to acquire what he needs by theft and little swindles. Above all, he likes to lie in the sun with his pals and revels in "dolce far niente" in convivial amusement. [35]

The Negro, that is the masculine sex, has a lusty humor and loves to present it. He can give a hearty laugh over the smallest matter. One rarely sees anything serious, let alone a sad face, when more of them are together. The black slave is dependent on his master and his family. He grows up with their children and is their playmate, although likely seen by them as their inferior. He is used in relation to his age and sex for diverse duties up to the age at which he will be assigned a particular profession as worker, servant, craftsman, maidservant, cook, laundress or such. His inclinations extend first to the already mentioned sweet idleness and jawboning. Then comes his grooming, at which he has developed, as I have already described, a hilarious taste which is not of elegance and taste but which comes down to eccentric forms of clothing and gaudy combinations of colors. Furthermore he likes every ostentation: dance, music, church service, funeral, etc.

For the most part, Negroes are Baptists or Methodists whose customs and doctrines such as baptism by immersion, the calling of the Holy Ghost and His utterances given by one or more of God's children make a particular impression on their mind which is very susceptible to such things.

As a consequence of their constitution and their routine life, they in general enjoy quite good health. In only the rarest of cases are they susceptible to climatic nuisances such as malaria and yellow fever.

Considered and taken together, the essence, the character, the outward appearance and the good and bad traits lead one to the conclusion that he, as a human being, is entitled to the enjoyment of freedom. In his former condition, however, as is still true today, he could not cope with the associated rights and obligations and first had to be prepared for them. Finally, nature imparted to him a subordinate role in which he makes some gain and is comfortable. He must, however, all the while like the canary which one frees in our

---

35 The Italian phrase means pleasant idleness.

climate, degenerate because he does not know how to use the blessings of freedom for his own good. How long will it be before the black race is extinct on the North American continent?

What had been only a threatening danger became acute in 1860; and in order to keep this at bay and in order to preserve its ancient rights, property and prosperity, the South had to quickly and energetically take measures.

This 19th century lithograph by G. Lehman depicts Charleston as seen from Castle Pinckney. Wikicommons.

Chapter 3

Charleston, the Cradle of Rebellion

Approximately in the middle of the coast of State of South Carolina, rich in bays and islands, a state called according to its hallmark "the Palmetto State," just below the 32 degree of latitude north lies the metropolis of this state: the old and famous Charleston which was at the time of my portrayal yet a flowering trading city. She was old in comparison to many of her American sisters, some of which, however, had outperformed her; and she was famous because of her consequential engagement in the fight for American freedom and independence. Until that time, always a pillar of the Union of pure democratic hue, she was now again the first, which as the representative of her state rejected with indignation the policies of the North; and with this, since a settlement with the brothers of the North was not to be expected, she sundered herself from the Union. That is why, during the war which resulted from this step, she had gained the appellation "cradle of secession" (Cradle of Rebellion), which filled her with pride.

In a bay, created by the mighty rivers, the Ashley and Cooper, she lies outstretched on a small tongue of land, approximately three English miles from the Atlantic Ocean from which this large bay is sundered by two islands which approach one another—Sullivan's Island to the north and Morris Island to the south. The connection between the ocean and the Bay of Charleston[36] and the two islands which almost connect consists of a strait which separates the two islands. Between the two

---

36 Conrad means Charleston Harbor.

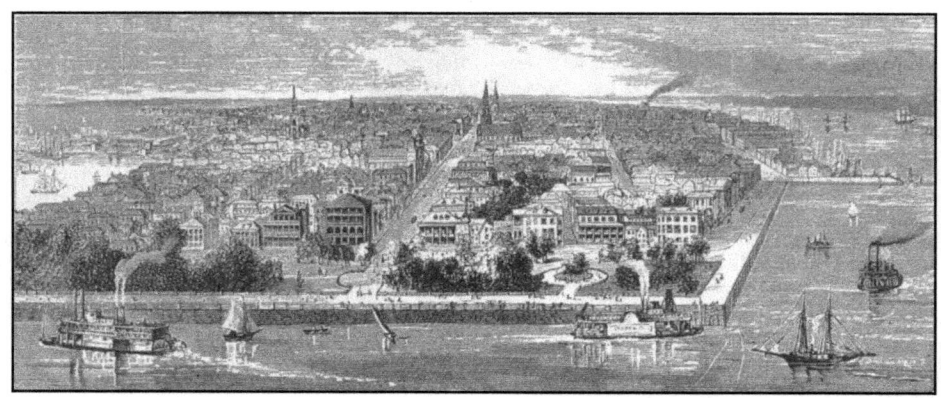

A view of Charleston, 1872, engraved by Harry Fenn. Wikicommons.

islands stands Fort Sumter, often referred to, and Fort Moultrie on Sullivan's Island which dominate this channel or approach. These two fortifications of the waterway, advantaged by nature, are reinforced in strength by Fort Johnston and Castle Pinckney which lie on islands inside the basin or bay.

Sullivan's Island has a beautiful bathing beach and is populated in high summer by town folk who enjoy the fresh and healthy sea air. They can, however, at the same time take care of their business in the city because there is regular transport made possible by steamboats. In contrast, the neighboring island, Morris Island, consists of a large sand dune which allows for no further use than a lighthouse beacon which can be seen for miles and which shows to the oncoming ships their destination and which serves as a guide around the sandbanks.

Across from the city on the east bank of the Cooper River, which at this spot is several miles wide, north of Sullivan's Island, lies the lovely village of Mount Pleasant surrounded by a tranquil forest, likewise a favorite summer sojourn for the inhabitants of Charleston. To the south and west, on the opposite bank of the Ashley which flows around the city, the view is limited by thick woodland out of which individual groups of evergreen live oaks, palms and pines protrude. Farther inland and along the coast begin the cotton plantations and the rice plantations. Here Sea Island cotton is cultivated, a cotton of incomparable quality which has the toughness of silk, which is used in a blend with silk, and which realizes a high price, along with the likewise unsurpassed Carolina rice.

The city of Charleston itself has no particular points of interests. It made, however, in peace time, a very friendly impression with broad streets evidencing bustling activity, partly shaded by rows of sycamores with intermittent plazas. The lower southeast part was dedicated to wholesale trade and shipping. Located here was the customs house, the post office, numerous warehouses and places of business. Approximately eight banks carried on their lucrative trade in authentic palaces. From East Bay Street running along the Cooper River, docks jutted out into the river. Steamships and sailing vessels of every nationality were anchored here in order to unload their goods and to take on the products of the South to transport to distant parts of the world. Here, thousands of working men practiced their professions. Black and white workers, sailors from many countries, businessmen, customs officials, and so forth, among large and small ships, innumerable cotton bales, and barrels of rice and resin which are transported on a peculiar cart (dray) pulled by a mule made a colorful picture which the singing of sailors, without which they could not complete any difficult work, brought to life. Only on Sunday, when all over North America each and every work ceases or evenings, did this bustling activity die down. No one lived in this area, and one could take walks without catching sight of even one person.

The middle part of the city mainly serves retail shops and commerce and was in general inhabited by the middle class while the upper city was composed almost entirely of private homes. These, in contrast to the massive somber commercial buildings, were usually made of wood in a light but elegant style. They afforded, with their piazzas and gardens, a charming sight.

At the southern tip where both rivers meet the city ends with a small park called the "Battery" which is protected from the rising tides by means of strong stonework which is built out into the bay and rises about four meters above sea level. From this point one has a beautiful full view of the bay, the majestic rivers which create the bay, the distant evergreen banks, Sullivan's and Morris Island which appear to seal the basin, Fort Sumter dominating the middle of the basin, and Castle Pinckney lying on a little green island. This park or garden, surrounded by water on three sides, has a pleasant location. Regrettably, the trees, standing on a fill bottom, barely thrive because their roots combine with saltwater. There was always a refreshing sea breeze here. It was a magnificent spot for pause with a view to the coastal waters with their boundaries and interruptions and, lying beyond them, the vast ocean on which waves played and stormed as well as the ships and the sails brought by them. It always produced new charm and made manifest the vastness of nature. Here after sunset white residents in need of repose gathered by foot, by wagon or by horse on the wide promenade paths. After the prosaic tasks of the day, the undulation and the hustling and bustling, elegant women and girls with charming faces again produced an attractive and refreshing picture. Evenings, concerts often took place, the cost of which by optional contributions was often contested. As darkness set in, everything living disappeared from the location, save for a few nature lovers for whom it was previously too noisy, who waited for the rising of the moon and who enjoyed by its wonderful illumination the still evening peace and the refreshing cool of the night.

In schools, instruction was free, a very charitable and exemplary feature which had as its purpose that the children of the poor could enjoy an education as good as that of those with well-off parents.

In the upper city, surrounded by large open squares, was the Citadel which was used as exemplary institution of education for mature pupils. There they received a solid science curriculum and at the same time a military training. They, however, dedicated themselves after they had finished the course of study almost entirely to state service or commerce, only seldom to the military profession.

In addition to the numerous rivers and natural canals which cut through the low country and facilitated the procuring of native products, three railroads connected commerce to the interior of the state and to that of the farthermost south, west and north so that one could reach

New York in 48 hours, while a steamship journey took 60 hours, in spite of which the former was used because of greater comfort.

Numerous large hotels, guest houses and boarding houses offered to the traveler shelter and comfort.

A theater and numerous large halls for concert productions and for expositions were available. They were, however, used intermittently by traveling companies or only moderately by German music bands. There was a lack of interest on the part of the solid and religious Southerner and little success for the entrepreneur for regular or frequent pleasure and amusement in the arts.

On the sole land side of the city only one road next to the railroad led to the interior of the country. Because of the lack of cobblestone and because of the inexpensiveness of wood, the road was paved with wood for a distance of several miles. Then, as the peninsula widened, it divided into different sandy paths leading in different directions. In the immediate vicinity of the city, there were numerous farms which were traversed by this same road and which provided the inhabitants with vegetables, milk, butter, eggs and so forth. Where these farms ended began the primeval forest, inexhaustible with firewood and timber and rich with game as in romantic Parthia. In the middle of this unending forest lay, after reclamation, newly developed plantations and, many miles apart, smaller cities or villages. Between the aforementioned road and the Cooper, within sight of the towers of the city and the life which they overlooked, the homestead of the dead had been provided for. This walled cemetery, bathed in the tides of the river and crisscrossed by many rivulets, was a complete paradise: part forest, part park, meadow, flower garden with small rises, ponds, canals, bridges, shady places to sit, winding trails and paths on which one could hike for hours with constant change. The place is called "Magnolia," the same as the huge tree which gives its shade in grand specimens. Here in this romantic place rest Americas after the joy and suffering of life. (The Germans had their own, and the colored were in yet another acre of God.)[37] They lay spread apart, not in narrow rows

---

37 Many persons of German descent were buried in Bethany Cemetery, located near

A photograph of Magnolia Cemetery taken around 1900. Library of Congress.

near together as is the case with us, in pleasant irregularity with their splendid and precious monuments; here, one family rests in a tightly hedged park with places to sit; there, one in forest shadows; here again is a monument overshadowed by a live oak; over there, another on a free rise with the view to land and ocean and into eternity.

Here one could allow oneself to sleep in eternal peace. It was, however, uplifting and quickening for the living to walk and to rest within view of magnificent nature, of art advantageously adapted in recognition of the transience of this world, in the acknowledgment of piety and the honor of men who prepared such a paradisiacal place of

---

Magnolia Cemetery.

rest. I spent many Sunday afternoons here in such contemplations and found repose, joy and satisfaction.

However, from the dead back to the living. In happy times, Charleston had about 60,000 residents of which freely the half belonged to the colored race who were held in slavery (but not languishing as such.)

The white population consisted in large part of born and bred South Carolinians (geborenen und erzogenen Süd-Caolinern), but also many Northlanders (Yankees) and representatives of European nations were among them and endeavored to profit from the thriving commerce. In particular among the last group there were Germans and Irishmen, with the latter serving mainly as workers and the former, with few better exceptions, as craftsmen and in particular merchants who were as such called "bacon cutters."The Germans of the educated class, which maintained their own German newspaper and a German and religious parish, belonged to the estate of businessmen. In addition, they had exclusive control of apothecaries and drug stores, in the dignity of which they immediately acquired the title of doctor.

This group among our countrymen enjoyed high esteem because of their sense of reality and their financial soundness while the previously mentioned retail dealer or Low German because of his profession often came into conflict with penal law, because, contrary to them, he often sold liquor to Negroes or because he acquired from them stolen merchandise and masked it. These so-called "Dutchmen" were a people unto themselves and were not recognized by their own countrymen and by all other nationalities as coequals. They were placed on the same level as Irishmen, and they preferred commence with the colored though whom they sought to enrich themselves. The native white South Carolinians, nota bene from the educated class, are the consummate gentlemen and ladies who with certainty quickly acquire the esteem of the foreigner, who without personal knowledge would view them only as slave barons and tyrants. There is no trace of tyrant in them. They were naturally defenders of slavery out of principle, because of custom and because of interest. One would indeed be allowed to call them barons if one considers the proud measured character which each one has, but completely free of egoism. They are aristocrats through and through in their physical poise as well as in their demeanor, thinking and action. They were kind and polite toward their countrymen and toward every foreigner, but were filled with a nationalism and patriotism which later broke out in blazing flames. Among them, however, as it is the case in many other nations, no stranger needed to suffer. They were affectionate toward slaves and subordinates, and they were betaken with warm hearts for the poor and for unaided suffering. They were steeped in religious appreciation and were thoroughly conservative in their faith, their views and their habits. They were, however, very tolerant toward every religious and political dissenter. This I learned to value in the years of my association with them and am certain as with me so has each one who has lived among them.

It is therefore quite natural that the city of Charleston and its residents, as generally all South Carolinians, awakened a warm interest in me and left behind aroused and pleasant memories which, to be sure, were considered through other circumstances and allowed the advantages of my German homeland to be recognized, but of no fault of the country or the people.

For example, the climate in summer was almost unbearable for a northlander. The high temperature during the day was only somewhat eased at night after relaxation with a little refreshment. At the same time, one had to suffer through swarms of vermin, namely mosquitoes and bugs, against which no doubt every possible repellant was used which however in no way sufficed. In contrast, the winter was the more pleasant, during which the temperature moved toward the freezing point but only seldom fell below it and then only for a few hours. The sun, which was so bothersome in the summer, made the winter days cozy; and evenings one took pleasure in a gentle hearth fire. In the winter, roses, violets and Camellias bloomed in the gardens, and with them a man lifted his head which the blaze of summer had lowered. Ice and snow and the pleasures associated with them were naturally unknown, only if at all through a quick moving occurrence. Ice which was used in great quantities was brought from the Northern states in numerous shiploads and created in spite of the relatively inexpensive price a meaningful article of commerce.

Another mischief was brought to Charleston by the summer climate: the prevalence of yellow fever which was a very dangerous and, in most cases, a deadly disease which almost every non-acclimatized white was subject to. At the appearance of the disease, everyone who somehow could went inland or to the islands; but many who were not in the position had to remain constantly exposed to the danger and stare death in the face. The danger was, however, considerably lessened through a careful way of living. I escaped the consequences through strict observance of these ways.

In addition, that which I felt to be unpleasant in this otherwise interesting area and in the generally pleasant circumstances was the complete lack of mountains, or even hills, in a range of several hundred miles. Second only to the desire to be with relatives and in a joyful family life, was, over time, an ardent longing for the mountains, a longing which could not be satiated.

Above all, however, it was the outbreak of the war with its horror and deprivations which negatively impacted the pleasures of my sojourn there and greatly stirred my desire to leave this place, this country and these people to whom I owed so much gratitude. Perhaps adversity would have compelled me to follow these longings, had not fate been particularly merciful to me, and had it not with its graces so long have fettered me until the impoverished country was no longer able to offer me any advantages, such that I did not leave it until I was reconciled to it and had come to love it. One recourse remained to me, unlike many, broken in spirit and in means. Friends would have counted themselves fortunate to have been in my situation!

A 20th century photograph of the Confederate Home, formerly the Carolina Hotel, on Broad Street. Library of Congress.

Chapter 4

AMERICAN LIFESTYLE AND CUSTOMS

I was a seventeen-year-old youth when arrived in Charleston in November of 1859. I was induced to the move by the loving provision of my oldest brother and was surprised by and was pervaded with the many new stimulations of the New World: the strange languages, the many black people and the exciting life. I moved into the "Carolina House" in which he lived on a beautiful street planted with trees. It was close to the area of commence and had once been a hotel and contained all of the appropriate amenities associated with one. The lower boarding rooms were used as offices. The back boarding rooms were used as the kitchen, for domestic purposes and for Negro quarters. The two upper floors and the first floor contained a roomy dining area and a common social salon, the so-called "Parlour," with many living rooms for the guests, which were accessible by means of a piazza which ran along both floors of the house. The piazzas were in their length and breadth covered with jalousies which were used in almost all dwellings and which are a beneficial feature in the warm climate in that one can seal out the sun's rays; but the air can be allowed to circulate. [38]

The Carolina House enjoyed a good reputation in the city as well as beyond. It was almost always full with permanent guests and with strangers who were passing through. The owner, Mrs. Finney, a quite active, amiable and caring lady, understood perfectly how to be fair-

---

38 Jalousies are blinds with adjustable horizontal slats or louvers.

minded to her guests in every manner and to prepare for them a good home. These guests lived as families and as single men and women in one or more rooms accordingly. At times in consideration of costs, there were several men in a room but each with a bed when possible. In this regard, the American is frugal. It occurs quite frequently that in a hotel a stranger is approvingly placed in a lodging or bed which is already occupied by another, even a complete stranger. This and other facts appear to us Germans to be a sad fortune. Parents and several children live in one furnished room, or a couple spends their lives in this generally quite comfortable circumstance. This, however, corresponds to the circumstances found there. At marriage, American women receive no dowry; and they do not gladly submit to the preoccupation of housekeeping. The furnishing of a house is very expensive and is considered a luxury.

Whether at breakfast consisting of various warm dishes of meats and eggs, of hominy, diverse baked goods and coffee and tea or at dinner or supper with similar abundance, all of the tenants assembled at the table; and in the evening (or also during the day, he who had time and inclination for it), the entire company met in the parlour together, with the exception of the gentlemen who preferred alternative conversation outside the house or indulged themselves in their rooms or smoking on the piazza, for such was quite naturally not allowed in the parlour or at all in the presence of ladies. One had, however, less misgiving against chewing of tobacco which is highly unaesthetic by our standards.

At the clearing up each evening there was a jovial tone. All of the house guests constituted one big family. Worldwide it cannot be helped that among different elements, namely those of the fairer sex, differences come to light from time to time. Here in the Carolina House one was nevertheless tactful enough not to show or to display such contentions in this situation.

The parlour offered a colorful picture of gentlemen and ladies of different ranks, ages and nationalities, which devoted themselves to special dispositions of corresponding occupations or to effortless conversation. Here there was music and song. There were often quadrilles, dances françaises, and the so-called Virginia reel, naturally only contra since the American, at least in those days, viewed walkarounds or such which called for close contact of the sexes as thoroughly unseemly and did not allow them. [39] Guests of every age took part in the contra with great enthusiasm, however. Here, a chess match was set up; there, a game of whist with gentlemen and ladies, or other American card games such as "Euchre," "seven up" and so forth, naturally only for the honor since very card game for pecuniary gain was frowned upon and forbidden (nevertheless a few indulge this passion by playing poker, the game of chance, but in all secrecy behind locked doors). That was the everyday way of life in an American boardinghouse fireside which was so formed to bind the inhabitants to the house and to give them enjoyment and to keep them sound and healthy. In this matter, in the first instance our admirable landlady rendered outstanding service. She had an eye on the interest of every single guest. She supported herself and her children solely though the effort and activities of running this large establishment. Her further ascent was hindered up to today because of her opulent care of her guests at inexpensive prices, through the free room and board of those in distress, particularly that of several of her relatives, who took advantage of her kindheartedness.

She yet stands vividly before my eyes and thankfully remains indelibly in my memory. She was this honest lady, a true South Carolinian, as she presided over the long table which she and her Negro waiters watched. They immediately discovered and corrected every lack of food and every untidiness. She stood before either a coffee or tea urn filling the cups which the domestic staff handed to her; she took part in the social circle each evening and introduced every additional guest to the company, drawing him into the family circle and above all insured that the conversation suffered no standstill. She then, in the evening, dedicated herself in her room to her children and took care of her correspondence and needlework in order the she be the first up the next morning. Once breakfast was ended, accompanied by a Negro—the old house servant "Jim" or as he loved to call himself

---

39 Contra dances were arranged in lines or groupings of partners, and there was little touching except of the hands. What Conrad referred to as a "walkaround" was apparently a more intimate, face-to-face couple dance such as the waltz.

James Willie, Jr. (every syllable especially emphasized)—she shopped the market and other places and afterward in the house and in the kitchen brought order and redirected. She dispensed with these challenging tasks with such a calmness and adroitness, such that the greatest of respect was induced. In doing so, she had a friendly word for everyone who crossed her path and had a warm interest for all of her guests. The lady, noble in every respect, deserves a few words on my part, given her detailed attention, even love, in motherly care in so many cases of illness and her devoted correspondence over the years with one absent fourteen years.

In addition, many of my fellow boarders in Carolina House during those days left behind pleasant memories and made the stay of several years there very pleasant indeed.

Upon my arrival in Charleston, I had just completed my German commercial studies. My knowledge of English was insufficient, and I was not at all acquainted with the business relationships. My provident brother, however, adopting me as it were, gave me meaningful support in this way of life in an export business run by a German in which I had ample opportunity to fully learn the language and to acquire the nuances of the business. My quite nominal salary, the first of my own earning, was 100 dollars a year, nevertheless received on my part with great appreciation, with the possibility of a raise to 400 dollars for the next year. My income was certainly commensurate with my required performance. I was not required to do written work but only small tasks such as errands and assistance with the shipping of cotton. I came, however, into contact with all classes of men, seeing and learning as I did; and that was for my later professional development the main thing. My brother saw the necessity of polishing my German awkwardness and for that provided me with dance lessons which had the desired success such that I soon became an important member of the Caroline House quadrille. For my commercial studies, which I had neglected in Germany, I took a course in penmanship and in Italian bookkeeping. I must admit that in that short course with, however, an excellent methodology, I substantially improved my distinctive handwriting. In addition, I grasped debits and credit with all of its variations and bafflements and soon felt myself to be an accomplished bookkeeper.

My Americanization moved apace. Thanks to my almost complete association with Americans, I became after a short time fluent in English. One laughs, but I was able to use the language with poetic gushes. Naturally, the American teenage girls were the target of such linguistic outrages, although, oddly enough, the dance classes with these cute figurines went right by my heart without a trace.

The week was marked by regular commerce and high traffic. Only on Sundays was the lifestyle otherwise. All businesses and trades, even the most necessary, as well as restaurants and other such establishments were closed; and one abstained from every pleasure, sound and action which was not absolutely necessary for sustaining life. No trains departed; wagon traffic was completely suspended. Even taking walks, visiting or the desire to do anything else other than to busy oneself with God's Word were considered by the Americans to be irreligious and as far as possible to be avoided.

One attended church, if possible, three times. Most were always full and the members of the congregation made great sacrifice for them. Such churches were luxuriously furnished with chairs and carpeted halls as well as well-warmed in winter. Ministers, organists and singers received substantial salaries; and churches competed with others for the most beautiful voices in their choirs. Such an American church service, particularly those of the Episcopal Church, were uncommonly solemn and captivating through the ritual which was almost Catholic as well as through the wonderful, well-studied cantatas, motes, and pleasant sounding hymns, along with a short but pithy sermons.

During the rest of the time on Sunday, as long as it was not interrupted by the necessary meals, the pious American occupies himself with quite meditations, reads the Bible or other religious writings, and believes himself to be sinning if he occupies himself with other things or if he does not continuously fetter himself to metaphysical thoughts. There is a unity of all confessions in the principle of honoring the Sabbath.

As praiseworthy as this practice and celebration of Sundays may be – and it is certainly to regret the remainder of Christian nations (except for England) do not hold a little closer to the fulfillment of the Third Commandment – nevertheless, I was unable to completely tear away from my old habits, in order to accommodate this strict way of life. I allowed myself venial boredom or attempted to drive my boredom away. Nevertheless, I often visited the service of all confessions, almost regularly, visited lectures or threw myself, against all good manners, into playing cards in our well-protected room, usually with my brother and other Germans, with from time to time a rowdy American among us. Most of the time, however, I used Sunday afternoons to take walks to the Battery, to the previously mentioned cemetery "Magnolia," to the opposite bank of the Ashley over a long wooden bridge, or by steamboat to Sullivan's Island or Mount Pleasant across from it. I would allow myself to be put into a Sunday mood by the sublime nature and through the monotonous but captivating landscape. Spiritual music was usually played in the parlor; and thereby ended dead Sunday, which in any case had the charitable result that one had enjoyed complete rest and relaxation and could again begin one's work day joyously and with new strength.

That was an American Sunday. With the Day of Repentance and Prayer and other days of fast, it was a little different. These were privately celebrated but were not subject to other limitations. As to the first one, the churches were fully attended; and penance was done through fasting. As to the rest, one amused oneself as best one could and engaged in these differences, which I at first did not understand, in sacred acts of days of penance and Sundays as if they were given by God and had to be carried out as if they were one of the Ten Commandments, whereby they were only human creations with a religious sensibility but for which there were no biblical requirements.

The big, multi-day celebrations such as Christmas, Easter, Pentecost, Good Friday and Ascension Day to which we are accustomed did not as such exist because their celebration is not biblical which is of the most importance for the Christian American. They are understood to be merely events in the development of Christendom.

However, Christmas, New Year and the Fourth of July as a remembrance of the U. S. War of Independence are celebrated privately and publicly.

Our German ways of celebrating Christmas are completely alien to Americans, at least it was then. Their enjoyment is concentrated on luciferian rivalry, with a fat, if possible, wild turkey for dinner as well as a lot of noise in the streets and the houses, along with fireworks with which no little craziness and waste are produced. The constant release of fiery serpents amuses young and old alike throughout the day and often results in bodily injuries and damages to clothing.

At New Year's, Americans greet one another much as do we. They spend the day making reciprocal visits with the ladies well coiffed and dressed. By such visits, the guests are regaled with wine and mounds of pastry which cannot be turned down. A great honor is acquired to greet and book as many visitors as possible. For that reason, the visits to a given house are very short. The delicacies which are eaten on such a day are later reported by the stomach in its great distress. While Americans absolutely love sweets, they do not make any pretenses about drinks. Wine, they can take or leave. Beer, they absolutely detest. Some, however, gladly imbibe in strong drink such as whiskey (corn brandy) and cognac. Many complete avoid spirits of any kind. I have heard that the enjoyment of beer has, however, changed.

The Fourth of July is, however, the most important celebration. The sky is the limit. Everyone takes part, with each person, because of patriotism, obligating himself to exuberance. From very early in the morning until late in the night, there is wild joy. Firecrackers, fireworks, guns and small canons do their duty. One banquets throughout the day with every kind of fruit tart, ice cream and sweets. There are planned excursions into the forest and cruises around the harbor in sailing boats and steam boats. Everyone gives himself over to pleasure and amusement. On this day the entire republic portrays, through its residents, a picture of enthusiasm and pride that they are free Americans. On this day, no one thinks of business, political party or class differences. Negro slaves celebrate and enjoy the festivities along with the whites, using every opportunity to profit from the amusements of whites.

This parade serves as an opportunity for me to comment, for the purpose of situations to be described later, to comment on the constituent participants: in comparison to its population and territorial size, the United States have a very small standing army, not quite 10,000 territorial soldiers, recruited by the general government, which are used to man the important forts along the seacoast and on the Indian frontier.

By contrast, the individual states are obliged, in case of war or rebellion, to provide a certain number of militia to the general government; whereby every American citizen is obliged to serve a certain number of years in the militia or in the fire brigade. This obligation, although anchored in law, is, however, not considered as such, with military and fire brigade service being viewed as entertainment, with the former being found in every social connection during times of peace so that those obliged to duty remain well beyond the required length of service with their company. Foreigners and non-citizens volunteer for this service which has little impact on their business. In this way there comes to be in a city numerous military companies made up of Americans, Germans, Irish and other nationalities for which the state provides weapons but not the uniforms which must be privately maintained. These companies form regiments and brigades and are commanded by colonels and generals who have acquired military training but who like the common soldier belong to an unpretentious estate or office. Apart from training for war, and in a few cases an inspection, a parade or an exercise which force large contingents, each company is an independent society or club which bears its own name. The members chose their uniforms, make their by-laws and elect their own officers who, however, must have the ability to command the company. With the exception of the weapon assigned to him, each member can determine the style of his uniform, sometimes colorful, fanciful and even expensive. If with the cavalry, he must provide his own horse; and each member must regularly pay dues to the company treasury to defray the cost of renting a locale for meeting and drilling, locales which are usually furnished with gyms, bowling facilities and chess sets.

The fire brigades are organized in the same manner, save that they usually have their own firehouses outfitted with clubhouses and meeting rooms. They also must acquire their own firefighting equipment. They are, however, often well subsidized by the city and by the fire insurance companies.

In spite of the fact that the service is predicated on discipline, in that one subordinates himself to the authority of the elected superior and even immediately banishes a rebellious member, every superior is nevertheless a member of the company and is an equal member. The association is dominated by a cheerful, comradely tone as it meets one evening a week for exercises, and, at the pleasure of the company, goes to the clubhouse for entertainment. Several times a year, each company sponsors a parade through the city and engages for the festivities a band which has its own uniform for such purposes. The company struts its honor by marching strappingly with a quite noble appearance and with as many members as possible. The fire brigade appears with its equipment mirror polished.

Under these circumstances, this service gives much pleasure and is executed with great enthusiasm. I reference these military affairs based on the large, colorful parade on the 4th of July in which all of these uniformed associations take part. I do this to describe the country and its people as well as to relate them to future events.

Thus did I find Charleston and so did one live in the last year of flourishing and of sweet peace: 1859-60. I have described in advance the local conditions which I have observed and which I recall in order to turn to the difficult events of my future experiences as far as I can recall them without a specific record. Because of this, I must plead forbearance.

This 1857 illustration from Harper's Magazine *depicts the South Carolina Institute Hall in Charleston, where the Ordinance of Secession was signed in December 1860. Wikicommons.*

Chapter 5

The Die is Cast

The 20th of December 1860 was one of the beautiful winter days in Charleston, a day characteristic of the climate of that region with a bright and warm sun which makes the time outside so pleasant. I was busy with a group of Negroes at the wharf where I was preparing the load of a ship going to Bremen for one of my principals. I was measuring, through probes, the presumed quality of the cotton, marking it and ensuring that it was sent to the cotton press which would reduce the volume of the cotton by means of an enormous press, thereby compressing it to enhance the limited capacity of the ship. I spent the day with this routine activity which always brought new interests. Whites and blacks worked hand in hand as the ships were loaded and unloaded with the ever-audible songs of the sailors, with the orders of the commanders and with black sailors wandering through the rows of workers offering fruit, gingerbread and cakes.

The winter sun shone bright and warm. There was not a breath of air, and the never-ending surface of the water lay before us, mirror flat in its sublime peace which contradicted the moving events which were unfolding around it. The bay was a beautiful and colorful painting in which each loaded ship lay at anchor as if therein embedded, waiting for a breeze to develop which would enable it to depart. The distant wooded shore created a natural frame. It was a beautiful, but at the same time also an extremely important and fateful day.

The sun had likely just reached its apex when cannon roar from the Citadel Commons shook the air; the magnificent chimes of St. Philip's and St. Michael's and St. Michael intoned bright melodies; and with them, came the uninterrupted jubilation of thousands of voices. [40]

What did these sounds, certainly heralding a joyous event, mean? Everyone dropped his work and raced toward the city in order to be certain. Many already had a premonition as to the cause. Just now, the state legislature which had been called to Charleston, which was to counsel over the threatening danger to the South caused by the recent presidential election, had unanimously made the following decision:

"The State of South Carolina breaks the bands which link it to the United States of North America and henceforth becomes of its own an independent state. The great and glorious Union is dissolved!"[41]

Thus was the long-range declaration which the representatives of the state, the entirety of its citizens, and with few exceptions, all non-natives cheered over. Even the black residents cheered along without understanding for the matter, or more likely were ambivalent toward this special and important result of this event which involved them.

The entire day, the crowd moved through the streets in an excited mood with much noise to the front of the building in which the people's representatives had held their session and there gathered into an impenetrable troop, brought forth cheers a thousand-fold for the legal body, the new independent state, her governor Pickens and the city of Charleston, the source of this new fortune. [42] The enthusiasm was unbounded. Other matters were forgotten, the present events dominating every conversation. Friendly faces, decorated buildings and finely dressed ladies were everywhere to be found. The common

---

40   What Conrad refers to as the Citadel Commons was the parade ground for the Citadel, the military academy in Charleston. The area is now known as Marion Square.

41   The Secession Convention (not the state legislature), composed of delegates from every part of the state, unanimously ratified the Ordinance of Secession on December 20, 1860. Part of it stated that "the union now subsisting between South Carolina and other States, under the name of the 'United States of America,' is hereby dissolved."

42   The Ordinance of Secession was signed in Institute Hall on Meeting Street. The governor of South Carolina was Francis W. Pickens (1807-1869).

folk who could not afford this display, nevertheless, participated with gestures, handkerchief waving and shouts.

Indeed, the American ladies of the South abandoned with the day their traditional composure and nonchalance concerning things political and came out to the place of battle. Through word, pen and act; through patriotism, which kept them unbroken to the last moment; through their zeal for the South; through their burning hate of the enemies of the South; through their influence on the stronger sex; through their untiring good works and sacrifice for the wounded and fighting warriors, the Southern lady, indeed, played an important part in the coming events. She brought about both the blessed and the fateful. She drank the cup of sorrow to the last drop without flinching at it bitterness. Where the man threatened to fail, she would spur him on to steadfastness.

That day came to an end. Its wild jubilation hushed; but yet in the hearts of the adults, there was the beat of joyous excitement at the suddenly acquired independence, full of pride over the courage of the small state which had brought into being this exceptional position which promised so much; yet, at the same time, they were in suspense at what the general government would do on the one hand and how the fellow slave states would react to this step of their neighbor. It was hoped for and expected that other states would follow the example of this single state and would enter into a confederation with it; however, not too much weight was put on this consideration because it was firmly believed that the Union had no particular interest and certainly no right to challenge the secession of South Carolina from the commonwealth of states into which South Carolina had freely entered and from which it could and may secede. At this time, no thought was given to a war which could result from this step. Only gradually did the possibility, the likelihood and finally the fact of war dawn on the people.

The State of South Carolina viewed itself as its own independent state with no other federated peers. As such a power, the state pounded its chest. All measures were taken necessitated by its new foreign and domestic position. The state government, the representatives and the politicians became thoroughly engaged in the new reality.

The Flag of the United States—the beautiful and meaningful "Stars and Stripes"—was everywhere removed and replaced by the Flag of South Carolina with a golden palmetto tree on a blue field and a star at its crest. The high officials who had been appointed by the general government— judges, postmasters, tax officials, most of them Southerners – resigned from their offices with great fanfare, since the Union was dissolved, and they no longer recognized the authority of the federation, whereby they immediately took upon themselves the same offices under the authority of the State of South Carolina. The sons of South Carolina severed their service as officers with the U. S. Army and the U. S. Marines and made themselves available for service to their own fatherland. [43] As very quickly the other Southern states followed the example of their forerunner, South Carolina, the enthusiasm rose even more; and self assurance grew as did the trust in their own strength for victory in case a war would indeed break out.

Within a short time, all of the slave states left the Union with the same enthusiasm. The State of Virginia underwent a difficult struggle; however, after resolving misgivings about the withdrawal of this proudest and most aristocratic state in the entire Union, it was saluted and welcomed by the rebellious comrades. [44] Virginia proved herself at great sacrifice in this fight for "Southern rights." Maryland would have also liked to have taken her place among her peers; however, when her intent became known, it was hindered by the immediate action of Union troops to the advantage of the latter.

---

43 By "Marines" Conrad probably means the navy.

44 Virginia and three other Southern states did not secede until after Abraham Lincoln called for troops to invade the South following the bombardment of Fort Sumter. Virginia's governor, John Letcher, replied to Lincoln's request for militia troops from his state: "I have only to say that the militia of Virginia will not be furnished to the powers at Washington for any such use or purpose as they have in view. Your object is to subjugate the Southern States, and a requisition made upon me for such an object—an object, in my judgment, not within the purview of the Constitution or the act of 1795, will not be complied with."

These Southern states, insisting on their good right, characterized by their previous brothers in the North as rebels, united themselves in the course of a short time into a new confederation and created the "Confederate States of North America" and elected Jefferson Davis as President with Richmond, Virginia, becoming the capital and the seat of government. [45] It was generally believed, for good or for bad, that the United States would countenance this step and would recognize the lawful separation as well as the constitution of the Confederate States. The former nourished the sincere desire, although completely separate, to negotiate and to sustain the best friendly and neighborly relations with the latter. [46]

In fact, the general government in Washington reacted to this sequence of events, at least in the first months, quite passively and did not appear to know what position it should take on these matters. In any case, the mild and lethargic President Buchanan attempted to delay any action and undertook no measures which could burden him or his government in any way or other until his period in office had expired.

But even without any such decisions, the initial bliss developed more and more into an oppressive sultriness in which minor events gathered as little clouds in the bright sky until they gathered themselves, darkening the sunny sky, and discharged as a violent thunderstorm, destroying all of the fine hopes, laying waste to the entire country and plunging it into calamity.

A garrison of eighty federal troops was located in Fort Moultrie on Sullivan's Island, while, at the same time the much larger and much

---

45 Montgomery, Alabama, was briefly the first capital city of the Confederate States of America (not North America). The capital was moved to Richmond, Virginia, soon after Virginia seceded.

46 In December 1860 and January 1861 the governor of South Carolina sent envoys to Washington, D. C., to try to arrange an amicable and peaceful transfer of Fort Sumter and to offer the federal government monetary compensation for the fort. After the formation of the Confederacy, in March 1861, President Jefferson Davis sent three commissioners to Washington to offer the same terms about the fort, to seek recognition of the Confederacy as a sovereign nation, and to establish friendly relations between the two powers. Lincoln refused to meet with them.

stronger Fort Sumter, although not yet completed, as well as Castle Pinckney and Fort Johnson were outfitted with ordnance but were not manned. Before the State of South Carolina could make a decision or even come up with the idea to take possession of these unmanned forts, in the initial excitement of the moment, there came the surprising news on the morning of December 27th that the garrison at Fort Moultrie under the command of Major Anderson had left their position at Fort Moultrie under the cover of darkness and had transferred themselves to Fort Sumter with enough provisions for a limited amount of time.[47] This was the first incident which caused the Southern states to consider how such a move should be addressed. Major Anderson had immediately understood that he would not be able to hold Fort Moultrie were an attack, which he must consider given the prevailing circumstance, to come from the island and from Fort Sumter if the latter were occupied by the forces of South Carolina. Fort Sumter, on the other hand, would give him greater security. With or without instructions from the general government, he took these prudent measures which one might say was the first act of hostilities and immediately set about to make the accommodations inside the uncompleted fort livable.

This act naturally caused great excitement and concern, both in the city of Charleston and in the state which at that time stood alone; but it also created the necessity for the state to take countermeasures. For that purpose, the governor called out militia units to occupy the rest of the forts and to build further fortifications on Morris Island and Sullivan's Island in order to prevent a considered attack from the side or from Fort Sumter or to serve as attack points for a counterattack against the latter.

On the 11th of January 1861, Governor Pickens challenged Major Anderson to turn the fort over to the state; however, Major Anderson with marked politeness refused to comply with the demand, with the explanation, that he stood in the service of the United States, that he held this position for his government, and would and could not leave the post without countervailing instructions.

---

[47] During the secret nighttime transfer to Fort Sumter, Major Anderson's soldiers spiked the guns at Fort Moultrie and set ablaze the gun carriages.

Chapter 6

PLAYING SOLDIER

Everything remained peaceful during the first months of the year 1861. Neither in Charleston nor in the rest of the South were the events associated with Fort Sumter treated with indifference, nor was the interest in a possible defense neglected in the least. Everything which was necessary for the defense of the young republic was put in place; however, it was reckoned that the commander of Sumter would very soon leave his abidance on the orders of the government of the United States or would have to abandon his post once his provisions had been consumed which could not possibly last long. [48] This view was further strengthened by the fact that one after the other more and more former members of the Union were coming over to the side of the Confederation; and this itself strengthened the belief that the United States would not dare initiate hostilities, even if they had such an intent, which was little entertained. In case all of this consideration should fail, it was strongly reckoned that the European powers, namely England and France, would recognize the new republic because they would welcome an opportunity to break or weaken the American Union. With the independence of the South, the European powers would be able to further their own trade and compete with the factories and the industrial production of the North, claiming a substantial part thereof for themselves, indeed being able to make

---

[48] From late January through the first week of April 1861, Major Anderson and his men were allowed to purchase food and provisions from the Charleston markets. This arrangement lasted until April 7, when it was learned that warships were on their way to Charleston Harbor.

substantial profits for themselves. For this expected recognition and the eventual support of Europe, it was believed that the South was protected in all cases against possible, but unexpected, hostilities on the part of the North or the United States.

With this feeling of security, accompanied by political action, commerce in Charleston was in full bloom. The harbor was filled with transatlantic and American ships. As before, the North brought its goods and acquired Southern products. Fort Sumter allowed the ships to come and to go and appeared to be extinct, were it not for the fact that the flag of the United States waved daily over its ramparts. The fort itself had no connection to the outside world, neither with the coast of South Carolina nor with the North which seemed resigned to leave the garrison to its own fate.

I had gotten, thanks to the commercial training which I had received, another position in the overseas trading post with a German who was a friend of my brother. He ran and import-export business in which I at my position was able to better myself financially, and I was much more satisfied with the obligatory paperwork. My principal was at the same time the consul of the Kingdom of Hanover, an office which, however, brought very little income since there was seldom and arrival of a ship from Hanover, meaning that there was little work to do in that area. Through the increase in my income I was put in the pleasant situation of being able to completely finance my livelihood myself and was able to somewhat relieve my brother who had with much sacrifice cared for me. This situation made me more diligent in my profession and satisfied and full of life. I felt myself to be at peace with my fate, against which I had earlier complained because it had not immediately given me a particular advantage. I was now a "double bookkeeper" and a "consular secretary." I was merely lacking the desired fuzz on the upper lip so that I could command respect for my dignity which I myself extended to them.

At this time, there lived among us in the Carolina House a certain Mr. Chichester, an employee in a commercial book factory, with his genial wife who, in addition to an excellent education and her modest nature, had the rare and quite compelling ability as an American to speak fluent German.⁴⁹ This attribute initiated, between the charming lady on the one hand and my brother and me on the other, a cordial and lasting association based on mutual respect and animated interests. Since her spouse usually spent his evenings elsewhere, she entrusted herself to our special custody. Her husband was eager to form a new military company, which would not be difficult given the enthusiasm in those days for the fatherland; he was soon successful. Although he was a native Northerner, he gave himself loyally to the Southern cause. Without military training, he diligently took up the study of it and acquired a thorough knowledge of military science. In addition to a bit of ambition to acquire the post of captain, it was beyond that self-evident and completely justified that the huddle of friends belonging to the regulars of our company would elect him to that office for which he proved himself to be quite capable. He was committed to bring the number of men in the company to sixty-four which was the minimum required to receive a commission from the state. As previously stated, this goal was quickly reached. By inducement from the new captain, I reported for enlistment in his company and became, after unanimous approval, a fully entitled and zealous recruit of the "Charleston Zouave Cadets."The company adopted this name and took the French Zouaves as example both for uniforms and for drill. The addition of "Cadets" was earned by the fact that almost all of the members were between the ages of eighteen and twenty-two. It was a passel of green and cheerful lads, most born in Charleston. Among them, some also had German parents and could more or less speak German. There were, in addition to me, other "real" Germans in the group. So it was with my friend Laitenberger, born in Stuttgart but having lived a long time in Paris.⁵⁰ He was a bit older than average and was married. He was loyal and

---

49 Charles Edward Chichester (1834-1898), a native of Pennsylvania, came to Charleston in 1860 with his wife Jane Elizabeth Chichester (1833-1914). After his company of Zouaves disbanded, he continued to serve in the defense of Charleston. After the war he entered the Presbyterian ministry, pastoring in Winnsboro and Florence until he became the chaplain of the Port Society of Charleston. He was buried in Magnolia Cemetery dressed in his Confederate uniform coat.

50 Later in his narrative, Conrad indicates that Laitenberger's first name was Louis. Charleston death records list the death of an infant, Louis A. Laitenberger, in October 1861—likely Laitenberger's son.

lively as well as vain and "quite French." He was very entertaining and became my special brother-in-arms and my friend.

I became with body and soul a soldier, that is as long as the excitement lasted which this status guaranteed to me and my comrades and so long as there was nothing to risk which could put my life in danger. As a foreigner, I was not obligated to serve and could resign from the company if there were mobilization at any time. For our drills and social purposes we had rented a hall which was more like gym which was outfitted with training equipment, a bowling alley and other devices, as well as with chess and domino sets. (Cards and dice were forbidden as means of amusement according to the by-laws.) Our uniforms and weapons were also stored there. Each evening a large number of our members would gather for the purpose of training recruits, for exercise, for conferences and for uninhibited conviviality. I was issued like all the rest a musket, a bullet pouch on a white strap and a waist belt with a sidearm; but I had to provide the other parts of the uniform myself. This consisted of wide pantaloons, a vest buttoned to the top, and a wide and open jacket, everything from the same gray material with red-bordered flies. The jacket was richly trimmed with multiple, interlocking braid. In addition, there were brown leather leggings, in which the pantaloons were secured up to the knee. For headgear, we wore a bright red kepi with a straight brim, the crown of which angled forward and which had attached a golden palmetto palm. The backpack of different formats was wrapped in water-tight, black leather moleskin, held together with long straps carried over the shoulder. A rolled up red wool blanket was fastened on top of this improvised knapsack.

Acquiring the uniforms to be worn for this duty and paying the dues in order to serve as a soldier were a bit costly; however, I gladly made this sacrifice, and the costs were well compensated by the delight which the duty brought and the pride which filled me as well as those looking on wearing the conspicuous but elegant uniforms. After I had been trained by a sergeant, I was able to take part in the exercises of the entire company and in the public parades. In the parades, we all swelled with pride. When the Charleston Zouave Cadets passed through the streets in their colorful uniforms, along with a band

and black drummers up front, and with young men of the same age belonging to the better families imparting a very noble sight, windows opened everywhere. It was particularly the sweet and charming girls of "sweet sixteen" who waved their handkerchiefs and strewed flowers in our path. The public, black and white, gathered and accompanied us to the Citadel Commons where drills from the other companies with various and excellent precision were presented and observed with great interest. The public enjoyed a closing cheer of the Zouave's: One! Two! Three! Four! Five! Tiger! Zouave! with which we obliged them. I was never able to get behind the meaning of this cheer which we never missed giving at this event, or I have forgotten it.

Such parades and public exercises were always a great celebration for us. The next day, one could usually read the following in the newspapers: "Yesterday, we were again able to observe a magnificent spectacle: the Charleston Zouave Cadets in a parade with their unique drills under the command of Captain Chichester. When one is able to observe the stalwart bearing of the young men in their military attire and the precision with which they carry out their difficult maneuvers, then the company and particularly their officers must earn great praise, which would be supported by our citizens who took part in great numbers and with spirited interest. Charleston can be proud of such sons! And so forth." Whether or not those praises were justified, I cannot in all humility judge.

I therefore spent the evenings in the service of Mars and in the circle of my comrades and had little time for the amicable conversation in Carolina House. In addition, even there, politics dominated the discussions in which our ladies participated with great enthusiasm. Although all was peaceful and the businesses were running as usual and in spite of the fact that the North showed no signs of hostility, which was likely being fostered in secret and probably being prepared for, there, nevertheless, gradually developed in the South a dissatisfaction with the conduct of the United States which were expected to recognize the Confederate States, a demand which found not corresponding answer. The reality that the United States continued to hold Fort Sumter in the middle of Southern territory was held to be simply untenable if the fort were not handed over because it appeared to affirm the rule of the former over the South. The language in the newspapers and among the Southern people became more provocative and more vitriolic. The flag over Fort Sumter was a thorn in the eye. Each party attempted to put the blame on the other with each step and with each attack. Something, however, had to happen to calm the tempers, something which cleared the air which was growing ever thicker.

And the thunderstorm broke with all force to the elation of many who came to idolize the drama. With others, however, it brought dismay and worry at which consequences might come of the event.

Chapter 7

The Bombardment of Fort Sumter

By morning gray on the 12th of April 1861, sleeping Charleston was shocked from her peace by the fierce thunder of cannons which heralded nothing to revel in based on it irregular rhythm, force and direction but nevertheless something out of the ordinary. The first shot brought everyone to their feet. These followed with longer breaks and yet others. Then began a punctilious, pulsing cannonade. Any and everybody on the peninsula who could get out ran to the Battery to gain information as to the source of the thundering sounds and the reason for them. Certainty was in the eyes of everyone as soon as daylight allowed a complete view of the scene.

From Fort Moultrie and Fort Johnson controlled by South Carolina representing the Confederacy as well as from batteries set up on Morris Island and Sullivan's Island there was a continuous withering bombardment of Fort Sumter which returned the greetings sent to it with shells. The battery was quickly filled with thousands of curious onlookers, among which were women of all classes. From their mouths, since hostilities had finally commenced, came sundry curses and maledictions against the commander, against the garrison, against the Yankees and against Northerners, a demeanor which could be excused, given their boundless patriotism and their defense of the rightful cause of the South; nevertheless, it did not sound very edifying.

From the vantage point of the Battery, people had a clear view of the battle which was waged about three miles away and which one could observe without danger. It was an eerie day. The elements took part in the battle between men. A hurricane-like storm blew in from the east and drove the thunder of the cannons to us with full force. The ocean was in tumult. Waves fought with waves and billows slammed with great force against the walls of the Battery and drenched the gathered crowd time and again with their salty weapons. The sun, on the other hand, shone clearly and illuminated the background to which all gazes were fixed with interest, with tension, with enthusiasm and anger. One saw the initial blast from the cannons and the clouds of powder; then came the rolling percussion. It was difficult to see anything which would indicate the success of the shells on one side or the other. The people remained, however. They consoled themselves with the spectacle before them and expressed wishes and cursed with various expressions. The people waited eagerly for the result of the battle and for reports of its progress and what may have been the cause of it.

Within a few hours, there came from different sources the alleged cause and quickly became known to the public. At four in the morning, a transport steamer of the United States, "Star of the West" had attempted to enter Charleston Harbor, in order to bring provisions, munitions and reinforcements to Fort Sumter, which was correctly surmised by the observation posts. [51] There was perhaps no hostile intent in the move, and it was still perhaps possible that even if this plan had been carried out, no war would have ensued and the Confederate States would have taken their place as one of the major nations of the world. To the contrary, as Friedrich Schiller has pinned in his poem "The Song of the Bell":

With the powers of fate,

No eternal union can be braided.

And misfortune strides quickly.

---

51   Conrad was inaccurate in his memories of this particular time. The arrival of the *Star of the West* actually took place in early January 1861, when President Buchanan attempted to reinforce and provision Fort Sumter, sending a civilian merchant ship with armed troops and munitions concealed below her decks. Aware of its intentions and secret cargo, the South Carolinians fired on the ship, firing a warning shot first, and it reversed its course and steamed away. What in fact precipitated the bombardment of Fort Sumter by the Confederate defenders was the arrival of federal warships off the bar. Lincoln had sent notice to South Carolina's governor that he would send a naval expedition to resupply the fort—by force if necessary.

The aforementioned steamer had to take a course along a channel which went by Morris Island. It was observed from one of the batteries located there and was likely held suspect. This battery fired a shot across the bow which is a challenge well understood among seamen. The ship was to turn by and identify itself. The steamer did not, however, follow this command but continued its course at the original speed. The suspicion was therewith proved: if the intent was not exactly hostile, it could nevertheless not be countenanced. The battery fired directly on the steamer. As a result of this attack, the steamer deemed it prudent to turn about, which it did without any damage and reached the open ocean.

In the meantime, this first shot had alarmed not only the citizens of the city but also the adjacent forts. Fort Sumter, which immediately understood the situation of things, immediately fired on the attackers of its long awaited friends or providers, in order to silence them. Now, after the actual initiator had gotten itself to safety, all of the Confederate batteries opened up against Sumter which defended itself in all directions.

That was the first shot which was fired in this unholy war and which likely alone caused it to be. Who can know?

The bombardment suffered no break the entire day, and it did not seem possible that Fort Sumter with its garrison of eighty men could hold out against the challenging fire. As a result, however, neither party seemed to have success as a goal, at least there were no reports of wounded from the Confederate side; and Sumter, given the uninterrupted activity on its part, must have been in a similar situation.

Thus came the night during which many zealous patriots remained at their posts. Even though the combatants graced themselves with a little rest, the bombardment in subdued manner continued. The following morning, however, the battle started afresh with great intensity, and the interest of the public was, it was possible, even more pronounced through impatience in expectation of a change in the state of affairs.

Again, the battle and the elements rampaged. Fort Sumter rose up over the waves in its majesty and fired its guns in regular intervals

The bombardment of Fort Sumter, April 12, 1861, as depicted by Currier & Ives. Library of Congress.

from the various levels of its proud structure and the flag waved in anticipation of victory high above the ramparts. Not long, however, because it suddenly came crashing down after a round ripped it from its mounting. The fact that the flag vanished brought a never-ending full cheer among those there gathered; and they boasted of a great victory, that this proud flag, to which those there gathered had themselves earlier honored with enthusiasm, had been destroyed and humiliated. Soon, however, the flag reared up again, ever so bold, and silenced the victory shouts. The opponent had pulled himself together and renewed his defiance.

Until approximately noon of April 13th the struggle continued as well as did the excitement of the people who were watching it without their impatience being satiated. Then one suddenly saw from inside Fort Sumter an uncommonly strong and rising cloud of smoke which got thicker and thicker and out of which tongues of fire licked. There were new shouts of joy and victory and embraced different suppositions. Major Anderson wanted to destroy the fort and the garrison; he had to capitulate but first destroy the fort so that it could not be used when it fell into the hands of the enemy; he had taken to the boats which he had and had used the fire to distract his pursuers during the Confederate crossfire so that he could make for the open ocean. What was correct? It appeared that the inner structure of the fort was burning. Those inside must have been busy with extinguishing the blaze because at first the cannons had cease to fire. The smoke subsided, and the cannon fire began again, but subdued. The fort appeared to be disabled, and the cloud of smoke again became stronger. [52]

Then, the star spangled banner sank again, and in its place appeared a white flag, illuminated in the sun, a bright point shining in the dark scene, peacefully waving over the surging billows in a howling storm, over murderous battle, over human hate and anger!

Peace! Peace between us signaled Fort Sumter. Surrender with grace and with disgrace! So interpreted the crowd this event. And there was peace after thirty-six hours of battle! All participants ceased fire, and a boat was sent out from Fort Moultrie to Fort Sumter to receive the terms under which the fort was to capitulate. Major Anderson found this step to be necessary because a Confederate shell had set the magazine ablaze and the destruction of the interior of the fort and the provisions was to be feared. The garrison, already exhausted, had to be engaged to fight the fire and thereby made themselves venerable to the bullets and bombs which would have annihilated the small contingent, one man having fallen in just that attempt. [53] Major Anderson requested a temporary cease fire so that the blaze could be and should be extinguished and that with the surrender of the fort, a guarantee of an honorable withdrawal with march music.

The attack ceased and the fire was put out. During that time, there was a hurry to bring this compromise to the proper locale and place because the decisions concerning the capitulation had to be made by

---

52 On the morning of April 13, the shelling set fire to the fort's barracks. Several Confederate officers were sent out by steamer to Fort Sumter to offer Major Anderson assistance in extinguishing the fire, but he declined, telling them that it was almost burned out.

53 There were no casualties resulting from the bombardment on either side, but two garrison soldiers accidentally suffered mortal wounds after the surrender of the fort.

General Beauregard in Charleston. An officer from Fort Sumter was accompanied into the city to fulfill this duty. As the boat bringing him to the wharf landed, a large crowd had gathered there in order to find out what had just transpired. When it became known that the fort had surrendered, the victory cheers again broke out in full force. I felt sorry for the poor Union officer who marched through the street with a small cloak accompanied by a pressing mob and who had to endure many slurs of hate and contempt toward the Office of the Commandant. For the Negroes, this procession was particularly fun. Indicative that their understanding of the day was overshadowed by their blind patriotism was articulated by the words of a twelve-year-old Negro boy, "There we got the rascal, now we put him in jail," meaning, of course, Major Anderson.

The conditions of the surrender were accepted in their full form. The handover of the fort and the withdrawal of the garrison were set for the next day. On this occasion, the generous character of the South and of South Carolina was made evident. They only wanted to take possession of the fort which was on their territory which they held to be their good right. Once this goal was met, the previous anger against those whom they had hated because that right had been abridged immediately went away. At that moment, the animosities ceased. The previous enemies were accorded all honor and their bravery and endurance as they defended the isolated fort with a small garrison was acknowledged.

At the appointed hour, a steamer docked at Fort Sumter and landed the Confederate garrison which would relieve their predecessors with all military honors after the Union garrison had buried a fallen soldier. Finally, the Confederacy was able to grasp the hard-won pearl of the fortress. The retiring soldiers of the United States were transported to New York with all that they had and all that they had brought to the fort, which was not originally part of the fort itself. At the departure of the steamer, there stood on the beach of Sullivan's Island, which the steamer had to pass, a line of infantry presenting arms. From the forts, including Sumter, a salute was given and the flags were lowered in deference.

Thus one treats and honors a brave enemy! Now there was again peace! Hate had disappeared, and joy filled the hearts of all patriots. On the Southern side, not the least injury was taken. The first victory was achieved, and it was believed that a later would not be necessary. The soldiers rested after the difficult work, proud of the result of the hard battle. There was again a festive day of bells and cannon salutes which were dedicated to the taking of Fort Sumter. The anxiousness of the previous days gave way to a blessed joy; and few likely thought that the country could yet face such horrific events and devastation for which the battle which had just ended was a mere prelude!

The State of South Carolina and the Confederacy now had full authority and control of Charleston Harbor and need not fear Fort Sumter as a means to disrupt commerce. What had, however, been won?

The ice had been broken. The North, which did not take the fall of Fort Sumter lightly as had been expected, came off its reservation. Lincoln, in the course of time, had taken command of the ship of state and was running a tight ship. Before one could react, a fleet of the United States appeared before the harbors of the South and let the appropriate authorities know that, within a certain period of time, no ship would be allowed to enter or to leave and, with that effective date, a blockade would be in effect.

This communication had the effect of beating down thoughts of victory and peace. War was effectively declared with this decision, and the South had neither the material nor countermeasures to meet this threat. The entire fleet of the United States had remained with the North; and the South would first have to create its own if it was, in fact, for this purpose capable of doing so. As I have already mentioned, the commercial resources of the South were based almost solely on agriculture and the related enterprises of livestock breeding and trade while industry as such was almost nonexistent. Through the confiscation of arsenals on its territory, the South was supplied with weapons and munitions for a longer period of time; but against the fleet it was able to undertake nothing. For the building of a fleet there was an acute lack of material and infrastructure. The long blockade of the harbors was, therefore, a mischief with glaring consequences. If one were then able to produce the most necessary life necessities, such as bread and meat, there would still be a lack of clothing and all of the other articles of necessity which, up to this point, the North or foreign countries had provided.

How was the South going to procure such things? In addition, how were products to be traded if there were no markets? There were, however, only a few pessimists to whom the consequences were clear or who believed that the circumstances of the blockade would have a long duration. It was still reckoned with the recognition by and the eventual help of countries abroad, particularly since it was believed that England could not do without American cotton. Within the possibility to acquire the cotton, the textile mills and the thousands there employed would collapse. For this reason it was believed that England would not allow the closing of Southern places of export.

Nevertheless, the pressure of the blockade soon made itself felt. Once again, commerce came to life. The price for cotton on the foreign market rose enormously. With great bustle, during the sanctioned period of grace as much cotton as possible was exported. With the end of that period, however, the harbors were emptied of ships; and new ones were not allowed. Business stagnated. Even if one could reckon with a quick removal and lifting of the blockade, the exigency was, nevertheless, there. The banks ceased paying out specie, i.e. they held back their hard reserves. Gold and silver disappeared from public circulation and were traded only with agio, at first against the increased circulation of banknotes but later against the paper money created by the Confederate States. [54]

Gradually, the Southern property began to lose value all on its own and commerce declined in the entire country. More and more, the mistrust of the common cause grew subconsciously even though the patriots did not realize it, did not believe it and did not hold it to be possible; otherwise, their hope for a fortuitous end to the war which had broken out would have been weakened.

---

54 "Agio" is a commercial term meaning exchange rate, discount, or premium.

My principal, along with many others, used the supposedly "short business interruption" to travel to Germany with his family, where he would wait out the course of events with the intent of returning in the fall. [55] He left his business, the consulate and his house in the care of my brother which he, along with me, was to inhabit and to watch over and over which he was the legal agent, a duty which he took on with complaisance.

I continued to receive my salary which I did not earn because my enterprise in particular was completely shut down. Nevertheless, I spent the day in the office where I banished boredom with reading and with beginning and consequently keeping a diary. These notes, which I very zealously collected across several years and which would be of great value to me now, were, along with other interesting memorabilia, stolen from me.

Our lodgings were therefore moved to the private house and property of my principal in another part of the city on the Ashley River. For our minimal service requirements, we had one black female slave who lived with her husband and children in a side building. We provided her subsistence as proxies of our employer. We used only one bedroom since during the day we were out of the house, either at the office or at the Carolina House where we continued to take our meals and which we made into our headquarters.

At this juncture, a way of life without activity and combined with the knowledge that I was not earning my salary, was unpleasant to me. In spite of that, however, I concluded that I was in the meantime fortunate to have subsistence which many young folks had lost because they had been dismissed from their positions. The Americans showed themselves yet again to be a noble people in that those employers who could continue to pay the personnel which they no longer needed, particularly when such young people responded to the call of the fatherland and bore arms for it.

---

55 George C. Baurmeister was listed as a merchant in Charleston as early as 1851, and as consul by 1856. His name disappears from Charleston newspapers after the spring of 1861.

With all dispatch and energy the Confederate States organized the army and the defenses of the country which was made easier because of the enthusiasm of the people and the expectation of each born Southerner to make sacrifice with treasure and blood for the fatherland. Regular troops were recruited for one year with good wages. They were commanded by officers who had resigned from the United States Army. These soldiers mostly served as garrison troops for important points and defense positions. In addition, the previously mentioned militia companies all gathered to also participate in the action. Many of these were also mobilized and sent to the separate armies which had been constituted. For the time being, however, there was no use for them.

The Charleston Zouave Cadets, no little enthused to punish Yankees, found no satisfaction of their desires and continued for the time being in their peaceful drills so that for me there was no danger in remaining a member of the unit. Along with the interest in conviviality which membership or particularly drilling afforded me, I thought with heavy heart about the possible separation from the association when I was compelled by matter of reason to do so. I had no desire to be shot to death, even though I was committed to the cause of the South.

The opposing armies, prepared for attack and defense, began their murderous activities. The Confederates, without a doubt consisting of better and more courageous elements because the best sons of the country entered the fray with the warmest affection for their fatherland and with a sense of defending their good rights and homes, while the Unionists consisted of recruited foreigners, unemployed backwoodsmen and proletariats. The South had some success at Harper's Ferry, Manassas and Bull Run which emboldened its armies to march into enemy territory. [56] At Gettysburg in Pennsylvania, the South wrested another victory but in the face of consolidated enemy forces had to retire to Virginia. [57] During all of this, soldiers of the United States landed along the coast at different places, places which had very little or no fortifications. There they built their bases from

---

56 Manassas and Bull Run refer to the same battle, which was fought in July 1861.
57 The Battle of Gettysburg, fought in July 1863, was a Union victory, not a Southern one.

which they could further operate. In that manner, they took possession of several islands close to Charleston, inhabitants of which, sometimes without possessions given over to the enemy, fled to the relative safety of Charleston itself. [58]

In the Carolina House, we had many such refugees; and our good Mrs. Finney likely fed many through their impoverishment. The evening conversations were solely focused on the events of the day. Feelings ran high because of the bloody events, over won and lost battles and over what the future might bring. The ladies developed activities which for them had been demeaning, namely the production of cloth, of socks and stockings, of underwear and such for the wounded and for soldiers on the march.

Every moment used for pleasure or for musing appeared to be a theft or a crime against the fatherland. As the emergency worsened, the women then took up the professions of men, if their replacement was in the least sufficient, so that the men could take up weapons. They offered up their last jewelry to their country so that with the revenue from it their defenders could have some small amenities.

Because the sons and daughters of the Confederate States were in general willing to sacrifice, they suffered little financial distress. Had they been able to carry on free trade with foreign countries, they could have continued for years and without a doubt would have succeeded. Means for acquiring men and material for prosecuting the war were for a time available to them; however, they finally had to succumb because there were no means to replace men lost to death, wounds and capture and because they were cut off from the outside world without the possibility to get the supplies needed for the war and for commerce. Their assumption of the position of blacks toward whites forbade them in principle to send blacks into the field against armed whites.

In the summer of 1861, the beginning of the first period of suffering which influenced me with sympathy and great interest for the unfolding events which, however, caused me no material inconvenience. I was, however, visited by another great evil. I suddenly fell ill with typhus

---

58   Union forces took control of Beaufort and its nearby sea islands in late 1861.

and was suddenly fettered to the bed and to the little house in which we lived. Loneliness overcame me. My brother, who was very lovingly concerned for my recovery, had to be away to tend to business and that for the greater part of each day. The mulatto who was our housekeeper was a inadequate nurse and servant and was even less adept at providing the conversation which I strongly desired. Nevertheless, she brought good medical assistance which finally brought the desired recovery and the emancipation from the deadly imprisonment. The good Mrs. Finley sent daily provisions which were necessary for my physical wellbeing, and she cared in the utmost for my welfare. In addition, neighbors whom I did not know at all took interest in me and provided me with mountains of delicacies and medications, actions which were not merely of an individual nature but appear to be a part of the American character that at the first sign of illness he spring to the aid of the one in distress. I have experienced this many times on my own person. It can therefore be declared that in such a country real distress, which is either overcome or mitigated, rarely occurs.

As a convalescent, I received visits from acquaintances and from individuals among my comrades insofar as they could get furlough. The Zouave Cadets had been in the meantime and to their great joy put on active duty. They had been ordered to a very pleasant, comfortable and duty of little danger to Castle Pinckney where they were to watch an interred group of Northern prisoners. The description of this interesting duty awakened in me the longing to rejoin my company, which I, however, at the time could not do because of my health condition.

Chapter 8

Sullivan's Island

After I had been to that point rejuvenated so that I could leave the house and enjoy the golden freedom, I was ordered to seek better air for the strengthening of my health, and so I moved for a few weeks to Sullivan's Island. My brother accompanied me there, spending the evenings and Sundays with me, traveling into town each morning and returning in the afternoon. In this way, I could dispense with my business duties, for good or for bad, or at least easily take care of my duties. This circumstance created no problems for me. My stay on Sullivan's Island offered me a pleasant diversion after the long house arrest. In the fresh sea air I found the hoped-for strengthening and my raging appetite could hardly be stilled. We had found excellent quarters and meals in a simple, very honest family in whose circle the evenings passed pleasantly with conversation, including card games and chess. The lady, a born Alsatian, took her young patient very seriously and found it an honor to take good care of me and to feed out, and to speak "dütsch" with me which in this case put me in a bit of a dilemma because it was difficult for me to understand my own mother tongue. I took a great interest in the house and the yard dwellers, including the children and the numerous fowl for whose feeding I alone was responsible. For a change, the splitting of wood, which for them was a strange activity for a young gentleman, served to strengthen my muscles and to amuse my fellow house guests.

Our dwelling lay just behind Fort Moultrie and next to the parade ground associated with it. At that time, an engaged soldier provided me with interesting diversion with access to the various exercises on the grounds and the heavy cannons in the fort itself.

The west side of the island, which was overrun with Charlestonians who wanted to catch the sea breeze, had few particularly worthy points of interest. There were several churches and a grand hotel along with the aforementioned Fort Moultrie, at the entrance to which was a monument and grave of an Indian chief who had died in prison who had been feared and pursued for a long time because of the gruesome acts which he had committed against the white settlers until he was brought here under security. [59] In spite of the sandy soil, lush vegetation dominates the island, including palms, pear and other fruit trees, aloes, camellias, oleanders, etc. These offer, between the flat-roofed houses and their gardens, a pleasant tropical view.

The greatest attraction and worth which the island offered were the excellent beaches on the ocean side with their broad, flat and hard surfaces which the pounding of the waves had created. The beaches were not only excellent for swimming but also for promenading at low tide. Here, on the very edge of an endless world sea, under the influence of its clear waters, with its pure sweet air and with a full view of mighty nature, was a wonderful place to recover. It brought health to the sick and the infirm and quickened the healthy.

If in the earlier happy days the view of the sea was bustling with a brisk commerce of ships, among them the colorfully decorated freighters and the numerous white sails of the pilot ships and the fishing boats, it was now quite different. The gravity of the times made itself known even in the sublime peace. No vessel in the service of Mercury showed itself far and wide. At the most, there were solitary fishing boats up close to the shore under the protection of the fort, boats which provided Charleston and the island with excellent fish of all sorts.

The gulls hovered as always over the waves and played the perky game as in days past as they carried their treasures before our eyes and then away.

---

59 Osceola, a Seminole warrior, was brought to Fort Moultrie as a captive in 1838. He died there and is buried outside the fort.

The picture was, however, afflicted; and its otherwise beautiful and sublime motif was compelled to pique the eye of the observer.

To wit, there were manifest at a distance of several miles the various large ships of war which made up the blockade squadron which watched the harbor of Charleston and impeded all commerce between the city and the outside world, thereby denying the city and the entire country their sustentation by which they had become great and without which they must wither. They lay there unmoved, the ironclads, the sailing ships, the gunboats, threatening all who would dare come too close to them. They were, however, themselves not yet ready to commence an attack on the batteries of the fortified coast. Nor were they inclined to engage the strong forts and the harbor entrance well guarded with old ships and torpedoes. These stable but swimming monsters lay mute and soundless across from one another, each on his guard with proud frowardness for the opportunity to fulfill its purpose.

From the beaches of Sullivan's Island, one could get an overview of the harbor defenses. On the other side of the strait which connected the Bay of Charleston with the ocean these through the salient formed narrows lay the almost treeless and plantless Morris Island made up mostly of dunes. It ranged to the south along the coast as Sullivan's Island did to the north; it was, however, arrayed in lush vegetation. Both were separated from the mainland by a water-covered silt plain which built a natural protection of the latter which, even in the hands of the enemy, would hinder his being able to reach the mainland through the morass.

Morris Island with its sand provided the best material for its batteries which had been erected on various points on the island and hidden among the dunes. The island allowed only a dismal view which was only interrupted by a lighthouse with no function.

Between these two islands rose, completely dominating the entrance to the harbor, the majestic Fort Sumter built over many years at considerable cost since the foundation first had to be sunk and make to which other material which had to be transport would be affixed. Like a red boulder it rose up, visible from afar, out of the waves. Its resilience was put on display by the attack on the 12th and the 13th of

April with the dull glaze of the threatening cannons popping out of the ports on various levels.

Landward to the west was the elongated city of Charleston with its many steeples surrounded by the Cooper and the Ashley the background. Before the city, lay Castle Pinkney coming up out of the harbor basin. This now had for me a special interest. There my company trained and had authority. There I saw my comrades with their red caps with their bayonets glistening in the sun, walking their posts at the edge of the fort. There I affixed with love my gaze and my entire longing.

Chapter 9

Peace in War

After a few weeks on Sullivan's Island, I was completely recovered and returned in October of 1861 to Charleston. The work which was left behind for me was quickly finished because there was little business so that I was completely free of it. The state of affairs and the limited prospect of things getting better caused my employer to decide not to return, which he had intended for his work. In addition, the execution of such a plan to return to Charleston would have been extremely difficult, if not almost impossible, since we were completely cut off from the world.

Letters and news from Europe and the North reached us from the western states where the cordon to that point could not be so thoroughly laid down. Also, individual travelers succeeded in getting through to us by way of this uncomfortable and time consuming means, so that one remained at least a bit informed about what was happening in the world.

The conditions in the Confederacy had not changed much. There was daily and constant hope that England and France would intervene. Spirits were high with the success of our arms on the land, this in spite of lost battles which resulted in the loss of ever more coastal territory. There were still enough means and material to wage war as well as an adequate supply of manpower which attacked the enemy with fire and with a disregard for death. We were unhappy when the government could not use them all at once. The enthusiasm and the courage to sacrifice, if they did not increase, nevertheless remained very high.

In contrast, one became accustomed to the current state of the war which brought about austerity in many things and began again to take pleasure in the simpler things as far as this was possible.

My position and the attendant income remained the same for me. It would have been almost impossible to find another position and income. In this respect, I was one of the lucky ones who for the time being did not have to concern himself with these matters. It would have been extremely painful for me to have again become a burden to my brother who had made so many sacrifices for me and who also had for the time being no possibility to leave the country.

The situation in which I had no opportunity to make myself useful and the lack of activity could not be endured for very long. I was now completely well. The joy of military drills and the safety of the current assignment which my company had accepted finally brought that long hidden desire and choice to report for active service. So, on a beautiful fall day, I stood fully equipped for my military activities. The daily rudder boat and sail boat traffic between the city and Castle Pinkney brought me and my friend Laitenberger, who was in the same situation, not wanting to take his hide to market, but who was, nevertheless, won over by my example and was, at least provisionally, willing to participate as a latecomer to Castle Pinkney and the headquarters of the Zouave Cadets.

As the boat commanded by a corporal, who was our comrade, quietly glided toward its goal, there crept into my feelings both joyous and anxious expectations as to whether I was constituted for the completely different way of life which lay before me. I was filled with the hope and fear as well as curiosity and anxiety about the real life of the soldier.

As the boat approached the wharf, the guard posted there called the sergeant of the guard; and after he made the call, it echoed through the guards on the upper level of the fort and arrived at the guard house. The sergeant of the guard appeared and allowed the boat to land. Several comrades appeared with him on the landing and greeted us with great joy, with however a little kidding for being "shirkers" of duty. They were all glad to see us and glad to have us among them, raising their number by two.

We received a similar greeting from Captain Chichester and the three lieutenants. We were obliged to report first to the former who made us familiar with the main aspect of our duties, of the necessary discipline and such; but of most importance was the friendship of comrades.

The stalwart order and the joyful compliance with the commands impressed me. The hearty obligingness of the Zouave brothers made me feel at home, so that I immediately felt myself to be comfortable and gave myself over to the duties with body and with soul.

Castle Pinckney lies about a mile or two kilometers from Charleston on a small island in the harbor basin or actually in the middle of the mouth of the Cooper River. The island is overgrown with tall reeds and is under water during high tide so that it cannot be trespassed by foot nor landed on by boat. The island has no beach; however, it has rich oyster banks which are covered at high tide but are dry at low tide. There the indigenous species lead the amphibian life. On the south point of the swampy but always green island lies the castle for the protection of the inner harbor and the city. The castle is built of solid masonry which has been cleaned and painted many times. On three sides, the ten meter high wall constitutes a half circle and to the north a straight wall. The casemates were located within this half circle and were covered with masonry work and earth, building a flat surface on which cannons could be stationed. The outer wall, approximately one meter thick, had a height of approximately two meters extended out as a parapet and encircled and protected the ramp with steps leading up to the quadrangle with yet other steps leading from there to the enclosing wall which was supported with large building blocks which sloped outward. The north side of the fort was completed by a building the outer wall of which had the only door which served to provide access to the fort. From inside, there were several doors and windows which look out on a piazza which was connected to the quadrangle. This two-story building contained the barracks or living quarters for officer and of the men as well as the rooms of provisions and tools.

Charleston photographer George S. Cook took this photograph of the Charleston Zoauve Cadets at Castle Pinckney in September 1861. Library of Congress.

In the middle of the quadrangle encircled by bare walls was a small structure which served as a place to forge bullets in case that became necessary. Beside it was a tall pole on which the Confederate flag waved. From the entry archway closed off with a strong door was the access to the guard house.

The part of the island next to the fort was heightened by earth brought in and laid dry and ringed with palisades and thereby formed a larger outer quadrangle which was used as a drill ground. On this plaza there was a structure which was not used but which was intended as a small light house. Next to this structure was an even smaller house intended as a living quarters but which was used to store materials.

A broad stone path on which one could walk around the fort went around the half rotunda, of which, however, only at little was above the level of high tide so that the spring tide quite often covered it. This path, on the south side, ran out like a wharf where our boat and its gear were stored in a shed and from which all traffic to and from the city and the island was conducted.

So was the appearance and the construction of Castle Pinckney which would serve an entirely different purpose than the one for which it was constructed. Its garrison had never been this big and had never consisted of so many diverse elements as now.

At first, the fort held 160 prisoners of the United States Army or as one generally called them "Yankees." Approximately sixty of these were officers who were sent here because of the good quarters. Most of them were Americans and for the most part educated men. By contrast, the rest, non-commissioned officers and simple soldiers, consisted of all possible nationalities and characters, among them fellows who were raw and new, fellows who were kept in line by the strict discipline and from whom even their comrades separated themselves.For the purpose of taking in these prisoners, the fort had to be altered. All of the heavy ordnance was taken apart, and the parts were stacked in the outer quadrangle except for one twenty-four pounder which remained in the middle of the ramp with the purpose of giving alarm of danger in an emergency. The casemates were altered into cells by sealing entrances and openings by opening doors and windows, and by covering the floors and by furnishing them with places to sleep, tables and benches. The non-commissioned officers and common soldiers were quartered here. The officers who were prisoners lived in an entire wing of the barracks while we were assigned the other wing of the same barracks.

As stated, our company had been given the duty to guard these prisoners. It was an interesting, comfortable and easy duty. We were approximately sixty men strong, consisting of one captain, one lieutenant, two second lieutenants, one staff sergeant, five sergeants and a corporal and forty-four enlisted men, but as the Americans amicably say "privates." In addition, there were two colored servants who played the drum and fife and who in addition had to do the more menial tasks in the kitchen and such, which for whites appeared to be improper.

The four officers lived together in one room, and the rest of us had to spread ourselves in the rooms which remained vacant. Admittedly,

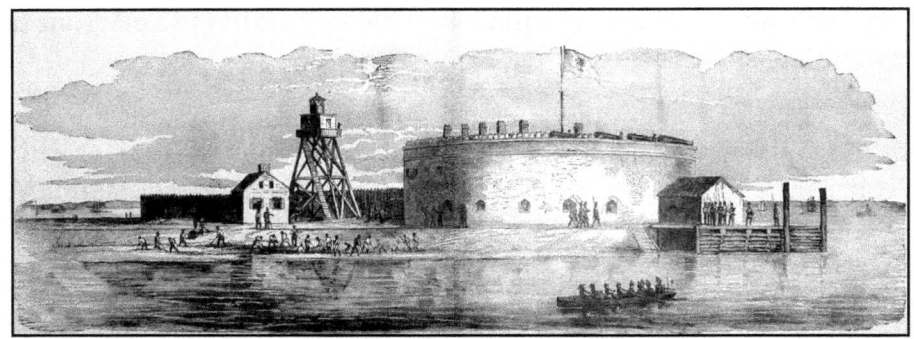

This image of Castle Pinckney was published in Frank Leslie's Illustrated Newspaper *in 1861. National Park Service, Open Parks Network.*

we lived in close quarters but were nevertheless very comfortable and merry. The beds, consisting of good mattresses, pillows made of sea grass and a full blanket provided by the state, were by two, one on top of the other, placed on the walls of the room, in each case broken up by a room which was filled with wall lockers in which each person could store his service materials and his private stuff. In the middle was a large table surrounded by wooden chairs which were assigned to each man. In this room there prevailed great order and cleanliness, both by order and by the inclination of each man.

Every such association had their own name such as Ripley Mess or Beauregard Mess. When I joined "the rebels," I associated myself with the Cave of the Rebels. By the otherwise prevailing harmony and friendship, a certain particularism emerged in the individual messes, insofar as each declared his to be the best. Each one was by private initiative determined to ensure that his table was well provided. It was routine that anyone who went to town brought back what the provost could not provide: fruit, cake, fowl, etc.

In truth, however, the state also provided for us in a fatherly manner. In addition to a substantial wage—if I am not mistaken, it was fifteen dollars for a private paid out in paper money which lost little value during the period when coins were available—everything was delivered which we needed for our service and our sustenance, just not our uniforms which each of us already had: bed, coat, wash pans, soap, hand towels, eating utensils and wares, and "last but not least" excellent and nutritious food which consisted of daily fresh meat, bread, vegetables, potatoes, rice, fish, legumes and syrup added to which there was served nearly every evening pancakes and hominy. At breakfast, at noon and at supper we came in goose step with our plates and tin cups to the kitchen window and received from the hand of the provost, who understood the art of cuisine and led the kitchen, the solid and liquid treasures. He was assisted daily by two comrades and two Negroes. The officers received the same fare as we. They did not have to get it themselves, however. It was brought to their quarters by the Negroes.

The prisoners were fed a simpler but nevertheless good fare. They received, in addition to the necessary cooking utensils and material, their rations for the entire group, delivered during a sequence of days outside. They had to prepare the rations themselves which lessened their awkward inactivity which they certainly experienced. The little house on the quadrangle which was for forging bullets was outfitted as a kitchen where they prepared meals for themselves and their officers. The officers enjoyed the greatest possible freedom. They could engage in conversations with us in the outer quadrangle. For walks, they could also use the stone walkway which went around the fort. They could tarry on the wharf. It is here that they liked to spend most of their time and pass the time with fishing.

It was a bit worse for the common soldiers. They were not allowed to leave the quadrangle inside the fort, except when it became necessary for them to seek certain locations outside the fort. In such cases, they were accompanied by a guard. The entertained themselves with all kinds of games, gymnastics, boxing, etc. Many of them busied themselves with various kinds of activities such as woodcarving, sketching and such. The necessary materials were provided to them by us. For each casemate, one man a day was singled out for the duty of cleaning. The entire group was responsible for sweeping out the quadrangle each day. One half hour after reveille everything was worked over and had to be in order.

Prisoners of war posed in front of Casemate No. 1, which they have named the "Hotel de Zoauve." Library of Congress.

These prisoners of war at Castle Pinckney were members of the 69th New York Infantry Regiment. Library of Congress.

From tattoo to reveille or from sundown to sunup, they were locked in their casemates. Even the officers cold not leave their rooms without permission or without the accompaniment of a guard.

At reveille, at noon and at tattoo, they all had to appear at muster so that their presence could be established. For the rest of the time they were left to themselves but were carefully watched.

That was the monotonous way of life for the prisoners. In reference to our own, I have only touched on the housing and the food; but we also had duties to fulfill, duties which all members without exception carried out with diligence and officiousness as if it were air and love.

The captain as commander of the post had clothed himself in a certain dignity which stood him well. With the prisoners as with all official relations, his dignity showed to his advantage because he understood how to maintain an exemplary discipline which in no wise offended us. He remained, despite his distinguished and responsible position, a comrade, friend and associate.

Likewise, the lieutenants continued this friendly attitude. The first lieutenant was elected to this rank only because of the great effort which he had made in creating the company, because of his age and because he was a well-respected advocate. He certainly possessed none of the competencies which related to the art of war, this in spite of the fact that he put out a lot of effort in the matter. There were funny episodes and outbursts when he had a mishap in commanding the company exercises. He was, however, a good fellow; and when he had dried the sweat of anxiety off his brow, he then made up for his mistakes by inviting all of the boys to something special and put himself through the mill. In such instances, the disorder which had occurred was discussed; and he was instructed by the common soldier in matters such as how the commands should have been given in order that such mistakes could be avoided. Such instruction our lieutenant also took without protest.

Both of the second lieutenants were competent officers by virtue of their training at military school. Their function like that of the first lieutenant consisted of the rotational service duties of the officer of the day. As such, they had to conduct the muster and the inspection of the prisoners and to oversee the watch.

The hero and the most favored of the entire company was the staff sergeant and secretary who was only twenty years old. In spite of his youth, he was the moderating member of the company who, when not in charge, was nevertheless busy, interested mostly in the welfare of the company, in their comradely demeanor and in the relations between officers and men. He was not only the middle point in his rank, but he was also the middle point in official and personal interactions. He was respected by both superiors and those of lower rank, and he was to them respectively kind. He was primarily to be thanked that there came from the top no pride of rank or no violations and from the bottom no disrespect or dissatisfaction could enter in. He ensured that each one knew his assigned duties and carried them out with pleasure. He understood the correct balance between discipline and camaraderie. He also knew the proper time to pay attention to matters.

Many would laugh at such rapport and declare it to be unpractical; but as difficult as it may seem, it existed in its bonny and homely form, without any disruption. It should probably be considered that no one was compelled to be a member of this company but had volunteered. Every superior was freely elected and usually unanimously on their record of service for the company and on their talents.

The older brother of the staff sergeant was also a sergeant, a fine and diligent lad, who had, for instance, trained me.

The activities of the company primarily consisted of guard duty which meant that for each private given the limited number of members the duty came around every three days. In light of this duty which in a certain way was exhausting, little time and concern was given to drilling. Usually, only about two hours a day were devoted to drills. The remainder of the time belonged to us which we passed according to our whims. We only had to remain in earshot of the drum beats.

Each morning at eight o'clock the watch was set by a sergeant, a corporal and twelve men. They were inspected by the officer of the day who took command from the retiring watch for the next twenty-four hours.

In front of the prisoners, the watch was formed up, the muskets were loaded and a number of bullets were distributed. In addition, loudly and quite audibly the instructions, repeated daily, were given. These instructions informed all how the watch commander and the guards were to relate to the prisoners and that if there were to be any suspicious incident on the part of a prisoner, there would be repercussions and the watch commander would be called for. An attack or an attempt to flee on the part of prisoners would give the guards the authority to shoot to kill or to stab with the bayonet.

Fortunately none of us was ever in the situation or the danger to have to execute this order. It may be that the daily reminder of the consequences contributed to the fact that the prisoners remained peaceful and acquitted themselves according to the prescribed rules.

The guard room which was always handed over and found clean and tidy contained a plank bed which could be converted into a comfortable den in the evening with a mattress and a blanket. It also contained a table, several benches, cabinets and a stand for the weapon which had to be immediately ready at all times for the anticipated call to action. The door of the guard house opened out onto the arched entrance of the fort, with several windows looking out on the inner quadrangle.

Four sentinels, who after two hours of guard duty were relieved, were placed at their respective positions.

Sentinel number one was responsible for protecting the guard house to guard the entrance so that no unauthorized person could enter the fort or leave it. He was also responsible for notifying the other sentinels of the approach of the commander of the officer of the day so that they could present their arms to him as he passed.

Sentinel number two guarded the inner quadrangle, the prisoners who walked there, the casemates and the barracks which could be seen. During the day, this was of no consequence; nights, however, every sound and every movement in the quadrangle had to be reconnoitered.

There were enough instances to cause him to call out. The prisoners appeared to have made a sport out of it by challenging the vigilance of the sentinel and keeping the sergeant moving because nearly the entire night they banged on their cell doors to be taken out. The sentinel would call for the sergeant. As he approached, he would be challenged and questioned. After he had identified himself, he was shown the affected casemate in which contained the needy prisoner. The sergeant opened the casemate, escorted the author of the disturbance out and then again locked the door. The challenge of the sentinel was again repeated, and as they approached sentinel number 1, the challenge was again made. The entire process was repeated as the prisoner escorted by the sergeant returned. Because of just one man, many words had to be lost. The watchwords had to be given with a strong voice. The footsteps rang out. The keys rattled on the keychain. The heavy doors clanged to. It was a heathen din the entire night through which a tired soldier could get used to over time. When the one was pacified, the same maneuver began again on the other side. The poor sergeant and the guards who had to escort these mischief-makers had almost no rest.

Sentinel three went around the fort on the parapet from which point he could look over the outer walls, the island, the nearby region, the large surface of the water, and the drawn-out city of Charleston, among other things. Because of this, the wide view and the changes during the day, the sentinel post was the most interesting, but not a hazard-free post. The wall which pitched outward and which was relatively narrow demanded by the walk around extreme caution and no fear of heights, so that one did not fall into the deep, particularly at that place where the barrel of the cannon standing on the ramp and jutting out over the parapet had to be crossed. No few of us were able to fulfill this duty. For me it was the best duty were it not for storms and rain which were quite common here. In such cases, the danger was even greater. In such cases, the sentinel was allowed to post himself on the top step of the stairs which led up to the parapet. From here he was at least able to keep an eye on the landing spot which was the most important part of the fort.

This sentinel had to simultaneously ensure the communication between the sentinel on the wharf and the one in the guard room since the distance between those two was too great.

Sentinel number 4 was stationed on the wharf and had to oversee both the officers among the prisoners and the possible landing or departure of the boats which could only take place when the watch commander was called and sanctioned the landing or departure.

Those were the places and the tasks of the sentinels which were manned with the highest sense of duty and which were taken up again after four hours of rest. When the morning hour marking the end of the watch arrived and the muskets were fired to ensure that there was no accident, then we had two days of rest before us, rest which was interrupted only by short drills.

Sweet idleness was never onerous for me despite the regimentation of our lives and the cramped quarters. There was always enough to do and to talk about. Cleaning and maintaining our uniforms and rooms which were inspected every Sunday took a good portion of our time. We also entertained ourselves with reading, with games and with gymnastics in the outer quadrangle. In addition, we told stories and entertained ourselves in various rooms or storage facilities on the ramp, at the wharf, etc. A boat was manned almost daily and sent to the nearby oyster bank at the time of low tide when the bank was laid dry. The boat was then pulled onto dry land and the best oysters were gathered. We built a fire from material which we had carried with us and roasted the best of our catch. The roasted oysters died and the shells opened; the contents could be enjoyed without the slightest effort. In this manner, the freshest oysters were prepared, half baked, without losing their jelly like character, and tasted best prepared this way.

When the tide returned and lifted our boat, we returned, laden with our rich treasure, to the fort. There the harvest was divided equally between the various messes, usually eaten together in joyous conviviality.

Sundays, as was the custom in America, one had to abstain from work and loud games. There was an inspection of all equipment and rooms. Midmornings and afternoons there was a church service in which the captain or the first lieutenant, both particularly godly men, read from Scripture and functioned as preachers.

On the day on which had for the second time been relieved of guard duty, almost every sixth day, we were allowed to visit the city. This leave was always used. This was again a nice change. It was just as much fun to sail or row over and to return in like manner in the evening. Quite often, extraordinary things were purchased and shared to the delight of those who had to stay behind.

I spent one such quite enjoyable day with my brother and in the Carolina House where I was royally served because of my uniform and because of my alleged patriotism as a Confederate soldier. I allowed my good friends to believe that and had no reason to tell them that I embraced this service not as a sacrifice but as a joy. I had to explain a lot about our life and about the enemy prisoners who were imagined to be manlike wild animals or at the least warped individuals.

My business left me lacking nothing, and I had nothing to lack from my salary which I drew and saw as the foundation for a large fortune of which I dreamed from time to time.

Yes, and when I on a silent night made my rounds on the parapet, there came to me thoughts of longings, hopes and fears. I would think of the tug of my old place of birth and home and all of the love which was there, which grew in my heart and went with me everywhere. Would I ever have the good fortune to see them again, to once again join their intimate circle? I was then filled with the hope that I had to fight and to struggle to achieve this goal. But how? Then the worries came again; the fear of how I could succeed in this now difficult time. I had to earn my daily bread, not to speak of the means to achieve such a costly pleasure.

All around me was silent stillness. Only the waves lapped at the feet of my high perch as the other sentinels quietly paced out their rounds. From the city, now and again, the chimes of the bells rang out, bringing the hour of our relief. There was no light and nothing to capture my attention.

My joyful comrades were sleeping and could not lighten my thoughts. All had been done for that. I had to work it out myself and busy myself with my longings, my hopes and my future.

But no! Not yet! The possibility of a happy future I had not yet discovered. Something scurried across the ramp along the parapet and brought me into reality, into the present.

"Halt! Who goes there?"

"The commanding officer of the sentinels!"

"Announce yourself commanding officer of the sentinels and give the password!"

With presented bayonet I awaited my esteemed captain until he had climbed the parapet and had identified himself with the password. Such a surprise foray which helped test the sentinels was quite common and could only be approved; however, just now I was irritated at the interruption which had intruded on my process of thought on earthly treasures and satisfaction. I was further irrigated that I was almost blindsided. Why did this fellow, just now, have to interrupt my daydreams? For that reason, I wanted to trick him. The opportunity and the place were ideal, and the right and the might were mine with the help of a loaded gun in my hand.

The captain had to appear before my bayonet. He gave the password and was recognized. I presented myself to the commander of the guard. I allowed him to about face. With dignity he stepped upon the stairs and was away; and I with dignity went in the opposite direction. As he took his time going down, I arrived at the other side of the fort. When today I admit that it was my esteemed commander, that was not my position in those days. I again challenged him, and the preliminaries were carried out again according to military custom. The captain had to make the round again and prove to me that he was not a fleeing or spying enemy. I presented myself, and we again separated. You would perhaps like to accuse me of a shiftless act, even a neglect of duty. Now you can give me some company, old friend, as a vessel for my day dreams. It was my pleasure to distance myself just enough from my commander so that I could no longer recognize him so that I would have to convince myself of his identity. I did this five or six times around the airy heights until the sergeant of the guard became aware of the situation through the duel of commands and came to find out about the situation. He found his captain here in a somewhat irritated mood on an involuntary promenade and accompanied him without protest to the barracks.

The next day I expressed to the captain my regret that my sense of duty and my ill-tempered shortsightedness had been induced by the boring walks. I could not have given criticism if he had accused me of a little chicanery. We, however, remained good friends and laughed about it. He did not test my sentinel duty again, at least not when it was on the parapet.

Soon the corporal appeared with my replacement, and I gladly exchanged places, the parapet for the guard house and sleep. Stretched out on the flat bed, I dreamed of riches and great treasures as prerequisites to earthly happiness and as a means to satisfaction of all wishes and longings. I was just about to return to my home country, but the shabby corporal would not suffer it. He demanded of me that I should take a damn Yankee outside. When I returned, everything had passed away and had disappeared.

Such scenes and such moods crossed through my life. When, however, the next day the sun again laughed and when I was surrounded by the expressed joy of my comrades, then everything was serene in my being. It was then that I lived in the present: a youth with no consequences out of which I, in the middle of war duty, joy and pleasure created.

They were all fine, jolly fellows, my comrades. There was not a rowdy sheep among them which disturbed the harmony of the corps or which needed to be disciplined with banishment. I recall no case of infighting which says a lot about young men in that number with different characters and with different ranks.

In counterpoise, there was no lack of jokesters and clowns who had the talent with their inexhaustible humor to keep all boredom and all dark moods at bay. We were not lacking in diligent and intelligent people who contributed to edifying and learned conversations through lectures and speeches. There were also those of less intelligence but with good natures who were the foils for those who were tricksters.

We had in my friend Laitenberger and excellent comrade who contributed a lot to our common amusement. His open demeanor, his lively spirit and his broken English, at least strongly accented with French pronunciation, make up front a highly inviting impression. He was already married and had left his "Madame" in Charleston as was the case with many of our number. His first youth was behind him, but he was the most loyal of husbands and a diligent soldier who stood his post like a statue and marched around with stiff legs in parade step. He followed protocols and orders to the last detail and would not deviate from them for the world.

It was a great pleasure to observe him as he ate. He would put each dish in a particular bowl which had to stand on a particular place. When the rest of us were already finished, he would have just finished his preparation by putting a table cloth at his place and artfully folding his napkin. He would then begin his frugal meal, divided into several servings which would be consumed as an elaborate dinner or supper and eaten with relish.

He had brought himself an entire trousseau of clothes, stuff for the table, eating and washing instruments, just about all of the different things which served as amenities and comforts. His wife was kept busy with his large demand for laundry, etc.

His attention to his appearance demanded the utmost care as well as a lot of time. He shaved himself daily; save for his Henri quatre, which along with the hair on his head enjoyed a special maintenance. [60] It was waxed, coiffed, turned and brushed until each hair had its intended place. This raven-black hair and beard were his entire pride. Woe unto him who dared assault his hair or beard, which happened often enough with or without intent. Our friend, particularly my friend, could become

---

60 The *Henri quatre* is a beard that surrounds the mouth, connecting the mustache with a short beard.

very angry, by Jove! There would thunder English, French and German curses on the head of the perpetrator. The mirror, the waxing and the brushing had to again endure an hour of restoration.

In this manner we spent several months after I was transferred to Castle Pinckney in a regular change between duty and freedom and in very pleasant company until an incident created a major change in our way of life.

On morning at muster a prisoner was missing which brought the entire fort, particularly the captain who carried the responsibility, into uproar and embarrassment. The evening before, he was allegedly present, which, however, could not have been the case. When his name had been called, someone else must have answered for him. The officer in charge of the muster must have failed to get the correct count and determine the identity of everyone. The missing prisoner was not to be found in the interior of the fort and could have only gotten by the sentinels in a manner which had at the time not been revealed. The entire area of the fort, every corner, and the entire small island was searched. The island was sailed around with boats. The deserter was still missing; and the manner of his disappearance, the direction which he went, and where he was remained a mystery.

The matter had to be reported to the high command in Charleston. The rest of us never heard or became aware of the accusations which our captain over this incident had to endure. If the captain as commander, the duty guards and the officer of the guard, who was charged with dereliction of duty, carried the responsibility for the affair, then, however, the honor of the entire company was involved and every member of it felt the imprudence which was caused by but a few and which was a dormant disgrace.

As a consequence of this an oppressive mood crept in and formed the only matter of discussion of the most recent occurrence, the consideration of all possibilities how the prisoner could have escaped and where he might be. The strictness and the watchfulness toward the other prisoners were intensified because at least some of them must have been aware of the intentions of the escapee. Many of the freedoms which they had enjoyed were taken away. The old rule that one locks the stall when the horse is stolen was put in play here.

After two days, the puzzle was solved. The deserter had been found on Sullivan's Island and taken into custody. He admitted to the following:

He had planned the escape attempt for several weeks. Daily, he had made use of a somewhat extended stay in a place with privacy to make the necessary preparations. For this purpose, the wisenheimer slipped in and out of a place which cannot be described and there had gone to the backside of a little house which was out of sight and pulled the necessary boards off the house and with them constructed a primitive, dangerous raft for which he had gathered the necessary material over a period of time. On the appointed day, which he had reckoned with the moon and the tide, just before the evening muster, he used just the right moment to pass the entrance without being seen by the sentinel. He gained his hiding place; and as darkness settled in, he pulled his raft over swamp and reeds to a protected cove where the raft floated.

During this entire process, with trained endurance, strength and thought processes, coupled together with daring thoughts as well as the tide and the dark night and by means thereof, he had hoped to let his vessel be driven into the open sea, where, once the light of day had broken, he would get the attention of the of the blockade fleet and be taken aboard.

All of these different moments were favorable enough for the success of the plan which had thus far suffered no disruption. The fugitive had successfully gotten out. The sentinel had not seen him in the darkness and partly because of his hiding in the tall reeds through which he transported his raft. The noise created in the reeds did not get through to the sentinel, and he could begin his trip by water. He also had good fortune with the current of the tide which pushed him out; however, the circumstance that the raft was difficult to steer, that the connection to the open sea between Sullivan's Island and Morris Island was very narrow and that he could not exactly hold course on the strait, had misdirected his vessel on the coast of the first island, from which area he could not easily distance himself.

During these efforts, surprised by daylight, he hid himself on the island in order to renew the attempt the next night. He was, however, discovered and taken into custody.

Explanation of this disappearance in no way contributed to the justification and rehabilitation of our company. To the contrary, a dereliction of duty in the guarding of prisoners was confirmed.

Was this the reason, or had one already had the intent for a long time; for shortly after this unfortunate incident came the order to transport the prisoners to Charleston and to house them in the jail there?

At the same time, it was determined that Castle Pinckney would again be converted into a defensive installation and that the Charleston Zouave Cadets along with another company to be transferred there were to be responsible for the maintenance of the fort and compose the garrison for the fort.

For all of us, that was a disheartening order because our way of life, until now, had been to us quite pleasant. We had even become so used to the prisoners that we viewed them and us as belonging together and we were sorry for our changed and common uncomfortable lot. The soldier must, however, obey. Some others and I in the same situation came to consider whether we should now quit our service instead of carrying out fortress duty. For me, however, such a decision was difficult given the perspective of other employment. What my comrades whom I had come to love would do I could at least attempt to do myself. I could not see a danger for my health, my life, or a wound to my honor in this new use of my strength. There was no other outside employment in view. These earnings and this position had to be taken into account. I remained with all of the rest with the loyal, jovial Zouaves.

On a certain day, a steamboat appeared; and the extraction of the prisoners took place under the escort of the entire company, save for a single sentinel. Upon landing in Charleston, we led those we were mandated to guard through the streets of the city to their new destination. Given the lively escort, the curiosity about the captured Yankees and the friendly greetings toward us by the public, it appeared that they did not hold any enmity toward us for allowing one lousy Yankee to get away. After we had made the delivery, the steamboat took us back to our posts. The fort appeared to us to be dead, eerie at the first sight of the empty rooms until we had become accustomed to this, until the rooms found their new purpose and until our fighting and work associates had moved in.

It appeared peculiar to us who were trained as infantry that we would be used to secure and garrison a fort and, in addition, that another infantry company had been appointed for this duty which we were all yet to learn. The entire artillery requires time at various points. The engagement of Castle Pinckney in a battle was quite unlikely and the service of artillery was not difficult; therefore, they did not hesitate to give us this duty.

All of us studied the craft, initially theoretically, with open eagerness. In particular, our officers had to inform themselves in detail over all the minutia. Afterward, they also had to master the practical drills. Against all expectations, things turned out well with this study so that we easily and quickly dispensed with our task.

Initially, we were busy with changing our quarters. The wing of the barracks which had been used by the captured officers contained more pleasant rooms than the part which we had used. We laid claim to the better of the rooms and left the darker rooms to our associates whom we were expecting.

We were now able to move. I got the most comfortable room with three comrades. Among them, including Laitenberger were two sons of German parents, humorously called "the Dutchman's Mess" by the rest because we had introduced the German language as obligatory in this private circle. Captain Chichester moved into the small house in the outer quadrangle after the material which was stored in it had been moved out and after it had been made more or less livable. There, separated from the comings and goings of soldiers, he quartered his lovely wife who was the pride and the joy of the entire company.

After some days, the Emerald Light Infantry moved in. As the name already implies, this was a company of Irishmen which had about the same strength as we. The company consisted mostly of older men. Judging by their estate, they were mostly craftsmen. They were all true sons of the Green Island. In age, education and character, they did not fit well with us. Dealings with them were limited to the most necessary interactions. The only advantage which they had over us was in their physical strength. This played to our advantage with the work which lay ahead.

Our captain remained the commandant and now commanded a small battalion. We, however, felt ourselves to be superior to the Emeralds in every respect and created for ourselves a certain respect and privilege. We were particularly superior in the precision and bearing in the drills where they quite wreaked often battered disarray. In spite of much effort on the part of our officers, they made little headway.

The work of reconditioning the fort was begun. For this purpose, a captain of engineering was transferred to us to oversee and to guide the work.

The walls of the casemates were demolished. The openings were widened and the furnishings were removed. The parts of the cannons which had been stored were brought up. There in the casemates they were put together and mounted. The many workmen and the already mentioned physical capacity of the Irishmen made the work for each individual easy. Everything went according to plan. Things were not too hurried so that we did not lack in free time or hours of rest.

Although not obliged, the officers regularly worked with us so that the last complaint which one could make of this business was nullified. The engineer was a master at giving orders in the correct tone and by his own engagement and thereby kept along with his inexhaustible humor the boys in good spirits.

This mechanical work did not make me mad. To the contrary, I felt healthy and satisfied. Food and sleep conferred a double pleasure. The joy of the camaraderie was, if it were possible, better than before.

Guard duty was substantially reduced by the loss of two posts on the wharf and in the quadrangle and through the number of men now available, and it was made easier as the special attention for observing was no longer necessary.

Enjoyable hours which I more often experienced based on a long special acquaintance were granted to me by the cozy evenings at the captain's, where a number of comrades regularly gathered and paid homage to the small and friendly commander's wife. The others treated me both with respect and jealousy when this attractive lady made use of the German language with me, the foreigner, or when she singled me out for some other reason. We were, as you know, old acquaintances; and I imagined that a small part of the interest which I nourished for her was valued by her.

When, after several weeks, the preliminary work had been completed, all cannons were on the ramp and in the casemates and finally mounted, and after the necessary supply of munitions had been acquired, the artillery drills and the garrison duty began.

The armament of the fort consisted of ten twenty-four pound cannons. Five stood on the ramp, and five were in the casemates. In addition, on the ramp, there was a gun of a larger caliber to be used for counterattack.

With the allocation of the men to the individual cannons, I was assigned one in a casemate where was in case of an attack by the enemy, in any case more secure because the bombs which might explode over the fort were less likely to make their destructive effect there as on the open ramp; however, it was less pleasant than under the free sky during the drills, particularly the firing of the cannon, because of the heavy air, the powder smoke which only gradually dissipated and the blast which worked severely on the eardrums.

The practical drills were eagerly carried out; and within a short time, we had so acclimated ourselves to the duty that we passed with complete satisfaction an inspection by General Ripley as it pertained to our knowledge of the parts of the cannon, the execution of the individual hand movements, quick fire and target orientation, whereas our Irish comrades, to be honest, essentially remained far behind us. [61]

This new profession, which did not mean that our infantry drills were neglected, was for us a great pleasure. Some voices were even raised in our circle to wish a battle with the Yankees to demonstrate our capabilities. Although the stay and duty in Castle Pinckney were so pleasant, the sons of Carolina were not satisfied; they wanted to actively assist their fatherland which need their service even more; however, this post could not be abandoned; and someone had to assert its presence because one indeed had to always expect and attack by the fleet or an attempt to sail into the harbor such that, if successful, Castle Pinckney would have to enter the fray and play a very important role in the defense of the city.

I still have to mention a festival that our company carried out which took place at the dedication of the big cannon which had never been used in combat.

The beautiful wife of the captain, who was often present with great interest at artillery drills and infantry drills, had declared that she was prepared to be the godmother of the cannon and to give it, as she fired it, her name. This was the unanimous wish of the men. For this purpose, a special committee was nominated to get various decorations from the city which would adorn the huge cannon on the appointed day. In so far as the movement and loading of the cannon would not be hindered, it was covered with garlands, flowers, ribbons and ties. Everything was ready for the celebration. Under the command of the first lieutenant, our company marched out in parade uniforms and muskets. (The Emeralds avoided the celebration; and we did not challenge them to come.) We surrounded the object in a half circle while the operating crew took their positions.

Then a detachment under the command of the lieutenant was sent to the quarters of the captain. A little surprise was prepared for him. He was escorted along with the dignified godmother to the proper place so that the act could be consummated.

---

61 General Roswell Sabine Ripley (1823-1887).

As inconsequential as the act was, the very successful arrangement which proved to be a surprise for our friends, provided us great pleasure. It was a sublime observance: the black instrument of death arrayed in a colorful dress and the company in full dress uniforms standing straight and proud to see that instrument so presented.

The command ensued. The loading and the orientation were likely never again carried out with such precision. The friction lanyard was placed in the vent, and the cord decorated with Confederate colors was placed in the hand of the beautiful godmother.

With great gravity the first lieutenant gave the command over to the captain who, up until that point, had remained passive. The captain took command, drew his sword, and "Fire!" billowed out of his mouth. Proud, calm and with a charming smile his new recruit carried out the order. Trembling and rebounding, the monster roared his first sound into the world, a sound which boomed as a powerful wave over the surface of the water. The company presented arms. Our black tambour beat its elegant rolls. The flag was lowered and raised three times. A sign with the name "Jane" was affixed to the candidate for baptism. The activity was ended with three cheers and with the Zouave cry: to the welfare of the cannon, to its godmother, and to the company.

For the surprise which had been prepared and for the standing ovation, the honored couple believed that they had to respond in kind, so they invited us to a super that evening of the celebration with copious and tasty delicacies from the city.

All of us were gathered there, save for those of our company to had to pull watch, who were for a portion of the time relieved to that they too could profit from the enjoyment of the evening. We were united in high spirits, thereby showing the comradely relationship between officers and privates. In spite of the close quarters and the primitive furnishings, perhaps just because of that, the entire party was in the best of spirits. Tables and benches had been brought from our own quarters. We could not complain about place settings because we had brought our own eating and drinking utensils along ourselves. The entire party was completely satisfied and entertained itself with speeches, toasts and speeches into the late hours of the night.

This company celebration was, however, at the same time the end of our military service, at least mine.

For the Confederate States of America, the situation was becoming more serious and more doubtful. The possibility of a longer war had brought the Confederate government to a directive that the militias which to this point had been independent would have to pledge themselves to active military duty for three years or until the end of the war. If these militias by the established deadline were unable to recruit the necessary number of men, then said company would be dissolved and their members, if possible with the same rank, would be taken into regiments being formed.

Our company and the company which was garrisoned with us were caught up in this mandate since the legal strength had not been reached. In such instances, the strength was further reduced by those who left the company, particularly by foreigners who were not compelled or who did not want to remain for a longer compulsory time.

In order to give the Zouaves and the Emeralds time to recruit the men which they lacked, they were ordered away from garrison duty and were replaced by a company of regular artillery.

I was thus compelled to leave the realm of interesting and playful activity, the bloodless duty of war, from the places where the terrors and sufferings of war and the worry and the distress were unknown. I had to cut myself off from happy times and youthful blood and my fine comrades whom I had come to love during the long and intimate communion, comrades with whom I had known peace in war.

As difficult as I found the separation and as I apprehended an uncertain future as it related to other employment, I did not want to obligate myself to war; and I did not want to put my life into an earthwork. We would not have been able to stay together. The Zouaves indeed attempted to complete their ranks, but there were not enough by the legal deadline; and after it had passed, the company was dissolved. The members went to other companies in which they had friends and which met the enlistment quotas. The officers and non-commissioned officers went for the most part as a unit to the new corps so that trouble could be avoided.

Everybody was scattered. They were made ardent by the impulse to fight for the sovereignty of their fatherland. They did not apprehend the loss of the easy duty which we had or of the good life together. They found their satisfaction in the stresses and dangers of war.

With but a few exceptions, I did not see them again, these humorous and lively boys. I did, however, manage to follow their fates, as far as it was possible, with friendly interest. Many of them remain on the battlefield, fallen as martyrs to their bravery. Yet more of them died of their wounds in field hospitals. Some few came home, sad because of the failure of their duty to the fatherland, a duty which they loyally carried out to the end. All of them, however, fought with courage and endurance. The news and the descriptions thereof filled me with true joy as the one and then the other had excelled in the course of a campaign with honor and with dignity.

There remains with me a pleasant memory of the joyous time I lived through, which next to the pleasure which it provided, also gave me the advantage that I found myself in excellent physical condition and good health because of a regulated lifestyle, fresh sea breeze and healthy food. I was also able to lay up a good some of money from wages and salaries because I did not have to spend money on living costs.

Portrait of William Cattell Bee (1809-1881) painted by Charles Fraser in 1848. Image courtesy of The Gibbes Museum of Art/Carolina Art Association.

Chapter 10

Promotion

I again moved into the Carolina House and entered the daily life. My director had decided had given up thought of a return because of the political and the legal situations. His business was completely phased out. Naturally, for that reason he released me from my engagement.

My limited savings, of which I was so proud and which appeared so considerable in my previous situation and imagination, would not suffice long to defray my cost of living; and I would again become a burden on my brother if I were not offered the possibility to earn something.

The following happenstance emerged, so quickly, that my worry about the future was strangled even as it arose so that I was completely spared its spawn which were boredom and moroseness.

Through a German house guest, Herr Müller, who provided this service of friendship to me and later proved to be very helpful to me, I was offered a bookkeeping position which he himself had held; he had recommended me to the owner of the respective business that I be his replacement. [62] When I was introduced, however, my youth, having just ended my twentieth year, raised no little concern. The director, nevertheless consented, trusting the recommendation of Herr Müller, and allowed me to make a test phase. I was engaged with a salary of sixty dollars for a probation period of one month.

---

62 This was C. G. Mueller, a bookkeeper for the W. C. Bee & Company.

The old, well-known firm, W. C. Bee & Co., still carried on a relatively lucrative factoring business even during the stagnation. They took care of the affairs of many of the planters of the state. For instance, they stored and sold their products and produce which came by rail or by boat and took on the management of their capital. When, for example, the enterprise with cotton was dormant because there was little opportunity for export, then rice became as the most important food item an important trade article; and they engaged the consignments, the logistics of husking and the sale in great quantities which were always a brisk activity of the firm.

The two owners of the company, Bee and Jervey, were noble men. They were gentlemen through and through, real South Carolinians with aristocratic points of view. Both were well on in years which was attested to by their white heads, which in turn imparted to them a dignified appearance, which, however, did not explain everything. The director, Mr. Bee, managed the business in a calm but steady manner. As a diligent business man, he enjoyed the greatest trust of the planters who for the most part were his personal friends. He stood in great esteem with his fellow citizens and the officials of the city. He held many honorary posts in the administration and leadership of non-profit and charitable institutions as well as banks, the church, public schools, orphanages, and other enterprises which he strongly supported with a selfless offering of time, work and money. As a zealous member of the church and other religious associations, he was a pious man who led a life beyond reproach. Out of principle, he denied himself every pleasure such as related to physical and worldly satisfactions. He lived simply and modestly with his family. He prayed and worked and let the blessings of his work go in large part to the poor.

I think now with the deepest honor, esteem and gratitude after such a long time and from a far distance of this man with whom I worked closely for several years. I very quickly gained his full trust. I learned to value his diligence in business and his personal endearing traits and virtues. His entire noble character, which is stamped onto me for all time, stands lifelike before me. I think of the few lines written by his hand which I was able to salvage from the shipwreck in those days. I have been so fortunate. I have yet even now received news from him and have the certainty that I, likewise, am still in his good memory.

The second owner, Mr. Jervey, was accepted as a partner after long years of service in the company. [63] He was also a man of noble and endearing character which earned from me, as from all others, great respect. It was through the trust of the director that he had risen to his current position. Several misfortunes in his family had diminished his energy, and his business performance was also affected. In addition, he was a zealous patriot. His thoughts and interests were only on politics and the course of the war. He wanted to prosecute the war personally from which he later could not abstain despite his old age and white hair.

I entered this business with some anxiety but quite soon felt myself right at home with the good folks who made it possible so that I quickly became acquainted with the forms and methods to which I was not accustomed. My punctuality and my zeal to understand all that was unclear and to satisfactorily finish the task which I had been assigned won over my superiors in short order. When the month ended, I passed my test by being able to lay before the American business man an authoritative balance. I was as a result permanently engaged for an undetermined period of time at the position.

Our office was bright and roomy and had an excellent location with a view toward the Battery at the southern wharf where the supply of cotton, rice, etc. was brought in and stored. There was also a wonderful view of the entire bay and ship traffic which was, however, limited to the rivers and to the harbor.

The active intelligence of my superior, who was quite worried about the contraction of such a yet important business in comparison to others, relative to its previous vivacity and flourishing and who was

---

63 Theodore Dehon Jervey (1817-1892) enlisted as a private in Confederate service at the age of 54 and served until the end of the war. After the war, in early 1866, "he was thrown into jail by Collicot, agent of United States" for refusing to turn over funds of the Importing and Exporting Company of South Carolina. He was imprisoned for six months and released in June 1866 "on a bond of $100,000." Salley, "The Jervey Family," 94. In 1868 the U. S. government dropped its lawsuit against Jervey.

quite aware that the existence of the planters depended on the cotton which was losing value, brought about the founding of a corporation, the purpose of which was to build or have built an appropriate steamer which could break through the harbor blockade and bring the products of the South, particularly cotton, to the nearest neutral port and then to bring back industrial products and such articles which were lacking here, again breaking the blockade. This was very daring, but if it succeeded, a very lucrative undertaking. It found support among the public because of the leading personality and the fact that another steamer had just been successful in getting in and then getting out, such that the purchase of ships and the operation of the project was quickly earmarked and produced.

Mr. Bee became the president of the company. Mr. Jervey was elected treasurer of the company; and the firm W. E. Bee and Co. took over the entire company management with commissions from the anticipated sales. The factoring business remained and was well supported by the new project in that the new company was a buyer for the cotton which could not be sold and which the factoring business owned.

I received more work for which I was compensated with a pay raise in that I not only continued to keep the old books of the original firm but also those for the new business as well as issuing share certificates which had to be signed by the president and the treasurer and which had to be altered when the ownership changed. I received the necessary help. As the business grew, so, too, the personnel which consisted mainly of married old men. This all happened to me just shortly after my entry and after my established trust on the part of the principals as well as my position of supervisor of my colleagues who assisted me in every way possible and with whom, without exception, I had very cordial business dealings.

For the purpose of the new founding of the business, it was at first necessary to buy the right steamer. Since the construction of such in a foreign country would take too long, Mr. Jervey was sent to Havana and my predecessor, Herr Müller, to whom I owed my position, was sent to Europe. They were to buy the ships which would most likely fit our needs.

In order for this to succeed, both gentlemen had to engage the service of a ship which could get through the blockade. A grave danger was always associated with this undertaking; for as soon as such a craft was discovered by the enemy fleet, the passengers were looking at being prisoners for at least the duration of the war.

*The blockade runner Ella and Annie,
a painting by R. G. Skerrett. Wikicommons.*

Chapter 11

The Blockade Business

During the preparations for our enterprise, the fortunate success of the first blockade breakers and the profits which we got from it brought more speculators into our orbit. It was primarily the English who zealously jumped into the blockade trade and furnished a number of steamers to the individual Southern ports. Several of those were successful in selling their valuable cargoes for a high price and fully loaded with return freight were able to get them to their West Indian ports. More of them, to the contrary, had the fate of being stopped by the blockade fleet or being overtaken by Northern cruisers on the open seas. The ship and the cargo were good booty; and the crew and the passengers, if they were not foreigners, were treated as prisoners of war.

Our friends, then, in order to reach their goal had to undertake this dangerous trip. They arrived without mishap on neutral territory and were able from there, without disruption, to begin further operations.

The blockade business, although it had driven the enemy fleet to strengthen itself and to conduct sharper watches, provided in general highly satisfactory results and was for the country, in particular the seaports, of great importance. The produce of the land, if nevertheless within limited scope, were commercialized. The public and the government received many necessary articles, weapons, clothing, etc. Only those items were imported which were absolutely needed and which consisted of that which was most necessary.

The steamships, which carried out this commerce and brought the people and the country these blessings, had to have certain properties in order to lessen the danger of seizure. They had to have the shallowest draft possible in order to remain close to the coast in still waters into which the blocking ships of war could not venture and so that they could remain a distance out of sight and out of the range of the cannons to avoid being hit. They had to be outfitted with powerful engines which were so constructed that they could run at a higher speed than the enemy vessels which followed them. They were painted gray, and they burned the best English coal so that they could not be seen at a distance despite their visible bulk and their black smoke. During the night, they could burn no lights so that they were not betrayed by the glow. They could only undertake their secret trips in dark and moonless nights. In addition, their construction had to provide ample room for the largest possible cargo to be carried.

Our emissaries were able to acquire steamships which met such criteria. In fact, those who went to Europe were able to secure the two twin steamers Orion and Girius which had, until that point, carried out the commerce between Lübeck and St. Petersburg. Mr. Jervey bought a steamer which had earlier run between Havana and New Orleans which got the name Ella and Annie. The other two were rechristened Alice and Fanny.

With these three ships began the actual business of our company, the "Importing and Exporting Company of South Carolina," which in the vernacular was called "Bee Company."

The nearby neutral port of Nassau, on the English island of New Providence, one of the islands in the Bahamas which could be reached in forty-eight hours, became the main destination and point of departure for the blockade runners. St. Georges in the Bermudas, which lay a little further away, was also used for such purposes.

In these situations, where we had our agents – in Nassau Herr Müller, already mentioned, functioned as one – the unloading and the loading took place as fast as possible. From there, the cotton was sent by ships to Liverpool where the cotton at that time was bringing a high price; and certain wares for the Confederate States of America were sent to the West Indies in return so that they, in turn, could be picked up by smugglers and brought to their designated ports.

The Ella and the Annie was the first of our ships to arrive full of cargo in Charleston, and Mr. Jervey happily returned home with the cargo. The imported wares were sold at auction for enormous profits. Afterward, however, with the enormous successes of the company and at the instigation of Mr. Bee, the sale of the imported articles, with a markup which ensured high profits, was made in small and single quantities with the engagement of an important business house. This mode of allocation had the advantage for the public that everyone could acquire the needed article in any quantity and at set prices. It was, therefore, not necessary to pay extravagant prices at the sale and then be subject to commercial buyers who then placed and pursued demands. [64]

This sacrifice brought our company to the public and allowed the public, up to a point, to participate in the profits. The other importers preferred to the contrary, even later on, to sell their wares at auction in order to anticipate a higher gain. Our enterprise in comparison to the others was, however, accompanied by more good fortune and success.

For the first outbound load of the Ella and the Annie a large part of the cargo hold was allocated to and loaded with the freight paid by independent persons because of the initial startup of the three steamers and the fact that the cargo had not been immediately sold had used up most of the available capital so that there were not enough means to acquire a full load of cotton. Even I, in common cause with my brother and a third man, undertook together a speculation in that we entrusted to this dangerous voyage five bales of cotton and consigned it with a contract with our agent in Nassau to invest, if there were a fortunate

---

[64] Many goods brought in through the blockade were sold to the public at the "Bee sales" in Charleston, which took place in a row of townhouses at 101-107 Bull Street, out of range of the enemy shelling. There were also such stores in Columbia, S.C., and Richmond, Virginia, which "provided customers with direct access to imported articles and eliminated the costs added by wholesale dealers." Skelton, "The Importing and Exporting Company," 30.

A 20th century photograph of 101-107 Bull Street in Charleston, a row of townhouses where the Bee sales took place. Library of Congress.

arrival, one fourth of the profit by buying certain wares to be used and allow them to be sent on the return trip on the same ship.

The steamer departed, and it was for me an anxious time until I knew something of the fate of it. I, however, did not long remain in this uncertainty and worry. After seven days, the ship was already back, and my speculative enterprises yielded brilliant results. We had gotten tenfold the value for our cotton and the same amount from the articles which came to us. A quite nice sum of money was the result of my share of the resulting surplus.

In the meantime, the Alice and Fanny had come and gone with equal results; and our personnel had their hands full dealing with the work on hand because of the hurried expeditions. Things had to be hurried because the few dark nights had to be considered. For that reason, it was possible that an arriving ship was unloaded on a given day and then on the next day loaded full, beginning its new trip the next night.

I grew more and more in my position, in my rank and in the estimation and trust of my superiors; and when Mr. Jervey soon resigned from his office of treasurer and secretary of the company, the duties thereof were transferred to me. With that I had secured a responsible and a respected position, with full disposal over the means of the company and in addition to that the authority of procurator for the firm W. E. Bee & Co. as it related to their private business. I was the co-procurement manager of this large-scale company; and since, according to Napoleon's proverb, sympathy is always with the spirit of success, I have to admit without self-promotion, that I enjoyed high esteem from the people of Charleston because everyone was enthusiastic about the "Bee Company" and all that was associated with it. After politics, the company was the subject of most interest. I was happy with all of the work and was thankful to Providence which had blessed and privileged me in this manner.

The investors could be quite content. One dividend followed the other in short order. After more trips with good fortune by the steamers, the full amount of the stock, having reached a dizzy height, which made up a given motive of speculation, had been paid back. Although the imported goods always found stimulating sales at their landing place which was Charleston, individual loads of cargo were, nevertheless, sold inland so that the people living in those distant places were given the opportunity to purchase the necessary articles, according to circumstances, at moderate prices. Individual loads were brought to Columbia, the capital of the state, and to Richmond, the capital of Virginia and the Confederacy, and were sold in the modified form of small quantities.

Occasioned by these arrangements, in order to establish connection to the different places and to raise the expected monies at the sale, I had to travel several times, which gave me a welcomed change from my desk tasks, despite the stresses associated with travel.

This 1861 cartoon map illustrates Gen. Winfield Scott's "Anaconda plan" to blockade the Confederacy. Library of Congress.

Chapter 12

An Anxious Trip

I had to take one such stressful tour among others to Columbus in the state of Georgia, which, because of a lack of time, had to be made as quickly as possible and which, without a break for the return trip, required two nights and a day and the same for the return trip.

It was my purpose to buy a large lot of cotton at my point of destination, cotton which was stored there and which could be inexpensively acquired. I was carrying for that transaction the necessary sum of money with me. The full amount I am no longer able to account for, but it was likely about $100,000 which completely filled a briefcase of medium size with Confederate ten-dollar notes well packed together. The briefcase, because of its weight, was not comfortable to carry. I was quite uncritically entrusted with this money. I could have easily been robbed of the money and of my life under the conditions prevailing in those days. I was, however, proud of the responsibility of my mission and did not hesitate for one moment in carrying it out.

I began my trip in the evening and was very happy to have captured for myself a double seat on which I could, employing my valuable pack as a pillow, sleep. On the next day, the trip began in Augusta and went straight across the fertile state of Georgia. The region offered little scenic charm; but there was, nevertheless, a certain interest, namely the large cotton and rice fields which alternated with primeval forests and morasses or swamps.

This landscape was in part cultivated but also for the greater part was still wild and swampy, obviously impassable terrain though which the train now peacefully hurried. Later, in 1864, this would be the stage for General Sherman's well-known war and victory "train."

I arrived in Atlanta in the evening and found as I boarded the train which was to take me farther that it was overloaded with the transport of Confederate soldiers, quite rude fellows from a distant place, which were likely full of patriotism but who were deficit in culture so that not only was every single seat was taken but also the aisles and the outer steps were occupied.

The American railroad administration does not limit the number of passengers and makes no consideration for the individual passenger, whether he finds a seat or not. They take as many as can catch the train. Under the circumstances, I could have taken a later train, so that I could have laid claim to a seat. In this case, however, it has to be considered that I would have had to wait a full twenty-four hours because only one train per day, as in most cases, ran this route. Time was of the essence for me. I kept up the hope to endure my standing through the night and that I would eventually get a seat as the train partially emptied.

Not only did this hope not come to fruition; things got worse. I had to endure the grim reality of foul air and terrible noise. It got worse through the vapors and the lighting of tobacco out of so many pipes, resulting in dense smoke. Furthermore, the soldiers were consuming more and more rotgut whiskey. In all of this, I was squeezed in with my briefcase which I could not let out of my hand and had to breathe in these fumes. I also had to listen to vulgar conversations; and since I was not inclined to enter into them, I found myself to be the target of derision. For hours, I had to endure these horrible conditions. I remained up and on guard in the necessity of defending my valuable assets. My knees became weaker; my strength lessened; my consciousness started fading away. Clasping my briefcase in cramped arms, I lost consciousness. Just as I had not dared to ask a soldier to give up a seat, none was given up for me in my condition. After a long time, I found myself on the outside steps of the car where the soldiers had placed me, a place where, this time, wind and weather brought healing. My first thought was of my briefcase which was not to be seen. The anxiety and worry about that brought me new strength. I was able to again push my way into the crowd where the item must have slipped from my hand or must have been slipped from my hand. Here, however, as well as close by there was no trace of it. A horrible fear took hold of me, a fear which rose to despair as all of my questions as to the whereabouts of my briefcase and my search of the entire car brought nothing. I was point-blank given the advice to get off while the train was moving and search the stretch of tracks in the dark night since the briefcase was likely placed on the steps with me and had slid off. This scornful supposition was raise to certainty by others. I doubted the possibility that I would again gain possession of the piece. Although I was overwhelmed with the disappearance which threatened to befuddle my senses, I could not, however, allow one word to be uttered about the value of the inconspicuous briefcase. I was determined to risk every attempt to find it again; and if the well grounded evidence of its whereabouts was known, no other person would make the trip with me. Had other passengers had an inkling of the value, they would have gotten to it before I did; and they would not have shy about taking it or my life, even if I had gotten it back because I would have guarded it with my life.

It was already my intent to stop the train. I would give the signal to halt the train so that I could walk back by day, anticipating the place where I had left the car. Several days prior to my departure, I had the opportunity to convince myself of the willingness of American engineers to stop a train at the wish of a passenger. A respectable gentleman, while looking out the window had lost his hat, an average hat; however, he did not want to do without it; so he pulled the signal line. The train stopped at the first possibility. The farmer got his hat; and after his return, which took a good half hour, the train continued its journey.

I could not, however, lay claim to the train waiting for me because the distance to the point where I hope to find the briefcase was too far. The possibility of finding it in the dark was impossible. The opportunity of a quick continuation of the journey or a twenty-four hour stay in the wilderness was under the current circumstances completely secondary if I only had enjoyed even the slightest hope for regaining my possession.

Before I could, however, execute my plan to stop the train and thereby lose every chance of finding the briefcase were it still on the train, I undertook yet one more time a thorough search, and –almost losing consciousness again – I found it, hidden in a toilet in the second car! With what intent had it been brought there? Did the culprit do it for the purpose of robbing me although one would have only been able to assume the usual content of such? Perhaps someone simply wanted to upset me and ultimately intended to lead me to it. I do not know; and, at the moment, I did not care at all. It was enough to have my treasure again and to be convinced that it was untouched and the original amount was there.

My uninhibited joy over my regained booty I could in no wise express. In my heart, however, I was overjoyed; and I thanked God for saving me from the horrible circumstances.

I clutched my booty even tighter and a set myself outside on the steps with a comfortable feeling in the storm and rain where the trip no longer raised any excitement.

Finally the hour of deliverance arrived which brought me to my goal. My tiredness had disappeared with my consciousness of security and safety; and during a hearty breakfast, I consoled myself that I had endured the hardships and the experiences of the previous night.

I was able to finish my business with satisfaction. When I had changed the dangerous paper money into cotton and had engaged an extra train, I telegraphed the fortunate completion of the business to Charleston and granted myself some rest before I began the more comfortable and better run return trip.

That was one episode in my otherwise worry free life. The memory of it was appalling to me for a long time. Such a situation cannot be portrayed. The only person who can empathize is the one who has experienced such commensurate feelings which have themselves been brought about by such despair. The aftereffects were, however, mitigated through the praise and the financial gain which the results of my mission brought.

Chapter 13

The Development of Doom

The successes which the blockade runners had by enlarged purpose with their regular commerce with the outside world was a taunt to the blockade fleet which was there to stop just such activity. This created quite understandably in the Union government a more heated zeal to control this nuisance.

The harbor of Savannah was already closed for some time through the capture of Fort Pulaski by the Union, although the city itself resisted to the end. Likewise, the Union had captured the strategic point of Port Royal between Charleston and Savannah and had there built large depots of the coastal fleet. From these stations, they were, however, not able to undertake anything; and attempts from there went for naught.

On the 7th of April of 1863, the blockade squadron attempted an attack on Charleston or the fortifications which guarded the city; however, the strength and the bravery of the defense and the torpedoes and obstructions which guarded the approach channels made the attack unsuccessful. [65] After a strong bombardment, the fleet had to turn around and limited themselves to their watch duty.

On the 10th of July, the attack was renewed with the same intensity and indeed this time with better results for the North. Within the course of four days, which the battle lasted, all batteries on Morris

---

65 The attack of the Union ironclad vessels was mainly directed against Fort Sumter.

Island up to the most important which was Fort Wagner were silenced and the batteries were vacated by the Confederate units and were, in turn, occupied by Union forces. [66] The remainder of the forts had given excellent resistance and had inflicted heavy damage on enemy ships. The enemy continued his attack on Fort Wagner itself from the newly won batteries. With the aid of the last gunboats operating there up to the 6th of September 1863, it likewise had to be abandoned by its garrison; and it fell into the hands of the Union.

With that, the Union had gained a very important position which controlled the entrance to the harbor as well as the fortification works in it. In addition, the position gave them control over the harbor basin and against all expectations over a portion of Charleston itself.

The blockade business and the commerce which flourished because of the important outcomes of the war were lost for Charleston. Even if the ships smuggling goods, despite the now greater danger, got through the enemy fleet and batteries, they were by day at their places of anchor in the inner harbor subject to a steady bombardment from whose field of fire they could not escape.

These ships had to seek other places for their gainful activities. Before I deal with this subject, however, I would like to focus on Charleston for a while and describe it through the events of unanticipated transformation.

The battles which were fought over the course of the last few years had brought much suffering to the land and to countless families, battles which at first were victorious for the South but later almost always to the advantage to the North. No one doubted, however, a favorable end. A suppression of the South was not deemed possible; and human strength and the willingness to sacrifice made it certain in this war as it pertained to the South. Pride and patriotism grew, where possible, with every loss which the South suffered. Again and

---

66   The First Battle of Fort Wagner was fought on July 10-11, 1863, during which Union forces took control of part of Morris Island, but not Fort Wagner. The second battle took place in July 1863, and was also an unsuccessful attempt to take Fort Wagner. Fort Wagner (or Battery Wagner) and nearby Battery Gregg were not taken by U. S. forces until the Confederates evacuated Morris Island in September 1863.

again young men and men up in years made themselves available for their fatherland in order to fill the thinned ranks of the army and to offer blood for the "righteous cause" on the altar of the fatherland. He who could not participate in the battles did his duty elsewhere as best he could: with spirit, with fervor and with money. Many, very many took their courage to sacrifice so far as to sell all of their jewelry and luxury items and bring the gain, beyond their needs to sustain life, to the country for the military and charity purposes. These noble folk believed that they had no right to such dispensable treasures as long as the fatherland and its defenders had need of them. The ladies were tireless in the nursing of the wounded, in production of knitted materials and sewing of clothing for the soldiers, through colleting of money and material and through the sponsoring of concerts, exhibits and fairs, among other things.

I have already stated that I as a good German was less enthusiastic for the cause of the South and I placed my own interests over those of the South. I used for this purpose many opportunities created by the aforementioned methods of putting the items into circulation: jewels, which were easy to make safe and to transport, inexpensive to buy, and could be invested in place of the rapidly debased paper money.

In spite of the serious situation of things and the demonstrated mettle of resistance, people slowly became accustomed to this condition and began again within certain limits to pay homage to pleasures and well as to others such as political interests. The joyous change of attitude was certainly made possible through the resurgence of business by means of the blockade runners in which many participated and in which everyone was more or less interested. Concerts and other entertainment for charitable purposes served as a positive effect on the otherwise joyless lives of the people.

When my otherwise short supply of time allowed, I did not allow myself to miss such pleasures since I made strong efforts to spend my live as comfortable as possible, although the temptations to these extravagances were precluded at the outset by the dominant circumstances. My old quarters, the Carolina House, with its mostly long-term guests, offered me comfortable dealings and excellent hours of relaxation after strenuous work of the day. At the games of whist and chess with ladies and with music and entertainment, the evenings passed in almost always merry ways, much like the long-gone times of sweet freedoms.

Only the quadrilles were reduced in their frequency because it was deemed that they did not correspond to the gravity of the situation. The entertainment in the Carolina House was interrupted through attending a concert or walks to the Battery which the young ladies of the house loved to take and for which I gladly functioned as companion and security. I also spent pleasant evenings from time to time with my old friend and comrade in arms Laitenberger who like me had chosen to leave the militia; he was still employed in the same business in which he had been involved where he was waiting for back pay. We allowed the great time of our military strolls in Castle Pinckney to pass in review and amused ourselves with several reminiscences of events which happened there. His good wife was, however, happy to have him back: Louis could now be better taken care of, although she had borne the long solitude without complaint.

Sundays I dedicated, in addition to visiting churches of all confessions, exclusively to my brother in whose company I usually took long walks in the area in order to enjoy nature and to satisfy my sitting lifestyle with the necessity of movement. This was also the only time in which we could talk without interruption in our mother tongue, for which I had little opportunity. Sometimes I used the peace of Sunday in order to communicate to my distant homeland with those who loved me about my work and activities in my advantageous position. This written communication with them who were so dear in my life created the link which fettered me to my old homeland which often became taut through a powerful longing. The knowledge that by means of my goal I would again experience a homecoming and that I could get closer and closer to it filled me with infinite joy. In the meantime, however, I would have to be content with the hope of reaching that goal. Since I had finally seen the light before me and since I could no longer fail to apprehend its source, I did not needed to hurry in order to take possession of it but could, on the contrary, collect the treasures which came my way in its glow.

Chapter 14

The Bombardment of Charleston

Thus passed the summer of 1863 in distress and losses of battles and territory but also in the hope of a final success for the country which manifested itself in brisk business relative to the times and in a quickening of courage and endurance in the best possible mood possible for Charleston and its citizens, and for me in strenuous but gainful activity and satisfaction with the imposed conditions—until the capture of Morris Island by Union forces which brought about an existential change.

A threat to Charleston with its fortifications and their seeming invincibility was considered unthinkable, and this feeling of security remained despite the most recent attacks. People did not anticipate any further objectionable consequences, as bad as they felt about the capture of Morris Island and its loss. People believed that the assaults on Fort Sumter, Fort Moultrie and others would continue but would be repulsed. These attacks actually took place. The bullets and the shells flew without ceasing from one side to the other, without extensive damages on either side. For Sumter, which lay closest to the enemy batteries and which was quite visible by its masonry, indeed suffered during the course of time various breaches and small collapses of the walls; but that did not cause it to lose any of its resilience.

What had not been, however, foreseen; and what had been considered unbelievable, and had, however, put the citizens of Charleston in agitation and anxiety was the fact that the Union forces could reach the city with their newly acquired batteries after they had, for this very purpose, installed large caliber cannons. [67]

A panicked terror and an intense bewilderment seized the populace as the first shell flew into the city. Now no one was safe in his own home and had to leave it and flee. Many who were able to do so closed their homes and resettled with their belongings into the countryside. Those who remained behind crowded into the upper part of the city which still lay out of the range of the enemy guns. The lower, southern half of the city was evacuated as soon as possible and lay after just a few days barren and abandoned so that the shells and bombs which landed there made the only noise in streets and buildings which would have otherwise been bustling.

The city took on a completely different physiognomy. The streets were transformed into a green lawn. All of the apartments and public buildings, the warehouses, the offices, the banks and the churches stood empty and unused and showed more or less the effects of the bombardment. Not a few magnificent buildings became in a short time ruins. It is here that the shells made their mischief. Each day brought new reports of the damages which they had caused.

The bombardment was kept up day and night until the end of the war or for one and one-half years. [68] Often, there were irregular pauses which usually lasted for twenty-four hours. At other times, the shelling lost during the pauses was made up for by a faster tempo of shelling. One was never safe in the range of the murderous tools when one dared to trespass on this eerie landscape. On the other hand, despite the destructive effects of the shelling, almost no one could resist taking a look at this uncommon, interesting and brawly play when, after a time, the troubled waters of the mind had been stilled and one had become accustomed to the regular pace of the bombardment.

---

67   Enemy cannons on Morris Island could send shells into the city of Charleston over a distance of about five miles. The bombardment began in the middle of the night on August 22, 1863, and continued in varying degrees until mid-February 1865.

68   The bombardment of the city ended in mid-February 1865, about two months before the end of the war.

The battery offered an excellent point of observation and with a little care was completely safe. To begin with, one heard the roaring sound of the cannon on Morris Island (as an aside, when it pleased the gentlemen laying siege to satisfy the presence of the observer) which quite naturally covered the three and one-half miles in a tempo quicker than the shot which it heralded. One had then with this notice enough time to catch sight of the shot, to determine its direction and, in case it was heading toward the observation point, to leave the spot or to get to safety. Man gets used to everything, even to the murderous bombs; and here the danger was by far not so large. How it must have appeared to those who were unable to catch sight of the cruel and brawly appearance and the entire line of flight of the projectile from its source to its target!

As soon as the huge projectile, announced by the blast of the cannon, was sighted, and one had nothing to fear for his person as a result, which was rarely the case, one could follow it on its course with the naked eye. Lightning swift it hurried through the air and brought about in accord with its size a whistling or howling sound which change its tonality in relation to the lesser or greater distance from the observer or the direction and the speed of the wind, this until it arrived at its determined destination and completed its mission with a powerful report either through its impact or explosion.

In the houses and streets as well as the routes to the battery a stay or stop over was more dangerous because one was not able to determine the direction in enough time and could not withdraw. I will never forget when I was undertaking a walk with a young lady to the previously mentioned observation point when we were informed by shot and roar of the arrival of a shell which without a doubt had providenced the obliteration of our young lives. By instinct, we ran a few steps forward and pressed ourselves against a house; and on the place we had just left, the shelf hit and exploded. It was a miracle that we were not hit by the fragments. We, however, gave up the pleasure of enjoying a wonderful moonlit night for this evening.

Although it was to be assumed that the enemy targeted the steeples and spires of the city, they were, if by Providence, neither hit nor damaged. The damage was not as bad as one might have believed and as the enemy intended. The purpose was to force the city to capitulate; however, no one was in the least inclined to yield to this demand. The lower part of the city was yielded to the bombardment; and we found ourselves, in the end, in this new adversity. It was a wonder that more lives were not lost to the murderous bombs. It was only seldom that such occurred, and those killed were mostly Negroes who were caught by surprise while lingering and moving around in the abandoned district, quite often to steal useable items which they found in the houses standing empty. [69]

Sometimes, however not very often, a shell reached the inhabited area of the city because of a propitious wind or after-pressure and caused alarm and created almost always greater harm. In one case, for example, a colored barber, just as he was about to set his razor to the cheek of a client, was completely beheaded by a shell coming through the window. The soaped up gentleman was thrown out of his comfortable seating by the shockwave but came away with nothing but sheer terror.

The effects of another shell in an inhabited house, which I was able to view myself, was completely astounding. The projectile went through a window on the first floor in which, fortunately at that time, no one was to be found. It flew toward a mirror on the other side of the room and slid on it without breaking it and then bored through a wall to a third room without exploding, this after it had passed through another wall and struck a pianoforte and had ripped it into a thousand pieces.

Otherwise, as I have noted, the bombardment was bearable for those who, if required to remain in Charleston, had the good fortune to own a house in the upper city or to find someplace to dwell there. It was nevertheless barren and dead in the old, otherwise, lively Charleston, dead through the migration of so many of its residents who had moved to more peaceful regions and dead through the businesses which were

---

69 The Rev. Anthony Toomer Porter, an Episcopal clergyman of Charleston, estimated that about eighty civilians were killed by the shelling of the city. He also recorded that two Episcopal churches were struck by shells. Other Charleston churches, houses, and buildings were also damaged by the shelling. Porter, *Led On,* 146.

completely closed. It had become still and quiet in the houses, in the streets and in the hearts of the people which had become subdued by the gravity of the situation. Even the bells of St. Michael's and St. Philip's were silent as were those of most of the churches. The bells had been pressed into another service for the fatherland; they had been transformed into cannons; and their sounds of joy and praise had become a war cry. It was very painful to me when I could no longer hear the beautiful, harmonious melodies; and it pained every Charlestonian to give them up; however, one yielded to the needs of the fatherland for which one gladly brought every sacrifice.

No one lost courage despite the tests and despite the losses which most of the residence suffered through the destruction of the houses and through the devaluation of property as well as the debasement of state, industrial and bank currencies which the people had to bear. Residents lived in the confidence that times would change and that Southern arms would prevail or that the United States would realize that they would not succeed in suppressing the Confederacy and that they would eventually abandon their scheme. At the same time, one continued to hope that foreign states would intervene. It was believed that these powers would wait until the last minute, once both parties were weakened, to recognize the sovereignty of the Confederacy.

The behavior of the Negro was completely satisfactory. Nothing was to be feared from them in the least. To the contrary, they were in their own way good patriots and remained as before loyal to their masters and wished and cursed the "Yanks," who were indeed guilty of every possible evil because there were no longer any celebrations for them to enjoy and there was a lack of meat for the pot. I must, however, assert that such sentiments on the part of the Negro were in word and thought rather than in the compulsion to act because the Negro does not like to put his life in danger.

For the owners, the slaves had become a burden in these times because they had no work and rendered no service, but they had to be maintained and supported. They could have been armed and used for military service which would have been a great service to their country. Such a move was, however, against the law and against the sentiments of Southerners. Thus, midst the greatest distress, the South forewent this measure which could have been used against the hated enemy. [70]

Our mistress of the boarding house, Mrs. Finney, had to exchange her roomy hotel for a smaller house in the upper part of the city. Several of the permanent guests followed her there, particularly those who had not moved out or who were not so situated as to leave the city, finding themselves in the same situation. Even in this situation, the good lady knew how to make it comfortable for her guests.

The bombardment influenced our business in that the ships could no longer use Charleston as a regular port because of the heightened danger upon arrival and departure and on the loading and unloading which could only take place in places with less danger. It did, however, occur in isolated cases that a ship being chased, cut off from its port of intent and attempting to avoid enemy fire, would avail itself of the possibility of seeking escape into the harbor. These few risks and distress moves were blessed with good fortune.

---

[70] During the war, there were repeated calls for the enlistment of black soldiers. In March 1865, a bill was passed in the Confederate Congress authorizing the arming and emancipation of 300,000 slaves. Around the same time, President Davis had sent envoys to Europe who were to offer the emancipation of the slaves in exchange for foreign recognition— but all this came too late, as the war ended in Southern defeat in April 1865.

Chapter 15

WILMINGTON, NORTH CAROLINA

The port city of Wilmington in North Carolina was the suitable Confederate harbor after Charleston after it had been as good as sealed off by the Bombardment. Wilmington lay on the Cape Fear River about forty miles from the mouth at the ocean and could be reached by deep ocean vessels. Up until this point, commerce had been of little importance. The soil conditions of the surrounding area consisted of swampy areas and sandbanks covered by thick pine forests which produce only wood, resin and turpentine. These products, based on their limited worth, were shipped by smaller boats to other ports which lay close by where the resin and turpentine were used as necessary ballast for ships carrying cotton.

For these reasons, this port became of the utmost importance. It could be used to import and export valuable articles of trade. Wilmington had likely never seen such lucrative times than those of the war and the blooming of the blockade trade. The ship owners, however, acquired a disadvantage because the goods, arriving and leaving, had to be transported far and wide before they could be sold of offloaded. For that reason, there emerged disagreeable delays because the necessary load of cotton did not get through on time, and "time" was in this case not only "money" but "a lot of money."

The railroads in the Confederacy could no longer carry out, depending on the circumstances and area, the commerce requirements because they used up more and more of their operating resources but were not in the position to replace them. In part, they wanted to put the blockade businesses under pressure in order to participate in the good profits. That is to say that the railroad companies which we planned to use for our commerce made quite demanding claims. In addition to charging high freight costs to transport our goods, they also had other prerequisites for fulfilling their requirements, namely that our ships would carry a large batch of cotton for their bill and that they had to bring back the necessary machine parts and materials. For that reason, the business lost a large percentage of its own room and usage. Nevertheless, one was obliged to yield to this demand and had to overcome the various inconveniences which went with doing business in Wilmington.

The city which lay high above the lethargic and murky Cape Fear River offered nothing worthy of note or captivating if one overlooked the painful theater of war which exacted its toll on the newly created life of the city and the bustle of strangers. It was an old city with about one thousand residences but without any noteworthy structures. Only a few of the streets were paved; most consisted of loose sand paths which were barely passable with a wagon and which were transformed by the least wind into a cloud of dust. The only thing in which I had an interest was the inconspicuous presence of a "spring" which supplied fresh, cold water and which provided me with a great treat which I did without for years in Charleston which had only other costly beverages, save for the collected rain water in collected in cisterns.

The region, as I have already stated, consisted of sandy soil overgrown with pine on the one side and abysmal swamp land on the other. There was not the slightest variation; and there was nothing which would allure a lover of nature.

The proximity of the previously mentioned swamp had adverse influence on the climatic conditions throughout the year; in summer, however, a malarial fever dominated Wilmington in a form which was extremely debilitating or terminal. As new arrivals, we were particularly vulnerable to the disease; and we consumed enormous quantities of quinine which was the best although not the most dependable medication against the disease. With this treatment, we entirely escaped the disease.

Although the place, the area, the climate and life outside of business offered few pleasantries, I liked the residents of Wilmington even less. They were, with few exceptions, simply culturally backward and deviated significantly from an aristocratic South Carolinian or Charlestonian. They seemed to place no value on higher education. By and large, they were a simple and plump little people who made no demands on life and appeared to feel perfectly at home in their simplicity.

By means of the commerce which was transplanted there from Charleston and the parade of strangers who were drawn there with it, the reserved North Carolinian was aroused and became more civilized. The desire for riches and the opportunity for such which offered itself had its effect.

In order to carry out our expansive business, we had sought out the storage and work spaces which best met our needs. We rented the best which was to be had. Everything was, however, quite defective, and our places of trade were primitive beyond measure.

With regard to living quarters, we were more fortunate. We rented a spacious house, dedicated as a parsonage, from an unmarried Methodist pastor born in Ireland. Our seven-man personnel, including Mr. Jervey, quartered ourselves in the house at the expense of the company. Everything necessary such as house needs, tableware, cooking utensils, beds, etc. were put on the ledger of the company; and a complete household was established. For the preparation of the meals and for service two Negro slaves, one a man and one a woman, belonging to Mr. Jervey were engaged.

As compensation for the use of the house, the pastor who had reserved two rooms for himself received all of his meals from us. Our group at table was now eight, counting the pastor. We, otherwise, had little to do with him; and neither he nor we felt attracted to one another in the least. The gentleman, as unbelievable as it might seem, was truthfully too liberal for us. None of us were grumblers. He was particularly worried that none of us visited his church. Even curiosity aroused by his orations and table talk was unable to induce us to go there.

Household affairs were managed with excellence by a member of our company, Ravenel, the son-in-law of Mr. Bee. [71] For that purpose he received in abundance all of the necessary assets. As a reward for our very stressful work, we lived opulently. Our ships provided us with both necessities and delicacies which others relative to the times had to do without. There were two to each bedroom, with Mr. Jervey having one to himself. In addition, we had a dining room, a parlor and the required rooms for doing business.

The completely collegial relationships made our domestic and business cohabitation very pleasant. The desire for rest and relaxation after a strenuous day was easily fulfilled so that the lack of outside entertainment outside of the house was not tangible. In addition, we had the church and the theater during the week if we wanted to take advantage of them, which, to be honest, seldom occurred.

Mr. Jervey, however, had no peace in his comfort. He could not reconcile his comfort while soldiers were offering their lives and their health and were subject to all kinds of inconveniences. One morning, after the wind had rattled his window during the night and had given his conscience a prick, he announced his decision to hurry to the front in Virginia. Thus, the courageous, white-haired man joined a regiment as a common soldier. He gladly suffered the deprivations and, as fortune would have it, later returned home without injury.

I became the only director in the Wilmington office and acquired greater responsibility, nominally, of course, since up until this point I had been taking care of the most important affairs myself, naturally in constant communication with our director in Charleston.

---

71 This was Wiliam Parker Ravenel (1832-1887), the husband of Bee's daughter Ann Alicia Bee Ravenel (1832-1874).

Our fleet now consisted of five ships. Immediately after our first successes, we had commissioned the building of more ships in England. Two of these were now on line and ready for action. The last of the commissioned ships was supposed to leave its English wharf just as the war and with it the blockade business ended.

We, ourselves, did not get away without losses. The Ella and Annie on her third homeward voyage was overtaken and confiscated on the open sea by an enemy cruiser. The crew was held as prisoners until the end of the war. One of the newer ships, "the Ella," had made three successful trips back and forth. In an attempt to enter the Cape Fear River, she was spotted and chased and would have likewise fallen into the hands of the enemy if she had not been quickly steered onto a sandbank at the mouth of the river and set ablaze so that the enemy missed the chance at capturing very valuable commodities. The crew, without their personal belongings, managed to get to make it to shore without being hit by the bullets which were whizzing past. These two losses, as unpleasant as they were, could not be compared to the other successes which we had planned. It was not only that these two steamers delivered double if not threefold their costs, but that the other steamers brought even higher gains. If I remember the total correctly, the Alice made fourteen double trips; the Ella and Annie, three; the Caroline, four; and the Ella, three. When one compares our successes to those of companies who came after us, one can conclude that about one third of the attempts failed, primarily with the loss of the steamers. The "Bee Company" was alone in its successes, its renown and its reliability.

We could also take pride in the diligent and determined captains and pilots in our service, who, with in view of the dangers and the responsibilities which they faced, received high salaries, likewise the rest of the crew in relation to their duties. In addition, we offered them the opportunity for private investment by transporting and selling articles of unique value for their own profit. These men earned thereby a very satisfactory fortune; and they probably said "good-bye" to the sea after the war.

One of the captains came regrettably into conflict with the law because he felt that his business success gave him the privilege of making three ladies happy at once. The first wife lived in England; the second, in Nassau; and the third, in Charleston. The lady of Charleston considered herself to be the mistress of his life. One would have never suspected a Don Juan in the modest little man. For a while, things went well for him. The West Indian and the American were overjoyed by the regular return of their spouse who always brought home a rich bounty. His wife in England, however, appeared not to have enjoyed the long separations and the riches which came with his visits. One fine day, she surprised our friend in Nassau and made a visit to our Christian Mohammedan in his house. I never knew whether the arrival of the third wife constituted a peaceful marriage of four or whether no few eyes were scratched out. I only knew that we had to lose our very diligent captain because the court demanded his presence for quite a while.

The work load was systematically divided. Each department worked independently of the other. Ravenel, previously mentioned, took care of the declaration of cargoes received at the customs house where he paid the entry tariff and received permission for the cargo. The gentleman in question had acquired this post in a very sly manner so that he got the first view for the investors and could inform them of the content of the cargo. Articles which would have the highest use, he revised against the established sale price and therewith accommodated his friends who had need of a cheaper price. This was of no consequence to us since there was no downside to the company; but with great anxiety our colleague kept any knowledge of his accounting from his father-in-law, Mr. Bee, who would not have allowed it and who was not so well disposed to his son-in-law. Except for the few simple services already mentioned, he did little for the company. He was, therefore, even more engaged in his private matters for which he made himself useful.

A colleague, Kittel, was responsible for receiving the arriving goods and for matching the crates, bales, etc. with the investors and for ensuring that such was properly sent on to Charleston, Columbia, Richmond, etc.

Another colleague, Downey, was responsible for the timely acquisition of cotton and was in control of thirty Negroes under a white overseer, Negroes whom we had rented from a Mississippi planter who had been driven out of the state. [72] They were well taken care of and gave us the best of service.

The rest of us took care of the paper work which was often very pressing for a pending expedition of a steamer. In such cases, we worked until late in the night.

When the dark nights which had to be used for the blockade had passed and the ships were either here or in the West Indies waiting for the next opportunity to again begin the trip, we could enjoy a little more rest; but there was always enough work for the office personnel in order to take care of matters which remained.

My earnings matched my performance. I was in the fortunate situation to acquire even more savings. The only means of payment was Confederate currency which lost more and more value. Since I was in doubt of the success of Southern weapons and of a rise in value of Confederate notes, I changed my income into solid currency which I sent to known firms in Europe in order to at least have something secure, but not without loss. Among other things, I enjoyed the privilege to load for myself one bale of cotton for each ship. My friend, Downey, who undertook this task for me, made sure that the heaviest bale was allocated to me. I indeed suspect that he had two normal bales pressed together for me because my allocation always weighed between nine-hundred and one-thousand pounds. Such as bale got a very high price in England or in Nassau, since the price of cotton there had become very high, but was very cheap for us to get. I transferred my returns to my friends overseas and accrued interest.

In addition, I did a little business with Confederate bonds, which, depending on the exchange rate, did better in England than in the South itself. Since the ships on which I sent the bonds as well as the cotton

---

72 The name F. T. Downey appears in the records of the Importing and Exporting Company of South Carolina.

successfully reached their objective, I was in this matter also quite successful, even though one had to always be aware of the risks of a loss.

The capital which I however invested in Southern goods, which my always optimistic brother talked me into, was a total loss: tobacco, bank stock, railroad stock, etc. because they were either destroyed by fire or stolen, which in spite of this would have been worthless as a result of the ruin of the institutions involved.

While our business was booming, the enemy was winning more and more territory. He had already made several attempts to land on the coast of North Carolina and South Carolina, so that he could attack and occupy the hated places such as Wilmington and Charleston which had proved to be impossible to overcome by sea. He had, nevertheless, to that point not been successful; but one had to daily fear a "better result" of his efforts. It was therefore decided to transfer the capital and the main books of the company to a more secure place. Columbia appeared to be the appropriate place. It was located almost equally between Charleston and Wilmington where Charleston banks with whom we worked had domiciled themselves.

I was assigned to open a main office in Columbia and to manage it. In the spring of 1864, I moved to Columbia. On the important days of the month, when our ships arrived in Wilmington or when they were quickly sent out, my presence there was necessary so that I had to regularly make the unpleasant trip there and back.

It was an unsettling life with the trips back and forth, with each trip taking about twelve hours of overnight travel. When one had the misfortune, which was often the case, to miss the connection at the trunk station of Kingsville, one had to stay a full twenty-four hours in this place which lay in the middle of a forest and which consisted of a primitive hotel and a station house. There one lost valuable time and was bored to death. That gives an indication of the unpleasantness of such trips.

Those were the conditions in the South in those days, and they may well still be that way. Some people asserted that it was a plot between the hotel owner and the conductor in that the conductor would ensure, with a payoff, that the train would arrive too late to connect so that the passengers had no other choice but to stay in the so-called hotel and to eat there. I also had to travel to Charleston, as I did earlier from Wilmington, to meet with my director about important matters. After a night trip, I arrived there in the morning, took care of business during the day, and returned to Columbia the next night. Although it was strenuous, there was no connection to miss. Such a trip also included the amenity of seeing Charleston, which I loved, my brother and my friends. Even the thunder of the cannons had a certain appeal to me.

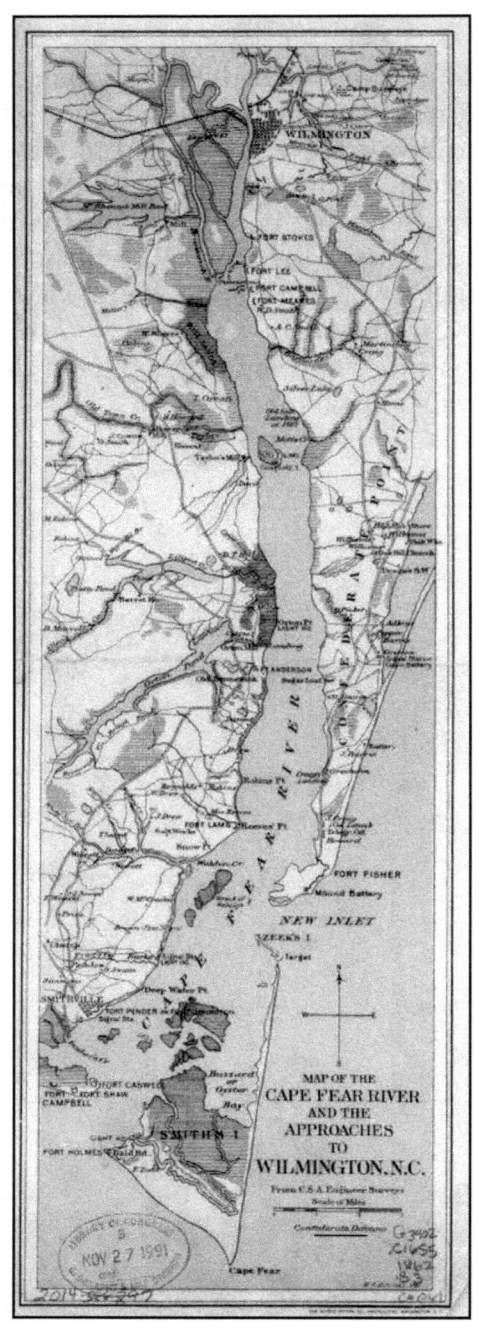

This Confederate map shows the Cape Fear River region of North Carolina, and the city of Wilmington. Library of Congress.

Chapter 16

Columbia, South Carolina

Thus Columbia became my headquarters where I managed the business, first alone and then with the assistance of several colleagues. The individual revenues from the sale of arriving goods came here to be paid out as dividends to the stockholders. It was here that the transactions of the businesses in Charleston and Wilmington were reported and recorded. In fact, all of the internal affairs of the company were carried out here, with the written collaboration of Mr. Bee who always remained in Charleston.

The amenities induce me to take time with the description of the place and to waken to memory the beautiful and the painful recollections, this despite the frequent trips and the hard work to which I had accustomed myself and despite the happy and the cheerless days which I experienced there.

In a certain manner, the war had had a positive influence on Columbia as well. As the capital of the State of South Carolina, Columbia had long been the seat of state government and the chief administration center as well as the courts of justice and other authorities. It was also now one of the privileged points allocated by the Confederate government to house its various departments. So it was that from Columbia, the country was flooded with the newly created paper money with many hands responsible for it, for the most part the hands of ladies. [73] Columbia was a main distribution point

---

[73] There were several printing plants in Columbia producing Confederate currency and

for provisions and war material with which the individual theaters of operations were supported. In addition, there were military hospitals and other installations which were necessary for the administration of the country and the prosecution of the war. All of this necessitated a large number of personnel. Since there was a lack of men because of military service, ladies were the main workforce in the previously mentioned department. According to their situations, they worked gratis or for compensation, usually in the less strenuous positions.

As a result, the city experienced a marked increase in population, in the expansion of business and of traffic through an enormous immigration from Charleston and through the refugees driven from the coasts because banks and larger businesses were relocated here.

The usual number of residents was about twelve thousand.[74] Now there was a much higher number with many seeking shelter. All apartments and hotels were full. The streets were filled with hustle and bustle, and businesses were booming. Our ships ensured that the fairer sex was always supplied with the necessary European fabrics, ribbons, buttons, shoes, etc. Men, on the other hand, found the ordinary commodities of local industry to be sufficient , an industry which with inferior fashion attempted to satisfy the needs produced by the distress of the times.

It was indeed very lively in Columbia and quite noble. The best families of the state had taken refuge here in their capital city. Most of the time, they were well situated and included many extravagances in their lifestyle and their public appearances with carriages and horses. So it was that though all of these circumstances, the horrors of war were here less evident.

The city had, in comparison to the other American cities which I knew, a romantic setting. The city lay on an elevated plain with hilly terrain and fertile soil. The plane sank rather steeply to the southwest into the valley of the Congaree River which had an attractive appeal. It was a thunderous

---

bonds. Many women worked as clerks in these plants and were known as "treasury girls."
74 The population of Columbia in 1860 was a little over 8,000 residents.

river as it flowed over boulders of rock into the Saluda about one-half hour from the city. The railroads which connected Charleston and Wilmington and points south and Greenville and the Blue Mountains to the north ended in this valley. [75] Those collecting Charlotte and Richmond had their stations on the eastern side of the city.

The city was constructed according to the American system in spacious and regular squares. With its wood-constructed new and quite inviting houses mostly painted bright colors and its numerous gardens and broad streets lined almost their entire length with trees, the city made a homey and pastoral appeal. At the south end of the city was located the majestic capitol made of white granite. [76] It was in every way a magnificent building in solidity, in style, in external form and in inner furnishings. From this point, the main street ran in a straight line through the middle of the city. On it were all of the department stores, the hotels, the city hall and other public buildings. Its big-city traffic stood out against the peace of the rest of the streets.

The city also had a large number of churches for the different confessions of its residents; however, none of them had a particular distinction architecturally. By contrast there were three institutions with such distinction: the university which was closed at the time because the students had traded their seats in the lecture halls for those on the battlefield; the state asylum; and the convent of the Ursuline Order which was a well-known school for young women.

On the west end, the city rose to the so-called Arsenal Hill on the crest of which was located the state arsenal which had a now empty weapons depot and which served as a cadet school for boarding pupils. A large reservoir was also located there from which the city received it good spring water.

Around the arsenal was a small suburb consisting of villas and gardens. This high point offered a pleasant view of the city, its houses hidden among the green trees, the buildings which ranged above the

---

75 "Blue Mountains" means the Blue Ridge Mountains.
76 Conrad is referring to the new South Carolina state house under construction.

trees and the steeples of the otherwise mundane churches. Farther into the valley of the Congaree, the river itself was visible in places through the trees; and its turbulence was audible. It gave life to the charming picture. On the other bank of the river were the heights which in part fell off sharply; and in the further distance, was a beautiful landscape which mostly consisted of woodland which for the greater part of the year was resplendent with varying shades of glorious color. At the foot of the hill and falling away from the city itself, the city park trundled along the creek in compliant manner, creating a cauldron which opened itself to the Congaree which there captured a roaring creek which sprang up in the park and flowed through it.

This park, which was actually deeper that it was long and broad in its expanse, consisted of luscious green meadows and groups of trees through which comfortable footpaths snaked into the dale where the aforementioned creek had its origins and which had been ordered into small basins and falls. [77] In the summer, the cauldron provided very refreshing cool air because the rays of the sun were very rarely able to reach the shaded ground.

As pleasant as a walk in the park was, it was not, however, the only destination of those going for walks. The entire area around Columbia offered to the nature lover rich variety and opportunity to enjoy himself with diverse landscapes, forest and water games, and the forms and cultures of the terrain.

The climate was pleasant and healthy. Although on summer days, the sun exerted the force commensurate with its degree of latitude, the nights, by contrast, were cool and refreshing. The winters there unburdened us from northern cold and destruction.

It is, therefore, no wonder that a large portion of the refugees sought their asylum here and that I myself was content and satisfied with the same. In addition to matters of climate and nature, the lifestyle, the people, the dominant tone, and the commerce which I shared with the good folks contributed to my comfortable feeling.

---

77 This was Sidney Park, and is now known as Finlay Park.

I had found a very comfortable accommodation in a large boarding house owned by Mrs. Rutjes or "Madame" as she allowed herself to be called according to the custom of those who served her and by her guests. [78] Her first husband had been a Frenchman with whom she had spent some time in his homeland. She appeared to have so enjoyed French life that she used that acquired style in every possible way and spiced her English with many French words. Her second husband, a Dane, was either unfaithful or ran away. After this episode, which occurred with the exile from Charleston because of the bombardment, she founded the boarding house in Columbia which had wide popularity and which gave the owner a good income.

This "Madame" ruled as a despot and tyrannized the entire house, whereby those guests who submitted themselves to her authority had nothing to suffer. One could without question be quite satisfied with the excellent meals and lodging but gladly close an ear to the curse words which she used to keep the colored servants well disciplined or when "Madame," her anger kindled, dealt singlehandedly with an unruly guest or one that had not paid. She drove the business with a steady rein, supported by an intelligent Mulatto by the name of "Major" who embodied in one person the wide-ranging services and capabilities of a boot polisher and a house superintendent in addition to the many kinds of activities which lay between those two talents.

The house had the best reputation and was always full. On overlooked "Madame's" little caprices and found certain exhilaration in them. Our landlady did not get involved with the business dealings of her guests: perhaps because she was too busy or perhaps because she knew that she did not belong to or fit into their circle.

It was a nice and fine fellowship which I had found and one to which I came to belong during the duration of my long stay. The fellowship including families which I had superficially known in Charleston, families of planters driven from the coast and many employees of offices, both men and women, from all parts of the Confederacy.

---

78 This was Theonie Marie Louise Alexandrine de la Riviere Mignot Rutjes (1819-1875). Her husband Adolphus Johannes Rutjes was likely a native of the Netherlands.

It was a colorful mix of people among whom I was probably the only foreigner. Nevertheless, all were in perfect harmony. When we gathered in the parlor in the evenings and divided into individual groups according to inclination, be it politics, card games, music, or other, it was always a picture or harmony, of cheerfulness and peace. Those who were able to live in this house did not need to worry about subsistence. He who had once suffered this, the chaos of war could no longer oppress him, as long as his heart had not been traumatized.

There were, in our fellowship, no few talented people who could offer rich material and special enjoyment through instrumental, vocal or rhetorical recitals as entertainment. Indeed, quite often charming parties, amateur concerts and dances were arranged in which, depending on the available space, non-residents of the house could participate. In such cases, our "Madame" displayed excellent hospitality.

I felt right at home in this circle and was a regular participant after a completed day's work.

My brother delighted me with his visits which his business located in Charleston allowed. I was likewise comfortable in this friendly and lively place in which folks were more carefree than in Charleston.

Among the other house guests with whom I was on friendly terms, I had special acquaintances with whom I interacted with fondness. First among them were two ladies! Who would laugh! Although they were single, they were born four years before I was. They served in the department of finance. They were amiable and educated ladies. One of them was very diligent with her German. This probably kindled mutual interest between us. It was also likely that I dedicated my attention and my gallantry to them because they were unattached and possessed charming character. It was to them that I owed access to many of the esteemed families of the city.

I made another friend in the person of a young businessman who had moved there and with whom I shared a neighboring table. I later moved my office into his business location. It is with him that I took longer walks on Sunday in the region, with a fondness for the Congaree on the banks of which, our both being of a rather quixotic nature, we listened to and watched the congenial dancing of the waves of the river over the massive granite boulders.

The observation of such water life, of its effervescing, the eternal coming and going of the body of water without any meaningful change in form had for me something captivating, sublime and exhorting for thought, not unlike the life of a man, hurrying, not aware, often clear, often dirty, often useful, often destructive to the environment, often animated and happy, then creeping as its purpose was being fulfilled and finally sinking into infinity. In the solitude of the forest into which the hustle and bustle of the world does not penetrate, one can hang onto such thoughts. There one is not disturbed; one is not ridiculed.

One of the most interesting fellows to whom I was originally drawn by curiosity but later by his extraordinary intellectual talents was a young deaf and dumb Charlestonian who was the son of a well-situated patrician. He had been reared in Paris and was, even in his regrettable situation, one of the most intelligent men whom I had ever met. With the assistance of a writing tablet which he always had with him, he was able to thoroughly discuss every topic, both in English and in French. He gave deputations, theorized matters of great consequence, developed newly minted perspectives and maintained with all of that the lustiest of humor, such that he was the darling of the fellowship, a status which he also owed to his fine manners and his captivating gallantry toward the ladies. One could learn from this man, who never showed himself to be unhappy, a lot in various matters. In chess and in cards he was as feared as he was loved because he was superior in observing every move and every mistake.

Those were the regular associations of the house which vouchsafed for me comfort and joy. What made my time in Columbia so meaningful and that which keeps alive my unquenchable memories of the wonderful time was the encounter with such admirable human beings with whom I am yet bound after fifteen years in such an intimate friendship which regrettably, because of the great distance, can only be nourished through a regular exchange of letters.

A lady whom I had known in the Carolina House in Charleston introduced me, after I had settled in Columbia, to her brother, Mr.

Groning, and his family which consisted of his wife, two small daughters and siblings. [79] They owned and lived in a small villa, the so-called "Cottage," with a garden in a most pleasant setting on Arsenal Hill. So it was that in this charming little house I spent many happy hours sitting on the veranda. After a few visits, it came to be an intimate home for me with loyal, happy and joyful people. It was a true, sacrificial friendship which was free of all egoism. It was a place of cheerfulness and joy while the days of good fortune were with us and a place of peace and comfort when the days of terror came upon us.

The family life which I found here but which I had previously completely lacked while in America, a life in which I counted myself a member and was so counted, pulled me with force into this comforting circle in which I could enjoy engaging conversation, often with pleasant company which also felt welcome in this most hospitable house, while I enjoyed warm interest in my own person and all of my affairs.

Among others there, I also got to know the family McCully with whom I also had acceptance and warm inclusion. [80] They possessed an elegant house which was all that remained of a large fortune which had been lost through unfortunate investments by a man who had suffered a stroke and who was now a completely broken man. His wife and four grown daughters were well educated women. The oldest of the sisterhood worked along with the mother in the Department of Finance in order to earn a living for the family. An additional income was added by the house itself and slaves who were rented out. As modestly as these good people lived and as submissive as they were to their fate in the loss of their wealth, they, nevertheless, never denied, free of all pride, their aristocratic dignity. I count myself fortunate to have found very pleasant interactions in this genial circle.

---

79 This may have been Lewis Groning (1818-1884), a refugee from Charleston. His wife was Sarah Groning (1826-1903).

80 This was the family of John McCully, whose wife was Eliza M. Haraden McCully (1814-1892). The 1860 census listed John McCully as a man of 60, with a wife and several dependents (children) in his household, as well as an elderly lady named Susan Haraden, his mother-in-law. Susan Devericks Haraden (1796-1865) was the widow of Nathaniel Haraden, a native of Massachusetts who served as the sail master on the USS *Constitution*.

Another guest of the House of Groning left her mark on me. She was a very charming, young English woman talented with noble character of intellect and heart with an enchanting voice. She was, however, unable to stay, having given her hand several years before to a rich South Carolina planter of seventy years. This step meant the loss of her life's joy. The elderly spouse persecuted her out of jealousy which, I am sure, she did not deserve. Completely despondent, she had fled to this place, a house where she found refuge and recuperation until she finally submitted to her punishing fate of enduring the broken promises of her husband. I can still see this angelic figure and can still hear her sweet voice with which she sang songs of melancholy and longing. I was struck with great sadness when I learned afterward of her death and therein her deliverance. She died of a broken heart. [81]

The year 1864 passed thusly in a busy but most pleasurable manner. The memories bring the good things with them, suppress the small cares and worries of the past, greatly weaken the considerable sufferings, and keep alive, perhaps even heighten, the joys and pleasures.

In the meantime, my brother had left the theater of business and war and had taken one of or steamers to Bermuda and from there on to our homeland. [82] The longing for the pleasure for the good fortune which he had helped to bring about and the feeling of abandonment at being separated from my only kinsman crept over me; but I would not and could not leave my good position; and I rejoiced again and again that he and my love for him had been granted a time of solidarity.

This solidarity transferred to me for the duration of his absence the management of the Consulate of Hanover in the State of South Carolina and for the processing of papers of some of his yet pending business dealings as well as his paper fortune which he through his optimistic view had almost completely put in Confederate or state bonds.

---

[81] This English lady may have been Julia Clara Rowcroft (1841-1866), who married Charles Warley (1797-1877), a Colleton District planter (Antwerp Plantation) in 1858.

[82] The following notice appeared in the *Charleston Daily Courier* on July 8, 1864: "During my absence from the state my brother F. A. Clacius, for the present at Wilmington, N.C., will act as my attorney; he will likewise attend to the business of the Hanoverian Consulate. Charleston, June 18th, 1864. C. Clacius."

The consulate now entailed a lot of work which consisted of filling out certificates for the subjects of the Kingdom of Hanover once their claim had been verified. The reason was that the holder of such a certificate was freed from the duty of military service which was required of every man from sixteen to sixty who had not yet volunteered. The exceptions were being an invalid or holding a position which could not be filled with the female workforce.

Yes, the existence of the South was becoming ever more doubtful. In Virginia, the enemy made steady gains; and when in the fall of 1864, Sherman's army penetrated into Georgia and laid waste to the defenseless landscape, with the expressed purpose of moving against Charleston and Savannah, they were poised for an attack on the rear of the South. The loss of these cities was calculated and no longer in doubt. With these things, the authorities and the public were filled with grave misgivings, even if they were not uttered in public.

With an array of weapons by all combat-capable forces, a last attempt would be made to stop the progress of the enemy if not to win back already lost territory. Each state took measures commensurate with its own situation in order to defend its own territory. Even I had to put out effort to be exempted from military duty with reserve forces. In a real moment of distress while away in Wilmington, I was almost picked up by a military patrol which had the duty to retain each male for service. My office of consul in South Carolina was not recognized in North Carolina; and with the distress of the times, little consideration was given. For that reason, I remained hidden in Wilmington on that disastrous day. That evening, with the help of a pass which I had previously acquired, I happily made it to a train which "kidnapped" me to Columbia.

The business still moved along, but it became ever more unsettling with the daily threat of losing places with harbors and with the even greater attention of the blockading fleet of the United States. It occurred more and more that a ship attempting a landing was discovered and pursued by the enemy and had to return to the port of origin. From time to time, ships even made it into Charleston and were fortunate in avoiding the risk of their destruction through the bombardment.

Chapter 17

On Post in the Woods

Early in December of 1864, I was informed by telegram that our steamer, the Caroline, in order to escape the pursuit of the enemy, had found shelter in the little port city of Georgetown after failed attempts to reach Wilmington or Charleston.

This place, which in the good old days had provided Charleston with raw rice which was cultivated in the region and along the rivers which discharged into the ocean there, was now completely cut off from trade; and its coastal shipping had been forcibly suppressed which was often the only means for transporting the local product. This gave us numerous inconveniences and worries with regard to the further transport of arriving goods and to acquiring new cargos for the errant steamers. The next railroad station was approximately fifty miles away; and the transport of the important quality wares to and from this place was very difficult, given the lack of transport means. It was very time consuming and quite costly. Along with colleagues from Wilmington, I had to go to the location in order to secure the expedition. It was not possible to transport the goods from the locale or get cotton to the locale by means of wagons because the vehicles which could be found were not in the condition to move the goods in time required. All that we could do was to have rafts built from the wood that abounded there in plenty and load them with the goods which would be transported on a long journey first up the Pee Dee and then up the Black River to the station located in Kingstree.

For the sake of comfort and for the lack of a hotel which met our standards, we took quarters on the Caroline herself, with good food and lodging. The enemy was aware of the presence of the Caroline in Georgetown. We could observe from our position as the enemy patrolled the entrance to the harbor, approached its entrance and took up position there. The harbor, which had been of no importance, was not fortified, save for a few mines which had been laid and of which the captains and pilots were aware. For this reason, we had to fear that the enemy, emboldened by the prize in the harbor, would attempt to come into the harbor with smaller vessels and kidnap our good Caroline since there was no defense to set against that intent.

In light of this threatening danger, it was decided in high council to go as far as possible up river with the ship. The fears of the present obstructions on the river and the shallowness suggested that such an attempt should not be undertaken. These were, however, allayed by technical experts and further considerations.

In addition to the advantage that the ship could no longer be seen by the enemy and be a temptation for him to kidnap, we managed an essential convergence to the railroad station.

The plan was executed without any incident. It was a wonderful winter's day or, better put, a late but beautiful fall day which was referred to as "Indian summer," this in these climes in December. The sun offered comfortable warmth in a cloudless sky. The air was pure and clear. No breeze stirred, and nature showed herself in her last allurement in her colorful glory of fall.

The trip up the broad Pee Dee and then up the Black River went very well indeed and offered to us great interest as well as to those gathered on the bank, both white and black, who had likely never seen a sea steamer and certainly not so far inland. The way on the relatively narrow, clear river with its twists and turns led through rice plantations and regions of vast forests. The ship's wake waters churned and threw themselves on the banks where they either distressed or disturbed the lush and flourishing reeds. Millions of wild geese were disturbed in their resting places and took flight in swarms like clouds. It did not seem possible to me that such masses of wildlife could exist in such limited space and could only regret that they would be lost to the human palate and stomach. About twenty miles from our starting point where the river was still wide enough, we stopped because a sharp curve hindered our forward progress. It was indeed a charming place for a longer stay in this solitary region. Although it was not foreseen, it put us in good stead. From our landing spot, the terrain which was otherwise flat rose to a steep, sloping high plateau which dropped on three sides into the river which snaked around its base. The plateau was covered with ancient, majestic live oaks in which moss and climbing plants lushly abounded. Grey squirrels in large numbers, frisky and fearless, played in their branches, looking for the fruit of the oaks as their nourishment. Farther in, the grove of oaks thickened into a primeval forest.

On the other side of the river, the land was cultivated for long stretches; however, the season of the year did not offer opportunity, which would have certainly been interesting, to observe the rice culture which was practiced there.

We settled in to this place of solitude as best we could. The rafts moved the goods which had been in part unloaded in Georgetown to their destinations and retrieved the cotton bales which had been ordered from the train station. In spite of the fact that the ship now lay half the distance between the port and the railroad station, the complete loading of the ship was several weeks away so that we spent the Christmas Tide in the stillness of the woods. It was not until that last days of December that the ship was ready to begin the voyage to the West Indies.

We had many hours to enjoy the muses. We hiked through the area and discovered many points of interest and explored the grandeurs of the forest. There was on board a plentiful supply of guns and ammunition. Since I was a poor shot, it fell to me to bag the squirrels, an act which required neither talent nor stealth. I was, however, very proud to provide the cook with a number of these little animals which the Americans view as a delicacy. My colleagues, who were practiced in the art of hunting, had the obligation of acquiring the more difficult game such as deer, rabbit and goose. Their skill made it possible that we have wild turkey for the Christmas table, a treat which the better-situated Americans could not dispense with. The river provided us with a large number of fish. The game, the fish and the provisions which we had on board ensured that we lived opulently.

From the nearby plantations, out of their houses and storage facilities, there came to us where we were positioned a delegation of blacks, both men and women, A mulatto woman who functioned as the voice of the group gave us an invitation to participate in a Christmas Negro Celebration at their quarters. Alone the sight of the doyenne delivering the invitation tempted one to attend. I would have gladly accepted because I was interested in Negro deviltry and wanted to get to know them in their lusty, ethnic environment. My white friends, on the other hand, felt it beneath their dignity to accept this offer. Thus, the delegation received a negative response; however, they returned home with delicacies which we gave them to spice up their festivities and were likely very pleased despite the failure of the mission.

After the Caroline had been fully loaded and after we had received word that the enemy was no longer asserting a full siege of the harbor, we returned there with the steamer. The moon phase at the time demanded an attempt at a quick escape. This took place on the very first night so that we were able to return to our different home bases.

Chapter 18

The Threatening Danger

My destination was Charleston where I was to take care of important matters with the owner. These duties and the unexpected arrival of the Fanny in Charleston harbor and dealing with her cargo held me there for several weeks.

Ever more threatening was the situation in Charleston through the bombardment in which the enemy perfected through bigger, farther-reaching cannons and by using other points which he had acquired through repeated attacks. The most threatening danger was, however, from the energetic advance of Sherman's "glorious" army, objectively spoken, of course. It was understood that the main objective of the march was to capture and punish Charleston, the most hated city which was the "cradle of the rebellion" which had continued stiff resistance and which had prolonged the war with the blockade business and the provisions which it had provided.

With the fearfully anticipated capture of the available harbors, which one considered to be but a matter of time, our business would have to come to an end of its own accord. It was important to figure out a way to safeguard the property of the investors.

As the catastrophe befell us, the ships had the good fortune of being in foreign ports. There, after a cessation of the hostilities which would end in the subjugation of the South, they could be commercialized to the credit of those invested. The cash which was in the banks and the pending gain from cotton sales in Liverpool, if not already divided, was to be paid out to all investors. It became my duty to ensure that these decisions were carried out by means of transfers and bills of exchange to our representative in London so that payments could be effected.

For this purpose, I again took up my post in Columbia. Mr. Bee wanted to remain in Charleston as long as possible and only leave Charleston in the moment of greatest distress when his own person was in danger, this after he had secured his family on his holdings in the countryside and after he had transferred the moveable property belonging to him to his firm and to the company to Columbia and other places.

On 23 January 1865, I left Charleston for the last time, filled with worry and doubt about the future, yet not knowing that I was leaving the place for the last time. I had likely taken the final leave of the people and the places which I had come to love.

In Columbia, my two colleagues and I were fully engaged in catching up matters which had been left undone during my absence and in changing Confederate money into sterling for the good fortune of our investors. The business claimed every bit of my time so that it was not possible for me to visit the families whom I had befriended.

There was nothing to fear for Columbia. To the contrary, one considered oneself and one's property more secure here than in any other place in the Confederacy.

However, misfortune marches quickly. Like a clap of thunder from clear skies, at first unbelievable but then even more convincingly, came the rumors and the reports that Sherman had suddenly changed his course and had brought his army about in the direction of Columbia.

A horror gripped the inhabitants at this news, doubted, of course, until reality burst upon us. If these reports were really founded in reality, then it would be only a few days until the arrival of the mass of troops. Many private persons, but particularly the bankers and authorities, took flight with such provisions that were in their custody. What the trains could carry was brought farther into the interior of the country. Madame Rutjes also took flight, and I had to find other quarters. I rented a private room and ate in a restaurant which was still open. Most of the residents could not or would not flee the city; and they did not know, if it were not safe here, where was one then to find refuge? It was also an unknown whether individuals would experience a lot of trouble at the capture of the city if this indeed occurred.

Even I covered myself with a misplaced feeling of security, betrayed as such as things actually turned out. I allowed myself to imagine that the enemy was not my enemy and my dignity as well as the things covered by the flag, and that the flag of Hanover itself would be respected. Without question, that would have happened if the command had been able to keep the mob of troops in a professional and disciplined manner. I was, however, fully convinced that no loss would be inflicted on my person and that I would simply remain here and see how things progressed. My colleagues left me and departed for points farther inland to places where their families were located. They took a large part of the books and papers with them since such might betray my participation in the prohibited business which could cause me difficulties.

The enemy came with force, and his anticipated arrival in Columbia eliminated all doubt. The Confederates had quickly assembled a militia of just over one thousand men to defend the city and had erected barricades made of the cotton bales which were present. [83] It had been decided to defend the city which was open on all sides, as meaningless and as detrimental as these measures were.

On 15 February 1865, doom was upon us. [84] This discharge of the thunderstorm did not itself cause as much terror as the mugginess which preceded it, especially since one did not know what consequences would result. One simply had no idea of the destructive effect. Despite all worries, the new drama which was unknown to all had a certain interest. The picture of war, for me since I did not fear for myself or for the peaceful residents, had a particular appeal. I expected a

---

83 There were several thousand Confederate troops who participated In the defense of Columbia against Sherman's forces which numbered over 60,000.

84 Conrad's memory is off by one day; the day he refers to here is February 16, 1865.

quick, unproblematic occupation of the city, the establishment of the authority of the United States, and a continued march of the army, ending in a peaceful and orderly execution of the operation.

On the day mentioned, the enemy appeared on the opposite heights and demonstrated before the unaided eye a most interesting picture of the pulsating life of the sixty thousand man army, their cannons, their wagon park, their tents and other things. It gave the appearance that the troops had settled in on that lovely place in order to rest from their strenuous march. The trees which crowned the plateau were for the most part felled and the earth was worked flat. Tents were put up, and a bivouac was erected such that it resembled an anthill from which flames and smoke of campfires rose and from which drum and trumpet signals sounded.

It has been told, that when General Sherman arrived at the point, he gave, in his humorous way, a speech to his troops which went something like this:

"Boys, over there lies a picturesque city. For a long time, we have not had good quarters. There we might find such. Would it not be good for us to take a closer look at it; and if it pleases us, to take possession of it?"

The "boys" were allegedly in complete agreement with this suggestion and with one voice yelled, "Hip, hip, hurrah!" They thereby gave their approval.

The day passed quite peacefully. They enemy could allow this moment in the certainty of his victory. On our side, the barricades were quickly erected, and time was won to move more things out of the city.

Chapter 19

THE OCCUPATION OF COLUMBIA

At the break of dawn on the following day, the fateful sixteenth of February, the scene changed. [85] As a consequence of the delayed surrender of the city, the enemy began to bombard the city, admittedly without any major damage but enough to rekindle the anxiety of the populace. I just managed to avoid death or major injury from a walnut-size piece of shrapnel from a shell which exploded above me and which then drilled a hole several inches deep at my feet. In spite of the momentary fright, I managed to retrieve it and keep it as a souvenir of the significant day and the danger which I had good fortune escaped.

The intended resistance, a defense by an insignificant military force, was nonsense, indeed a gross measure by the Confederate command which had no support from the populace given the reality of the situation. It could have been because the inefficacy of the plan became obvious or because of the request of the honest, old mayor; but the little band of Confederates withdrew and took their last wagons and equipment with them. The mayor went to the camp of the enemy and announced the unconditional surrender of the city and requested for it and its inhabitants fair treatment and protection.

In the meantime, I was able to order my affairs as far as possible. I had secured all of my business papers which had been left behind in a fireproof cabinet in my office. I packed my private things in a suitcase and left them in the locked room under the care of my landlady. The

---

85 Sherman's forces entered Columbia on February 17, 1865.

important papers of mine, of my brother, of the business and of the consulate I placed in part in a tin box and others in my pockets. I filled the travel case with clothes and other things which I would need so that, in any case, I could keep them with me. In addition, in case of a potential emergency, I had six-hundred dollars in gold coins and jewels of considerable value which I had purchased along with interest bearing coupons of considerable value which I secured in a long leather pouch around my waist and covered with my clothes.

Loaded with these valuables and carrying the flag of the Royal House of Hanover, I made my way to the house of a German woman whom I had gotten to know in Charleston. She had moved her circle of influence here through her talent as a music and voice teacher. She had invited me to serve as the protector of her house and her several small children, given my station and the authority of my office as consul.

Thus, it is here for the time being that I stored my baggage and unfolded the banner of the House of Hanover at the window. There I waited to see how things would turn out, believing that my apartment and office had been secured.

The invasion of enemy troops began around noon. First came the engineers and sappers who cleared away the obstructions blocking the main street since the purpose of these obstructions which would have meant a bloody street fight could no longer be served. The obstructions were quickly removed, and the carriage of the mayor along with some ranking officers moved through the street, now free, to the city hall. These were followed by the blue army in unending rows, led by the energetic and cold-blooded General Sherman and his staff and then by all of the blue uniformed regiments from the northwestern states of the Union: infantry, cavalry and artillery. The entire army marched into the city and spread itself into various streets or marched on through to camp in the area around the city since there was not enough room in the city itself.

I must admit that the drama bemused me: the unending host which had a long march behind it and a long march before it; the famous and feared leader with his general staff; and the fluttering flags of the victorious Union. This was all new to me and quite interesting. I do not regret having experienced it, even if I would abstain from the repetition of such in the future.

The soldiers were in the highest of spirits and sang and yelled in rank and file. They also cast longing eyes at the houses and were thinking, without a doubt, about the treasures which were likely there and which my fall to them as booty.

The citizens of Columbia had given themselves over to their fate. Few watched the entry of the enemy. The loss of the peaceful city, so important to the Confederacy, filled them with melancholy, with the thoughts of what was going to happen to them, and with worry. It is with patience that one has to face that which cannot be avoided. The streets were completely empty of civilians, and the new masters exerted their power far and wide in the city.

For the sake of the reputation of General Sherman and the entire nation of the United States, I suppose that the troops, as is the custom among civilized peoples and leaders, had been instructed not to misappropriate private property, not to destroy such, and not to harass citizens, especially not women, and that the command was serious that the promise of protection given to the city authorities as well as the protection of each person and private property was to be carried out. Nevertheless, however, the leader bears full responsibility for the misconduct of his subordinates, and his fame must be besmirched either because Sherman's army lacked the necessary discipline and bearing or in such cases because the commanders tolerated these infamous actions and perhaps even privately had a sense of delight in the deeds.

After the orderly occupation of the city, the highest officers, that being the generals and the colonels, quartered themselves in the best of houses, either those vacated by their owners or turned over to them by the owner. The rest of the host were left to themselves. The soldiers bivouacked in the streets or took over empty houses where they made themselves very much at home. Even inhabited houses were not spared. At first, they took their lodging in entry ways, foyers, and corridors. Up to that point, things were quite alright and were carried out with respect by the victorious enemy.

Even in the house in which I was having my stay, it swarmed with soldiers, among them several officers. They were to a point decent enough and respected the flag. The captain in command gave his assurance that nothing would befall us and that we should peaceably remain in our rooms. This quartering was, however, in no way pleasant. The taunting and raw speech of the soldiers, their entire demeanor, their insolent demands for food and drink to which they had no right made us not a little apprehensive.

They were generally a wild and gruff bunch who instilled disgust and fear in everyone. They were made up of the vulgar classes of mankind from all nations. Among them were not only the provincial Americans but also numerous Irish and Germans. To the disgrace of the German nation, I am compelled to assert that these sons of Germany who were members of this army were among the first and the most zealous in committing these foul deeds I will afterward delineate based on multiple opportunities to observe them.

With disgust, we were able to observe the wild, vulgar conduct from our windows which faced the main street. I was immediately convinced that nothing good would come of this and that Confederate soldiers, almost all of the sons of the country, were vastly superior to this curdle of hirelings in customs, in discipline and bravery.

I am being very impartial and freely cede exceptions when known to me by witness accounts or seen by me personally; but in general, this was a band of thieves and robbers, including the lower-ranking officers.

It did not take long for the mob not to be satisfied with the occupation of the streets and houses and with the freely given or coerced gifts. They initially began breaking into businesses and stores and plundering them. Only the money, the gold, the silver and other valuables were taken; the rest was ransacked, torn down, destroyed or strewn about. It was a dismal impression as one observed that items of all kinds, which the soldiers could not use or take with them, were thrown out of the various stores and lay in all manner in the streets, there to be crushed and destroyed. What could or should the owners do against this raw violence? For their protest and entreaties standing on the ruins of their property, they harvested only mockery and profane words. Above all, their appeal to the superiors who were present brought no results.

In light of this public plundering, I naturally feared a similar fate for my business papers and my personal things in the places where I had secured them. Worry and curiosity drove me out into the wild storm in order to find out what was happening. The office, which was partially hidden, I found undisturbed. It was not easy to imagine a breach of the money safe, which did not actually contain much of value since the books and papers had been sent away and the rest was protected on my person. Calmed by this, after I had emptied my packed travel case so that I could fill it again with things in the suitcase in my room, I made my way to my apartment. I had made but a few steps with the travel case, when a mounted soldier or robber stopped me and commanded me to give him the travel case. My objection that the case did not belong to him but to me, our hero did not acknowledge, but drew and swung his sword with the comment that I should not take up his valuable time and should rather concern myself with keeping my arm. I immediately understood the validity of his claim and made good on it by giving him, to my good fortune, an empty travel case. That was the first street robbery which I was to experience. Even better was yet to come!

In my apartment, a new shock awaited me. As I entered the courtyard, I found there the contents of my suitcase, to the extent that some of it was there, strewn about and mixed with other items which were not mine. Little Negro children were gawking and wondering at the photos of my relatives and were playing with the items which had been left behind by the thieves as useless. Letters from my family and friends which I had carefully sorted and packed, letters which contained words of love and of comfort, roamed around in the public courtyard, dirty and torn. Many of the things which I valued and which were irreplaceable were entirely lost. I was overcome by a deep longing at the loss of that which was mine, attended by anger and contempt for the worthless destroyers. I gathered from what remained the most valuable and relinquished the rest to destruction. It had been just as bad with my landlady. Her personal intervention was unable to protect her belongings or mine. Her losses were much greater than mine, save for the silver which remained untouched, buried in the garden.

I ran back to my provisional quarters and found surprisingly no damage in the apartment of Mrs. Volger although the shops on the ground floor had been looted empty. I do not know whom or what we had to thank: the protection of the flag up to that point, pure luck or a garrison which was somewhat decent. We gave, therefore, ourselves over to the hope that we would remain out of danger.

The noise in the street became greater. It was in part made up of the jubilation over the captured booty and in part made up of cursing because of it which I took to mean that they were dissatisfied with it. Headquarters remained quite passive in the face of this public plunder, even though some families which had the courage had complained about the outrages which were growing out of control and petitioned to have men posted to protect their houses. It was all merely pro forma without any effect. Either the posted watches did not have the commensurate authority, or they did not obey orders. Most of the protected homes suffered the same fate as the others.

I was not in a position to worry about the homes of my friends because of their remoteness. Everyone had enough to do simply caring for himself. I did not dare get to far from the place where I had located myself.

Thus ended the day for the noble warriors in comfortable and gainful work, but their day was not over. For that, the time was too valuable; and night fits much better those with dark souls and abets their dark craft.

Chapter 20

THE NIGHT OF TERROR

Night fell over the otherwise friendly city in which during the day tumult and disorder had ruled; over the evil enemy who worked with thousands of tools on destruction; and over unfortunate people who stared into the future with distress and worry.

With the arrival of darkness, the soldiers who were camped in the streets lit fires in order to prepare for themselves supper. I, therefore, brought to the attention of the captain of our house that this measure should perhaps be forbidden since such fires could easily ignite the bales of cotton and other stuff which was lying around close by which could lead to a calamity of the worst kind. O sancta simplicitas![86] How could I expect any regard from these people? The reply of the honorable captain as to why I might be concerned with the actions of his troops and whether I would provide them with a kitchen in which to cook their supper put me back in my place as one conquered. I could not afford to arouse the personal animosity of the man who had shown at least a spark of decorum and authority. I invited him and the two lieutenants to partake in our meager supper. Before supper had been put to table, however, a huge fire with a column of smoke rose up not too far away. The railroad station at the end of the city was burning and the cotton which was stored there gave the fire plenty of nourishment. That, too, just now today! In all of the confusion, however, this occurrence stirred little interest until flames began to

---

86 Translated from the Latin, this means holy innocence. Conrad was referring to his own naivete in alerting the officer to the danger of starting fires.

rise high in the other direction and when in a few minutes yet another house was burning, namely one just behind the one in which we were living. The realization suddenly dawned on us that this was planned arson with undetermined consequences, and this thought filled us with terror.

Since the enemy, loitering around the fires, made no effort to extinguish the blazes and since he seemed to revel in the sight with demeaning comments, our feeling was strengthened that the first were deliberately set. To this day, I do not know whether the riffraff was ordered to commit the arson from the highest authority or whether the command simply tolerated it.

Under such circumstances the rapid spread of the fire could not be stopped, and it became necessary for us to leave our quarters. The poor widow who had no possibility of saving her belonging was in disbelief. She pled on her knees with the commander of billeting to bring her and her children to safety and to allow some of his men to assist her in bringing some of her things to a family who lived on the edge of town with whom she was seeking refuge. Up to a point, he met her pleadings which would have softened a stone in that he accompanied the unfortunate woman and her children along with some of her belongings which consisted of silver which she could carry to her destination. More assistance than that he could not and would not give. What we were able to hurriedly pack in bundles, suitcases and purses we first carried down the stairs anticipating the assistance of the captain and his men. It was, however, immediately plundered by a greedy rabble and dragged away or the contents were scattered before our eyes. Every other attempt ended with the same results.

I was carrying my belongings, the entrusted goods and well as my private material in my hands and under my arms and was determined to reach my intended shelter in the closest house owned by Mr. Gully by whom I was befriended. I avoided the direct way via the main street in which a heavy throng of yelling and cheering soldiers moved and who gave themselves authorization to set cotton bales ablaze. I hoped by means of more peaceful streets to reach my goal without danger. The city imparted an indescribably grim sight. A much larger number of homes was burning in all directions, and the wind quickly aided the spread of this destructive element. In the houses and on the streets, the evil mob plundered, destroyed and rioted as if hell itself had broken out. Mixed in with this noise were the heart-rending cries of distress of people who had been plundered by these robbers, of people who had been attacked and of people attempting to escape the flames. Here and there, I saw these unfortunate souls with the children on their arms along with the little bit of belongings fleeing the devils and the fire, looking for any kind of shelter but only to find when they reached their assumed place of refuge the same loss.

It was horrible. The knowledge that these poor people could find no place of refuge made the circumstances even more horrible.

No one could offer help. Each was fixed on his own fate and on a possible safe place. So it was that I, too, was unable to take a care for the things happening around me but had to at least attempt to flee this theater of horrors and follow the slightest ray of hope offered by the privilege of Providence. I was at first successful in the course which I took through side streets and detours. I suffered the loss of a few papers which I could but carry under my arms and which were ripped away by soldiers whom I encountered. My cramped hands kept hold of their burden, and several attempts to relieve my hands of their charge were unsuccessful. By quick flight I was able to evade the several attempts which as if by a wonder did not result in pursuit and which hindered another successful robbery. Such attempts offered themselves en masse.

I almost reached my goal and did find the region where my refuge was located, still untouched by the fire. The glimmer of hope in rescue and of emancipation from my fear and distress grew to cheerful anticipation that I would finally find some rest. In my excited mind there were spawned all sorts of possible plans where I would bury my possessions and hide them from the eyes of the trailing hounds.

There at that moment a squad of soldiers led by a captain crossed my path in an orderly march. Without a doubt, they constituted an official patrol. With childlike naiveté, I viewed them, not as thieves, but as protectors of those in distress. I reduced my pace which had just about exhausted me and encountered this detachment on a street corner, hoping to complete the rest of the way which I was walking under their protection.

I was, however, stopped. The captain demanded to know what I was carrying. I made myself known as the Consul of Hanover and explained that my luggage to be partly my personal possessions and partly that of the consulate which I had packed together to escape the fire. With that, I believed that I had established my legitimacy and thought that I would be able to go on my way. The captain was, however, curious and wanted to convince himself of the truth of my testimony. The luggage was taken away from me, and I had to open the tin box which was in it. The entire enterprise for which I had worked was rumbling around in the things which were strewn all over the place. One would take this; the other would take that. Only the empty tin box with the seal of the consulate and some letters and worthless papers remained. Everyone profited. Pleading brought no results, and my cries of despair concerning this great loss, which I was actually not able to grasp in the moment of excitement, were silenced by the threat to beat me to death if I did not conduct myself peaceably.

The results of the robbery were not enough. The captain demanded my wallet and my watch. Humiliated as I was and in face of the threatened use of force, I freely gave him what he demanded, hoping thereby to avoid a more thorough search of my person.

That, dear reader, was the function of a patrol of the Army of Sherman which was accompanied by German sympathies, although not those of the English or the French, in their war of annihilation against the South, which to the contrary was nobler in thought and action than they. That was an example of the band of robbers and of their officers who had taken the field against a zealous but noble enemy and which had revealed by the light of day that their bravery was actually dastardly and cowardly robbery, cursing and defamation of defenseless people, namely women and children. I am not exaggerating as I give this description. The judgment of these matters is a matter for others. I gladly stipulate that not all of the Northern soldiers, perhaps only a small minority, were part of this sputum of humanity in that I

The burning of Columbia, by William Waud, 1865. Library of Congress.

later had opportunity to come to know well-disciplined soldiers of the United States.

I gathered up the case and a few of the papers left behind; and little by little, I became aware of what I had lost. In particular, it was the property entrusted to me by my brother which nearly all was taken in this last act of treachery. It was property which he had with great discipline earned over the years and to which he placed in his distant locale the peace of his financial security. This would hit him a particularly hard blow.

In addition, there was the larger part of the exchange in England, which I had written out as dividends for the stockholders of our company, dividends which had not yet been requested by them and which, if they were used, would represent a large fortune. For the purpose of annulling these dividends and thereby ensuring that they were worthless for the unlawful user, I had little opportunity for a long time. In the meantime, these dividends could be in good faith paid out to the thief or his accomplice.

The loss of the consulate documents and other private papers bothered me less; mine, in comparison to ones just mentioned, not at all. I was, however, downcast at the far-reaching losses and at the impossibility of being able to do anything to regain them. During that night and later once again, I experienced how much a man can bear. I also discovered that the presence of and the certainty of such a stoke of fate far less horrific is than the fear of such a fate when one has become convinced though such experience that there is nothing one can do about it and that one must keep still.

As I became conscious of this, my despair turned to resignation. There was little comfort in the knowledge that at this hour many people were beset by a much harder fate than was I. Despite everything which had befallen me, I could at the very least treasure that I had been able to save my life and the valuables consisting mostly of paper which were fastened to my body. I had, however, reason to fear for their future security.

With the little of what I had left, I arrived safely but exhausted and depressed to the house of the family McCully. In light of the grave events and the danger in which they also found themselves which they had fortunately been able to avoid up until that point, they were in a great agitation and greeted my arrival with great joy. The mentally and physically lethargic man sat sunken in silent brooding. An aged grandmother lay sick in bed. [87] With much effort, the grim happenings were kept from her. The wife and daughters were beside themselves with fear and worry, both heightened as I told of my experiences. With a lot of effort, I was able to convince them to begin to gather and to provisionally store their valuables so that they were prepared to flee

---

87 This was Mrs. McCully's mother, Susan Devericks Haraden, who was about seventy years old. She died on April 3, 1865, and her funeral notice, which was published the following day in the *Daily Phoenix*, mentions Mr. and Mrs. John McCully. Her husband, Nathaniel Haraden, who served on the USS *Constitution*, was commended for gallantry at the siege of Tripoli in 1804.

and take the most important things with them in case of a raid or the conflagration which was headed their way.

These fine people had the good fortune of having among the soldiers quartered there a courageous and educated young man who was not only considerate and kind to the occupants but also protected their property in word and in deed against the insolent and trespassing thieves. Among his comrades, he stood alone in his bearing documented by his natural strength of character which was rare. He opposed them like a superior as they attempted again and again to plunder the house and set it ablaze until his strength could no longer hold out against the violence. He himself declared the behavior of his companions to be undignified and ignoble and lamented the fact that among them was a useless pack consisting mostly of Europeans, particularly Irish and Dutchmen (Germans). He asserted, however, that these atrocities were contrary to the will of the highest commander.

The flames were already raging in this part of the city which had earlier been spared, perhaps after the richer houses had been emptied and destroyed. Stronger and stronger was the assault of the "brave" men, and it did not long last that our courageous protector was unable to thwart the predators storming through the doors and windows. Everything was beat to pieces; that which could be used was stolen away; that which could not be used was destroyed. With just a few effects, the poor despoiled family and I were barely able to gain the door as the flames were already licking out the windows. The greatest difficulty was saving the old grandmother who in ultimate distress escaped a death by fire, carried to safety by two helpful and loyal Negroes. One of the honorable assailants I was able to grab by the collar just as he was about to set the bed in which the old lady lay ablaze. I had heard her calls for help and was able to frustrate, just in the nick of time, a gruesome murder. In the struggle, for which I had no fear given the unimaginable act, and in the exchange of words which occurred as we fought, I became to my horror aware that this beast was a German, and he could not even speak English well! Such a son had our good fatherland provided to fight slavery but had delivered in truth a robber and a murderer. He was regrettably not the only one of his race who committed such despicable deeds.

The preferred method of the scoundrels to burn a house was to set the beds on fire. This best served their purpose. The fire spread easily and quickly. The rascals did not need to fear that a house would be spared.

Once again burned out and homeless, I left the house with the McCully family. Just as we left, the house exploded in flames at several points, thus lighting the sad and homeless way for its inhabitants of many years. Where should we then turn? There was no longer much choice. Only a relatively small number of houses remained unharmed; and these would be, based on prescience, visited by the same cruel fate. I wanted once again to seek my security by the family Groning. Arsenal Hill was still shrouded in deep darkness. The searing mob had not yet reached it, or they had not found the modest house worth the effort. My friends, at least at the moment, still had a home. Part of my band of refugees, including the old grandmother, two of the daughters and the suffering father found refuge with relatives not far from where I was headed. Both the grandmother and the father died within a short time of the night of horror, likely from starvation. The lady and two of the daughters went with me to my destination at which we arrived safely, not, however, without having lost a large part of the effects we had initially taken with us along the way.

I was completely shriveled by the repeated attacks and the blows of fate which had broken over me in the last few hours which seemed to me as an eternity as well as by the gorgeous and nightmarish view as seen from the hill of the flaming see which spread out below me and which advanced with a snarling voice! I now thought only of myself and my unfortunate wards for whom I was regrettably unable to offer but little protection and help.

At least part of the family was housed for the meantime, and I along with the rest had arrived at my friends' place. My friends, for some unknown reason, had up until now suffered nothing but fear and fright and had been able to fend off the numerous attempts of the intruders. It had been the energetic Mrs. Groning, a lady of the highest quality, who had understood how to fend off the cowardly rabble with a fearless stance, by means of well-formulated rebuffs and well-worded treatment of his curse-worthy behavior. She was herself a Northerner and repudiated the predators in connection with any people who would use such rabble in their service. Her fluent and powerful way of speech had a powerful effect on those who had not expected such resistance where they had otherwise encountered only fear, trembling and pleading. These negotiations, conducted through locked doors and windows always ended well with the withdrawal of the attackers, who went off to seek an easier field for their activities.

It was at an early morning hour that I reached my place of asylum and was given a welcome greeting along with my unfortunate companions. The nerves which had been tense up until this point refused to serve me further, and I was unable to keep myself upright. I found a bit of rest stretched out on the carpet in the living room, rest for the moment from that which lay behind me but also from that which was still before me. Again and again I was startled awake by new disturbers of the peace and was prepared for yet another eviction.

Little by little the unwelcomed visits waned; and with the coming of daylight, they stopped altogether. The unworthy subjects seemed to be satisfied with the result of their devilish works. Perhaps they were simply exhausted from their strenuous work during the night. It might have been that they were themselves startled at the view, revealed to them by the light of day, at the destruction which they had wrought. Enough it was. We were no longer being attacked. The streets cleared, and we took a deep breath! It indeed appeared that the friendly cottage enjoyed the good fortune to have been spared the general fate of the city. After all that we had been through, we were most grateful for heavenly providence who had left to our good host her home and her property and had at least provided us with a cheerful place of refuge while so many other unfortunate ones had to go without, this all in a very raw season of the year.

After I had gotten over the initial shock and after I had taken account of my losses, and in spite of the size of those losses, how fortunate I had been in comparison to many others, including the family McCully, since I had at least saved my cash and my valuables, I went outside to look for the other part of the family and for Mrs. Volger who had been separated from me earlier and to determine what their fates had been. I fortunately found her safe in one of the places of refuge which she had sought. Although barely alive because of the horrors which she had faced and the losses which she had suffered, she had also received by accident a great blessing.

This fact was, given the situation, nevertheless, a reassurance for me and for the family. When I had brought them this report, I took in the devastation of the previous night.

Chapter 21

The Results of the Destruction

The beautiful, friendly city of Columbia no longer existed. In one single night, indeed within a view hours, she had vanished, transformed into rubble. Only a few houses on Arsenal Hill and on the outer edges of the city remained standing. The center of town was totally destroyed. The routes on which the streets had crisscrossed the city were completely impassable and could only be recognized by the walls which jutted upward. Otherwise, everything was a pile of debris out of which smoke rose which befouled the air. With new horror, with disgust, and with hate for the instigators and the silent partners of this crime, I studied the ruins of this place which I had come to love, a place which in its new appalling appearance could no longer be recognized. So, too, lay my office with its contents, my apartment and many places where I often and gladly spent my time, in ruins.

What of the people who just yesterday were unsuspecting, calm and peaceful occupants of these ruins which were once houses? Many of them perished in the sea of flames and were now raising their complaints against their murderers before the Throne of the Most High. It required some time for their burned corpses to be found, retrieved from the rubble and be buried.

What of the rest? Where had they been driven by fear and distress? Those who were not as fortunate as I was to find shelter with friends, and relatively few could be taken in by those spared, were driven by despair into the forest. Consider such circumstances! How many thousands of every estate, of every age, black and white, had to wander

A view of Columbia after the fire, photographed in 1865 by George N. Barnard. National Archives and Records Administration.

around in the wilderness with no possibility to protect themselves from the cold and the wind, no means of nourishment, no clothing, barely having escaped with their lives? Families were separated. Mothers were searching for their children, not knowing whether their loved ones had somehow found safety or whether they perished as victims of the harsh elements.

Yes, dear reader, that is the gruesome picture. It seems unthinkable like an exaggeration; but so it was in reality, in our age and in a civilized country. This reality was brought about by those motivated by the love (?) of fellow humans who wanted to create for the slaves a golden age of freedom. These people who made use of such means in order to free their wards from the masters they hated but whom the slaves loved put both masters and slaves into a boundless suffering.

This incident in Columbia was a pivotal event in the American war. It was enough to besmirch the principle, the course and the success of the war. The hate of the South Carolinians would be passed down for generations against Northern brothers whose ancestors made them a part of this outrageous action.

I am judging as a neutral according to my own experiences and my own view of the horrible scenes; and I do not doubt that that a reasonable person will agree with my judgment of the methods of this Army of the United States, as well as I can recount the descriptions at hand, the hair-raising experiences and boundless suffering which was brought about by those methods.

What then about the slaves, who were to be freed from the yoke of their oppressors and for whose sake this war this crusade was fought? Quite simply, no one gave a care for them. They suffered the same fate, the same losses and the some burdens as did the whites. They remained true to their masters, and the masters fairly shared with them their last piece of bread with no obligation in the least to have done so. How much support are the Negroes likely getting yet today from their former masters without which they would perish; and how much support are they getting from the crusaders for a yet worthy principle and their liberators? Precisely these quietly turned their wards over to misery and suffering which they had brought on them and left them to continue to languish in slavery even as they had come as their deliverers. Their former oppressors took care of them out of human kindness so that they would not starve to death in a state of freedom.

And what of the noble warriors for freedom and the rights of man: the vulgar robbers, thieves and agents of murder and incendiary? The day after they had abandoned the theater of their outrages, they swarmed around in the region in search of booty, to get for themselves provisions and to lay waste to the land as well as to destroy the railroads for many miles around. Only a few were left behind to garrison the place and to support the headquarters. Theft and arson in the few remaining houses had completely ceased, likely on the order of the chief authority who perhaps had come to have a bit of compassion given the destruction which had taken place and who was now able to maintain discipline.

There were, nevertheless, a considerable number of these wild figures which remained on the site which was once Columbia. They were very busy searching the debris for melted gold and silver. They likewise dug around in the gardens of the few houses which remained in order to find the treasures which might be buried there. They were indeed very successful with this work. The booty which they took with them, consisting primarily of metal and valuables which required little room, is said to have filled an entire train of transport wagons.

I have attempted to describe, according to my experience of the events and the consequences which I observed, how they destroyed the city against all conditions of capitulation and against all laws of war as they destroyed the city, robbed the inhabitants of their homes and property, placed them in poverty and suffering, and even murdered them. Other hair-raising reports of individual incidents which I did not myself experience came to light publically. It was not only that the band of thieves demanded that money, jewelry and other valuables be handed over. For that there was not enough time. In many cases, they had taken possession of these things by force by tearing broaches from the breasts of women, ripping earrings from the ears of women so as to not waste time removing the valuables, thereby mangling the ears and tearing clothes. I myself saw a lady whose earlobes had been ripped open. Other indignities which the fairer sex in many cases had to endure, I refuse to tell. [88]

I place a veil over the grim past as if it had been in a bad dream had it not made a continuing effect on the future. If I am in the fortunate position to pull the veil back for an airing in order to remember those moments for my descriptions, so it was and likely at present still is for the larger part of those with whom I experienced these things not possible to veil the experiences of that night of terror and to overcome the consequences of those horrors.

---

88 Many outrages were committed by Sherman's soldiers against the women of Columbia. William Gilmore Simms wrote about these in his newspaper accounts published in the *Columbia Phoenix* in 1865, but withheld many of the "shocking details." Like Simms, Conrad was a Victorian gentleman, and was reluctant to publicly record such horrors. Dr. Daniel Trezevant, a Columbia physician, recorded several terrible rapes in a private journal, and named names.

The Results of the Destruction

After the first agitation had subsided so that I could consider the prevailing state of affairs, the worry about the future began to form itself and presented me with the dilemma as to as to which steps I should take. First of all, it seemed to me that I should inform my superior about the incidents and await further instructions from him. In addition, however, I needed to inform our representatives in Liverpool to register the theft of the stolen bills of exchange and to annul payment on them. [89] I then wanted to be certain of the location of our bookkeeper with the accounts of the business. Finally, I desired a place in which my presence there had no purpose in any way and could leave without being a burden.

I had no idea how a departure from here and communication with the outside world could be accomplished. I did not know whether the Union authorities were going to found a permanent headquarters here. Initially, therefore, I wanted to inform myself of their intentions. I went to their headquarters which was located in a house which had been spared, with the primary intent of gaining information over the city of ruins but also to file complaint at the way which I had been treated and perhaps to recover a part of my losses. I certainly could not let the authorities of the Union know about participation in the blockade business since such was viewed as being an open enemy of the United States and would have been so handled. It was only possible to appear as the Consul of Hanover if I wanted to accomplish anything.

I was warmly greeted by General Howard, the second in command under General Sherman. [90] Earlier in his career he had been a minster of the faith. He had lost an arm in the war with Mexico and had again distinguished himself in battles with the Indians. He intently listened to my complaint about the action which had befallen me as the consul of a neutral county about the theft of papers belonging to the consulate and about the theft of all of my private papers. The general expressed his regrets over the incidents of the previous night and also stated to me that if I could point out to him the regiment to which the captain

---

89 James M. Calder was the agent and treasurer for the Importing and Exporting Company of South Carolina in Liverpool.
90 This was General Oliver Otis Howard (1830-1909).

who had stolen from me belonged he would have him identified and to appear before me. Regrettably, I was unable to meet that requirement. The scoundrel is likely enjoying his miserable existence even today! What was then the crime of this one over against the obvious sins of so many thousands?

Whether this was really sympathy or sham sympathy on the part of the general I do not know. It, however, made a favorable impression on me. Even if I could not receive replacement or return for my losses, which I had not dared to actually expect, the general's suggestion seemed acceptable. He did openly share with me that the army would leave its present position in a few days and that no occupation force would remain here. He also informed me that they would be marching in a northerly direction and expected to reach a port city within eight to fourteen days. If I wanted to use the opportunity to go with them in order to reach the North or Europe, I could experience all of the amenities and austerities of him and his command and was duly invited to accompany them, whereby I was inclined to request a written statement.

This offer could not be rejected outright. Even if I did harbor an enduring hate for the band of robbers, I would not come in contact with them or have anything to fear from them given that I would be with the staff which consisted without any doubt of decent people. I, therefore, provisionally accepted the offer and received a written pass based on that acceptance.

After more sober reflection, I, nevertheless, declined this enticing opportunity. Were I to succeed in getting to the North in this manner, then I would very quickly, comfortably and securely get my very necessary report to England and then reach my homeland, since I already had this plan because the business was dissolved and I was no longer needed. However, with that step, Confederate territory was closed to me; and if Charleston was still a part of it, so was my way there where I still believed my director to be to whom I wanted to report my encounters. It was for me above all an absolute necessity to speak with him. It was, however, above all important to give him an account of my most recent conduct and the losses suffered. In no way did I want him to come to suspect that I had feigned the theft, that I had myself embezzled something, or that I had in any way neglected my duty. The need to personally describe these incidents made unproblematic my justification not to leave with Sherman's army. Afterward, with his blessing and with good conscience, I could carry out my plan to return to my homeland, which now pulled at me with a double longing to search out and to carry out.

So it was that I decided to remain and to await an opportunity through which the fulfillment of my desires could be made possible.

On the 20th of February, Sherman's army left Columbia if one still wants to use this term for the pile of rubble which was left. The day before, the arsenal which had been spared was blown up on orders of General Sherman. This was, however, no atrocity since it was the property of the state and the victorious enemy had every right to destroy it. The soldiers remained well-behaved and had made no further assaults on persons or property, if there were any persons left who had property, and limited themselves to the previously mentioned excavations.

The withdrawal of the soldiers was not a sensation and made little impression of those left behind. It was only after being completely free of them that one could be clear about the actual plight of the city and what measures for dealing with it should be taken. I saw the heroes departing who had picked their barren and foul-smelling laurels in this campaign. This was the victorious army which had contributed to the subjugation of the South, the end of the war and its goal. In addition to the bloodshed and the misery in which the South was placed, likely not yet having recovered from it even today, the means to those ends were to the highest degree reprehensible. As mockery, the national anthem of the United States "Hail Columbia Happy Land" rang out over the completely destroyed city of Columbia, sung as the soldiers departed.[91] It was a relief for each disheartened soul when the

---

91 "Hail Columbia" is a patriotic song composed in 1789 for the inauguration of President George Washington. It was considered an unofficial national anthem for many decades. Its first two lines of lyrics are: "Hail Columbia, happy land! / Hail, ye heroes, heav'n born band." One of Sherman's officers, Captain George W. Pepper, recorded that

blue figures and their endless wagon train disappeared and when one now had little to fear from them.

I allowed them to move on with their victory campaign in which I almost passively participated and would have thus likely spared myself much adversity. After some time had passed, we came to learn that they had conquered the entire territory though which they had passed, including Wilmington and the coastal region of North Carolina. In concert with the successes of the other Northern armies, they had subdued the South; and the Confederate States were again swallowed up into the Union.

---

some of the Federal troops sang the song during the occupation of Columbia, but changed the lyrics to: "Hail Columbia, happy land! / If I don't burn you, I'll be damned!" Pepper, *Personal Recollections*, 311.

Chapter 22

A Still-Life Under Constraint

I lingered, half compelled and half by choice, among the hapless people who were damned to lead a frightful existence and were driven to despair by pain, distress, cold and hunger. Although I myself was among the more fortunate who escaped this fate, I, nevertheless, was compelled to have compassion as I observed the prevalent suffering of the others.

My admirable friends, the family Groning, had taken me in so that I could in the meantime live with them without worrying about food. They had not had any loss whatsoever. To the contrary, they were well stocked with provisions and other necessities. One of the McCully girls was also staying with them. They were unable to house many refugees for any length of time because the house was too small. The other members of the McCully family found refuge with relatives. All of houses which remained were filled to every corner, and all that could be done to house and support the suffering by those to whom fate had shown mercy was done. There were, however, many, many others who could find no shelter and who were compelled to live outdoors or camp in shanties which had been quickly constructed in the distress. Some used cellars and the ruins of walls on the burned over area on which shelters could be most quickly constructed. This is the way these folks had to pass their days, genteel and humbled. They had counted themselves among the well-to-do just a few days before, able to enjoy all of the amenities of life. This blow was the hardest for them; they had to do without even the poorest of huts.

How did these unfortunate ones eke out an existence? Here and in a wide radius, wherever his ruinous army could reach, the enemy had destroyed everything. He had destroyed all food and cattle or taken it with him. Absolutely nothing remained with which a man could still his hunger. Even for hard currency, the necessary food could not be procured. What those few who had been spared had and would have gladly shared would have lasted but a few days.

In consideration of the horrible conditions, the Sherman authorities found enough mercy to leave behind a portion of the corn and cattle which made up the rich booty which they had gleaned from the area. It was placed in the hands of the diligent old mayor. The invaluable charity of the enemy, so received because of the circumstances of the recipients, consisted of sixty head of lean cows awaiting their fate in the city park and a certain quantity of corn allocated over several days. This gift constituted the sparse but adequate and eatable food for the entire population.

It was a peculiar scene each morning at 9:00 a. m. as the citizens gathered themselves in the "new city hall" in order to exchange the burning questions and ideas, to make some plans and to receive the rations for the next twenty-four hours which consisted of a frugal allocation of one quarter pound of meat and a pound of ground cornmeal for each person.

Actually, the "new city hall" did not even earn the name of a building. Gallows humor had simply given the name of the place for the distribution of provisions to the general gathering point of the people.

It was a tragic comedy at this time when everyone emerged from the most diverse housing and dens and wandered with great longing to the gathering point with all possible and even impossible containers in which they would put the expected present where in a tight crowd they took possession of the measured quantyty of foodstuff for their household which could only partly still their hunger. How these frugal meals were prepared and how they came by cooking and eating utensils I am not in the position to say. In hardship everything is possible. Under the prevailing conditions, one was not too choosy about the use of different means.

It is quite hard to believe that we were completely cut off from the world, that no support for relief was forthcoming, that those suffering did not move to more livable places, and that the reconstruction of the houses did not begin immediately.

For an explanation, I note that for miles around in the area, about two days ride, the country and the inhabitants had suffered the same fate. The railroads were completely destroyed. Supplies and news could not get through from points farther away. In addition, points farther away had more or less suffered the same fate. These outlying areas had few houses or inhabitants and even before the onset of this catastrophe had endured a considerable growth in population by refuges who consumed their already limited means. In this season, the few state roads were difficult to traverse and were considered unsafe because there were numerous robber bands made up of deserters from the army which roamed the countryside. The arrival of outside help or news or the evacuation of families on this side was thereby impeded or at the very beginning was simply impossible. Above all, it must be considered that money or something serving as money simply was not available, which for such travel is quite necessary. In the short term, money was of no use because in a wide area there was nothing that one could have purchased with hard money. There were no means of transport. All of the horses which did not perish in the fire were taken by the enemy. Only one man with three mules showed up who had been out in the countryside and had thereby escaped the plundering.

Naturally, with time, help began to arrive and the most essential commerce with the outside world was established. The condition of "hanging and trembling in a limbo of anguish" lasted for weeks.

This condition made itself even worse in that the people, in their greatest distress, could do nothing to change it, this in spite of the best of intentions. They could find no activity by which they were spared from and freed of the anguishing view and the contemplation of the situation. They simple had to take in the misery.

For the most part, it was women and children since most of the men were on the field of combat and had no idea of the fate of their loved ones. For these, it was twice as awful because there were not men to protect them and to offer them solace; and they could do nothing to better their situation and to divert their mirthless thoughts.

The Negroes who shared the same fortune as whites, often somewhat better than the whites, received the same rations. They were used to clear some streets from the rubble, at least to the point that these were passable. Everything was also done, as far as material and tools were available, to put locations which could serve as dwellings in the best possible condition.

Wretchedness dominated such that no one could describe it. One was compelled to view thousands of once joyous and happy people with deep compassion and with consternation toward their spoilers. I was in possession of a nice sum of money, the larger part which I would have gladly shared to relieve the misery, but even these fine gold pieces had for the moment no value whatsoever because it was impossible to find anything to purchase with them.

I had, otherwise, no hardship. In a certain manner, the present solitude after many years of demanding work and after experiencing the most recent incident of tension, was even beneficial to me. With my superb friends, a feeling of embarrassment or a sense that I was becoming a burden was simply not present. At that time, I lived in their intimate circle which became even more stimulating, worry free and, in a certain way, happier through the presence of my co-resident Miss Emma McCully, if one was able look away from and to forget, if just for a moment, the miserable circumstances and the suffering in the area.

Our excellent hostess freely shared her provisions with those who were without but managed to save a few delicacies for us. Her serene temperament had suffered little because of the terrible incidents. She quite cleverly knew how to share this serenity within her circle of friends. We were put in a good mood and were kept there. It was her husband who most needed her influence because he was by nature nervous and found himself in great distress since the most recent events so that his wife had to think and to act on his behalf. He was, however, a noble man and fair-minded. All who knew him respected him and loved him. He was a loyal and tender-hearted husband and father as well as a warm and dependable friend. As I was able to enjoy their invaluable charity, their cordial care, and an intimate home, so I am still filled today and for all time with great thankfulness toward these courageous people for their earnest and sharing friendship which is still cultivated through mutual written communication.

I spent the days being as useful as was possible for purposes of my own distraction and in the interest of my hostess. I cultivated the garden. I split wood. I unabashedly went into the forest with the wheelbarrow to fell trees for wood and to bring it to the house. These activities, which gave me great pleasure, had to be carried out since my friends had no slaves and no servants. Americans understood them to be a great sacrifice. My work, thus, served both our purposes. As spring began to break, I enjoyed walks, either alone or together with my housemates, walks on which I would daydream through the ruins with mirthless thoughts of the past, through budding nature with hopes of a better future, and on plans for that future. The Congaree splashed and frothed as it once had before the evil enemy had crossed it. It retained its old charm. It quickened the deserted country side as well as the downtrodden human hearts who here poured out their sadness and their worries. It offered consolation to them with its joyous example that life and the fate of man is an ebb and flow, that murky waters once again run clear, and that a new life will rise up among the ruins. The wonderful landscape and the sparkling waters have likely relieved much pain, have washed many wounds and poured some rays of hope into dark and sick hearts.

Each evening we sat in the cozy family circle and discussed the burning questions of the day concerning the futures of each of us or what needed to happen to change the unsustainable situation. We also read aloud or enjoyed music. The warm interest which all of us nurtured toward one another put us into a heartfelt communion and gave us a genuine sharing attitude. We indeed shared honestly both our dispositions of friendship and our earthly goods as far as it was possible. I possessed only the one suit which I saved that night along with my body. I, therefore, had to claim a part of Mr. Groning's wardrobe. Miss McCully provided me with a pair of socks. From Mrs. Groning I received a watch as replacement for the one which had been stolen over against which I unburdened myself of a little money which would later render service to the recipient. It was the family McCully who found themselves in the direst of circumstances. For a time they were compelled to find support among relatives, from the communal coffers and from charity until the deaths of the father and the grandmother, coming shortly thereafter, which were the results of the terrors and the associated privations. The oldest daughter succeeded in getting a position with the Department of the Treasury in Washington, a position which she still holds today and which made it possible for her to care for her mother and her sisters.

The Gronings were in a position to face the clarification of circumstances with greater ease even if the loss of position, the lack of income and the uncertain prospects created for the excitable husband no little worry. After several months, they were able to sell the little villa and find a new home in Philadelphia along with a satisfactory position.

I was the least damaged by the events. Indeed, I had to take on the liquidation of the business and, along with that, the loss of my well-earning position; but there was nothing to keep me there. I was determined to leave the place at the first opportunity and to remain in my circle of friends for the time being.

Several weeks passed in a peaceful still-life. There was no possibility for me to inform myself about the events in the outside world and in accord with that information to make a decision about the next steps to be taken.

The city of ruins was first visited by curiosity seekers from distant places who had heard of the calamity and who wanted to see the place where a beautiful city once stood. It was also contacted by those merely passing through who dared to come through a territory with no government with all of the associated dangers. There were also those who, with a lot of effort from places quite far away, got through with food and provisions for the hungry population. With these opportunities, news trickled in as to how thing were in the state and in the world. The most important news was that on the same day of the catastrophe in Columbia, Charleston, after years of resistance, had also given up to the Union and was under its control but without suffering the grim fate of her sister city. According to the custom of war, the conquest was peaceful. [92]

Knowing the intentions of my director, I had to assume that he had left the city of Charleston before it had been taken and had fled to one of his estates in the countryside, if he had been able to do that.

---

[92] Charleston was occupied by the besieging Federal forces in mid-February 1865, after the Confederate troops evacuated the area.

Photographer George N. Barnard titled this photograph "Ruins in Columbia, South Carolina." National Records and Archives Administration.

Sherman had obviously dwelled here as well with malice. The houses were, however, still standing and the sight of them had a calming effect on me and implied that I would at least find lodging. My first attempt was, however, a failure. I was outraged that I was denied lodging by a man from whom I least expected it. He was the owner of a business in Columbia who had profited well from the very lucrative sales of the import objects which we had provided him. He owned a large house; but he disdainfully showed me the door with the comment that he did not have a room available, that his wife was sick and that I could find quarters at the hotel. The man, who in "good times" had been the embodiment of manners to me, now rejected me. It could be that he was indeed right. I left with regret over the misfortune and with best wishes. I did not know then nor do I know now whether his excuses were genuine or not.

At the only inn, I was greeted by an honest old lady who gave multiple regrets that she was unable to take in any strangers since her provisions which she had rescued from the plundering were hardly enough to feed her own family.

At this opportunity, I must note that this refusal to give me shelter and those which I would experience in the future, quite contrary to the American character, were based on the fact that my coat had an unfortunate military cut to it. I was therefore taken to be a member of the Northern army. With all of them, given their anxious feelings caused by the most recent incidents, my coat marked me to be a robber and murderer and foreclosed to me, perhaps more than once, access to a convivial house. So it was the coat who was my old, innocent fellow traveler and life's partner.

Having been rejected, I determined to try my luck in other private houses. I had again mounted the dead-tired mule but made the following comment to the friendly old lady that I would have gladly paid for any service rendered to me in silver. That helped. Straight away, she came closer and asked in disbelief, "You said silver! That could earn you a night of assistance since you are already drenched!"

Fair and shiny money entices. The good folks had likely not seen such in years. Things were quickly made ready. The food at supper was plentiful and was the breakfast the next morning. The lodging, for which I had to give up but a small amount, was excellent. There was very cozy evening conversation with the simple but nice host family who listen in with great excitement to my accounts about the fate of Columbia. It was, above all expectations, a satisfactory end of the day and a strengthening for the next day.

My mule, which had been quickened by rest and good food, let it be known the next morning that he was in better spirits. Save for the malevolence of the weather, things went well. There was no change in the scenery and little enjoyment as opposed to the terrain which we went through yesterday. Along the entire way there was but uniformity and solitude. Hardly a human and no inhabited house were to be seen. There was the same evidence of the enemy's devastation in the disgusting sights and smells.

The concern began to rise in me that Chester had also fallen victim to the enemy and that this trip was therefore in vain if my colleague had taken refuge in a place which I could not discern. By and by, however, the evidence of the destruction got less and less and ceased altogether several miles from my place of destination. So it was that despite the pouring rain and after the exhaustion of two days of riding to which I was not accustomed, I was filled with hope at reaching my interim goal and with the joy after such a long time of entering a territory which had been spared the wrath of war and of seeing contented people.

I was indeed happy which this hope was fulfilled. Without any kind of mishap, I had reached Chester and there found a relatively robust village life and, above all, my friend Barbot who had managed to bring the business records to a safe place. With his family, I found friendly acceptance and dry clothes. We had a lot to report and to tell concerning the business and the reciprocal experiences since our separation. I spent an entire day making notes from the business records which were available after the loss of mine own. I needed them for the conference which I hoped to have with Mr. Bee and for the necessary nullification related to the stolen notes to be sent to England.

Where the director was residing was as unknown to my colleague as it was to me; however, by chance, a later refugee from Charleston had told him that Mr. Bee had left the city shortly before it fell. From this report, I at least gleaned that he had to be somewhere in the state; and since I was already on the pilgrimage, with the most dangerous part of the trip already behind me, I was aroused, without any doubts, to continue until I had reached my goal. The next place I assumed that he might be was on one of his properties near the city of Union which was about a day's ride from Chester in a westerly direction. That place, as well as this one, had been connected to Columbia by rail before it had been destroyed. From here, however, it could only be reached by foot, by horse or by wagon.

I got an opportunity to go there by means of a government transport of provisions which was supposed to leave the following day. After a conversation with the official leading the expedition, I was able to get a seat on a covered wagon and availed myself of this service. Because I did not know the way, because it offered protection from the drenching which I would have received had I gone by horse, and, in addition, because I did not know whether I would continue from there or return, I decided to reject the further service of the mule and send him back to his owner in Columbia. I found a gentleman who wanted to ride there in order to find his suffering relatives there. Both of us were assisted by this arrangement because were I to return to Columbia, which was my plan, returning by this route could not be assured.

I then rode farther into the world. Such a trip was better with companionship. The trip or better the march was much more comfortable than the previous ride since the weather had cleared and I now and again used my seat in the wagon for rest. Likewise, the region was more interesting with hilly formations, with greater variation of flora and fauna and with the lack of evidence of the enemy which would have accosted eyes and nose. The road was, however, quite sincerely terrible, and the transport made very slow headway. In addition, the trip was delayed for yet even more hours because of an incident which could have ended badly but which ended fortunately.

As we crossed a river, swollen by the downpour of rain, the horses of a wagon on the ferry went wild. The lead horses which, without proper precaution, had not be unhitched from the wagon, made their jump over the edge of the ferry and would have definitely carried the wagon to which they were hitched over the edge and would have definitely capsized the ferry on which we were standing had it not been for the good fortune that the hitch between the lead horses and the wagon broke. Thereby did we avoid drowning or a very perilous danger. It appeared that alone the horses in their high spirits did penance by drowning. The strong current quickly ripped the horses away. Since they were harnessed to one another, they fought without purpose against the flood.

The crew to whom the management and care of the horses had been entrusted hurried down both banks of the river in panic. Against all expectations, a happy fate determined that both animals, although they had swallowed a large amount of water and were thoroughly exhausted, were driven by the current into a curve in the river where they were able to gain ground and be saved.

We had lost of lot of time during the stop made necessary so that the horses could recover. We were, however, overjoyed that the incident had not brought about further consequences. For that reason, we arrived in Union late in the evening, but in good shape. This locale was also on the border of but was outside of the radius of the enemy's destructive rage. Up to this point, the railroad from Columbia to Spartanburg had been completely destroyed while the remainder of the line of about forty miles to the terminal at Spartanburg was intact and was kept in repair; however, there were only three trains per week in both directions.

In the hotel, in which I quite easily got lodging, I attempted to get as much information about the whereabouts of my director, whether here or elsewhere. I was overjoyed to learn that he had been in Union but had moved in the direction of Spartanburg about a week before. At least I had a clue, although I had to assume that he had made his way to a plantation which lay in a part of the state known as Pickens

District and that I was looking at a trip of several days. I used the first train to Spartanburg in order to gain further information.

On the trip, I enjoyed many scenic beauties of a kind that I had sadly not seen in America. Only Columbia with its romantic location had been a glorious exception to the prevailing flat terrain which I had otherwise encountered. Here, however, there were charming, alternating contours of hills and valleys divided by brisk creeks and rivers which crisscrossed them. There were woods, fields and meadows with industrious people and grazing cattle. Here and there the friendly manors and plantations could be sighted through the shadows of the live oaks. Near these houses were the Negro colonies whose inhabitants still led a satisfied and carefree existence. In the distance, the grand Blue Ridge Mountains, toward which we were traveling, overlooked the scene. Perhaps I would get the opportunity to get to know them more closely and in particular if I did not meet my intended friend. It was an alluring landscape which the advent of spring had adorned.

I reveled at the happy picture which did my heart good; and I regretted that I was not able to enjoy it with greater leisure. While I had ridden and wandered quite slowly through uninteresting regions, steam was taking me through this lovely locale quickly and away. It was, however, taking me to a place that was no less beautiful and providing me with a longer stay there.

The route from the train station led gradually upward through a high forest. At the top was also an imposing growth of trees, so much so, that one could not take it in. It was that the entire little city lay in a forest and thereby made a charming, idyllic impression. Many of the exiles from Charleston, Columbia and other places had retreated here, which made the place quite vibrant and in which I discovered many old acquaintances.

What I had hardly dared to hope came true. I was able to meet with my venerated director who had remained here longer than he had intended and thereby saved me a longer trip. I was overjoyed at the final end of my quest, at the reunion with this admirable man, at the disposal of all of my business duties, and at the disclosure of my actions and my fate. I found with him the appropriate recognition for having gone to the trouble of finding him. Although he very much lamented with his keen interest in the business the unpleasantness caused by the loss of important documents, he gave me no reproach because my choosing to remain in Columbia had been a mature decision and with the best of intent. The behavior of the enemy could not have been anticipated.

Under the prevailing circumstances our business was no longer viable. With the fall of Charleston and Wilmington, our ships could not be accounted for. The continued existence of the Confederacy appeared to be impossible. My presence in the South was at least for now without purpose. Mr. Bee fully concurred with my plan to travel to England to cancel the payment of stocks to illegitimate holders and to personally put the affairs of the business in order while there, since correspondence was not possible for a long time. He was completely in agreement that I might remain in my homeland to await the clarification of the circumstances. He made also a flattering proposal that I might wish to return to become a partner in his firm after peace was established. For the trip and for the interim stay in Europe, I would have gladly covered the cost; he, however, transferred to me a very hefty sum in the form of drafts on our Liverpool house, which I gladly accepted.

The agreed on plan was that I would first return to that which was once Columbia and from there would attempt to get to Charleston which appeared to be no problem for my status as a foreign consul. From there, I would be able to reach a Northern port and then travel to Europe.

Taking leave from my esteemed director, who had full faith in me, a fact which filled me with pride, and for whom I had come to have high respect after years of service, was very painful for me, in spite of the fact that I fully intended to accept his offer and very soon again work for him as a subordinate or co-equal and in spite of the fact that I was hurrying to those whom I loved and that the trip relieved all doubt about his judgment of my actions.

My intentions at the time were not fulfilled because I later decided to remain in Germany and never again saw the noble and honorable gentleman. I, however, must continue to remember him with sincere love and gratitude. He is one of the rare men, who do not overestimate their good fortune, who do not hesitate in the storms of life, who do not allow themselves to be tempted away from strict integrity, who are free from passions, and who endeavor to better the lives of others with modesty and charity. [95]

Even the deaths of his two sons in the battle for the fatherland did not shake for a moment his adoration for God. [96] He submitted himself to the will of the Most High and bore his boundless pain in silence.

My purpose had been fulfilled and my next goal had been meticulously laid out. I took leave of my benevolent friend after I had thoroughly discussed everything with him and then returned by train to Union.

Back in Union, I needed some good advice as to how I was to get to Columbia which lay two days away by the most direct route. The way there would again lead through empty territory and there were no travel opportunities available. I did not intend to go by foot. I succeeded in buying a horse along with saddle and bridle from a fellow countryman for a cheap price of approximately fifty dollars in coin. This animal had no resemblance to the blessed Rosinante for it was too well fed, young and without fault and afterward showed itself to have endurance and was powerful. [97] I had no interest in determining whether or not it had been stolen and was therefore inexpensive to buy. With this fine horse, which brought a double value for me as my property and the loyal service it provided, I determined to travel on to distant Charleston as I began my journey to Columbia.

---

95 A letter of April 18, 1865, found in the Bee-Chisholm Family Papers indicates that William C. Bee was in Aiken, S.C., where he wrote to his daughter that he had read a newspaper report that "Lincoln designed vengeance upon those who had through the blockade supplied the wants of our Army and people." Based on the report, he feared that if he fell into the hands of the enemy he would suffer "the death of a felon," and he prayed that God would spare him from such a horror.

96 William C. Bee lost two young sons in the war. John Stock Bee (1841-1863) was mortally wounded on Morris Island on July 10, 1863, and was taken to Union-held Hilton Head Island (S.C.), where he died about a week later. James Ladson Bee (1843-1864) was wounded at Cold Harbor (Va.) on May 30, 1864, and died as a prisoner of war on July 8, 1864.

97 Rosinante (or Rocinante) was the name of Don Quixote's old, decrepit horse.

As I rode out, the suspicion came to me that the previous owner, whose character suggested such, perhaps had the thought in the back of his mind to follow me and the reclaim the animal by force. It was easy to expect such offenses in this lawless time. Perhaps the previous owner was also capable of robbing me of my other valuables which I discretely carried with me. For that reason I set my horse into a trot and then a gallop as long as he and I could endure and came thereby very quickly away so that if my fear was justified, then I would not have to endure an attack.

The road which was quite obvious lead through flat terrain and gave notice of the same monotony which I had experience on the way out. Most of it was forest mixed with cultivated fields. It was deadly silent everywhere. No animal was to be seen, either stolen or killed by the enemy. There were no people on the fields which could not be worked because there were no horses and no mules. Seldom did I pass a house or farm building which had not been, at the very least, partially demolished. Even more seldom did I come into contact with a human being.

In the afternoon, I came to a village which consisted of a few houses, a church and a hotel. It was devoid of life. I was unable to see a living soul. It was only at the hotel where I would be able to restore myself, rest my horse and stay the night that I was able to find a Negro after a lot of knocking and calling. He told me that he was the only person in the place. Everyone had fled before the advancing enemy who had thoroughly cleaned out all of the provisions. He had been sent by his master to determine the extent of the plundering. Remaining here was not possible. Concerning lodging, I took some comfort in the comment of the Negro that I would soon find some inhabited houses and that they had provisions and would provide me with comfortable quarters. So after I had rested and after my horse and I had devoured the provisions which we had brought from Union, I again set forth.

Chapter 24

Hard Heartedness and Human Kindness

At sunset I reached a friendly property where a sedate looking house gave a tempting invitation for a night's rest. American hospitality gives every traveler the right to request lodging and food. The refusal of such is seen as inhumanity and is accursed. There were seldom exceptions, although I had to endure such rejections. Those, however, lay mainly in the conditions of the times in those days.

I rode up to the property and found several colored folk in the yard. To my questions on the matter they answered that the owner, Doctor M, lived in the house alone, having brought his family to safety and that he was at the moment making a house call in the neighborhood but should return shortly. They further said that I was guaranteed lodging since there was place enough. The most talkative Negro further told me with a joyous pride that they had tricked the Yankees in that they had hidden the greater part of their provision, animals, furniture and implements and were in this manner able to save them. I then awaited the return of the doctor. A Negro, without my knowledge, had already led the horse into a stall and given it food. I had, however, done my reckoning with the presence of the host. That is to say that when the host arrived, he rejected my request shortly and concisely. He had no lodging for strange rabble, and he hardly had enough during these times for himself and his people. I put my best foot forward, but he refused to accept rogues and vagabonds. I would go without any food for myself if he would only give my horse some hay. I said that I was ready to pay well for lodging but would be completely satisfied if I would be given a place in the stall, if only I could get quarters for the night. With this, the gentleman really got angry. Where was my horse? How could I dare to put my horse in his building without his permission and deal with the slaves behind his back? I must, he quipped, have a fine patrimony if I as a white man would sleep in a stall! He continued with such outbursts and demanded that I immediately leave his property; otherwise, he would remove me by force.

I gladly rejected further conversation with the kind gentleman as well as with his hospitality and preferred to quarter myself with "Mother Green," which appeared to be unavoidable since the night had already befallen us. The trembling Negro brought me the tired horse which had to be again disturbed from his peaceful rest; and I told the hard-hearted man, for whom the time was already too long for the necessary measures which I had to take to leave his yard, that I wished him a friendly farewell bound with the hope that if he came into the situation to be without lodging and help in a strange place, it was my deepest desire that fate would lead him to my door. It would give me the greatest joy to host with my means a man of his standing, but not according to his own heart.

That was also a "born and bred" South Carolinian, a proud and educated aristocrat who so completely deviated from the principles of his countrymen that he could bring it in his heart to drive me out into the dark night, into the wilderness. Quite likely, it was again my coat which gave him cause to fear that I was a robber who would during the night open his gates to my accomplices and then rob his well-provided quarters and murder him. I have forgiven him; however, at the time, it was a grave affair; and I thought to myself how it was that this man was able to fulfill his duty to mankind.

Fortunately, a good-natured Negro, whom I had secretly paid for his services to me, quietly told me that I would come upon a house about two miles further on. I wanted to reach this house and once again try my luck before I exposed myself to the unavoidable danger and discomfort under the stars by having to spend the night on damp ground. In the meantime, it had become very dark. The road could be recognized as a clearing in the forest. I had little hope that good fortune would allow me to find lodging. I, however, subordinated myself to patience. After the humiliation, I had become very tame. The collective experiences of the last weeks made me extremely humble.

I had a special compassion for my horse which had so well demonstrated his patience but was now quite worn-out. I had a bit of corn for him, but I feared spending the night in the open would be bad for him, and it would not be enough for the demands of the next day.

Nevertheless, we carried on with patience; and within the distance which had been indicated, I saw the glow of a light which animated me with new courage. In any case, our fate for the night had to be decided.

The structure lay a piece from the road. I would not have seen it without the light which shone from it was a modest house. Several dogs heralded my arrival, and an old man came toward me to whom I apprehensively made my request. He obliged me to dismount and to enter the house, likely to better see me. The impression which I made must not have been so bad. Then, with a cordiality which I had not expected but which did so much good for me, he gave me his hand and declared that as long as a roof was over his house and a piece of bread was there, no traveler would leave his door dissatisfied. I had to be satisfied with that which a modest home could offer that the enemy had left behind.

Who could have been more fortunate than I! My horse and I were well taken care of. We had a comfortable place to stay, and we were cared for in the most generous fashion. What a contrast this was to the attitude of the man who had driven me from his property with cursing and reproach and who, according to his people, was provide with everything. The inhabitants of this modest but attractive little house had lost almost everything.

The old man, quite honorable, was named Johnson. He was a man with an open and trustful face on which an inner peace and a noble character was mirrored. He was the head of the family which consisted of a daughter, a daughter-in-law and several children. All of them were simple, kind people. His sons had some years before followed the call of their fatherland and were now standing in the field of battle.

The good people were very anxious to care for me with the little that they had and to thereby make a strangers stay as pleasant as possible. The few hours which I spent with them brings a very pleasant memory and strengthens my experience that there are noble and selfless people who out of a sense of duty and grace of charity share their last possession with those in need and that the American nation rich with such examples is, regrettably elsewhere in general infrequent.

In the cozy communion of the family around the fireplace, we exchanged our experiences which were for both parties quite interesting. They had also come to know the terrors of war in their full violence. They had in fact found the time as the enemy neared to hide some food and things of value which the plunderers could not find. With that, they were able to deny the enemy their most necessary possessions, but everything else was taken from them. The worst of it was that a detachment of the passing riffraff hanged the old man in the literal sense of the word because he had stubbornly refused to give the location of the hidden items. He was cut down, just in time, by his slaves and brought back into life. [98] They were able to do this with great effort, but not until they had struggled mightily with the murderers. The next morning, the noble old man calmly showed me, laughing, the limb on which he had swung with the comment that God had protected him and had not allowed that he be taken away from his family for whom he was duty-bound to care. He had also come to the conclusion that his Negros had acknowledged his efforts to make their lot in life as comfortable as possible by showing him the same love. He said of his would-be murderers that he regretted that such misdeeds could spring from their hearts.

At my departure after a nice night's sleep and a good breakfast which strengthened me, I attempted to pay for the benefits which had been shared with me, motivated to that intent by the reality that I was quite capable of the offer and had only accepted the hospitality under such terms. The honest man roundly rejected my request. He said that were I rich and were he poor, I would still need his help if he were

---

98 Hanging men (both black and white), sometimes to death, was a common practice in Sherman's army when they wished to learn the whereabouts of hidden valuables.

in a position to assist. There was to be no recompense for his having done his duty; and he could not diminish the joy of have done his duty with even the least compensation. He further stated that they had yet a span of time to live; and until then, God would let them flourish. God had saved him and had allowed him to retain his strength so that he would be able to keep worry at bay.

I was powerless against such objections and was only able to secretly reward the Negroes who had served me. I had to take leave of these wonderful people with empty words; but I was overjoyed with a feeling of appreciation that through the hardheartedness of one man the gates of this peaceful and instructive circle had been opened to me. Thus it is that every evil has a healing effect.

He was a very noble man for whom I counted myself as fortunate to have gotten to know. His words, his sensibilities and his actions were a nice sermon and warning for those who heard and those who saw. He had a long and blameless life behind him. As experience had taught him, he had a charitable influence on his community which had hardly served as an example for his neighbor Dr. M.

My loyal companion had likewise profited very well from the friendly acceptance. He was as well-fed as he marched with courage into his day's work.

A seven-hour ride should bring us to our destination. In addition to the pleasant memories of the previous evening, on a trip which had thus far ended with good fortune, I already enjoyed the hope of again seeing my friends with whom I would remain for yet a few days.

The milestones gave ever-growing notice that I was drawing nearer to the former capital of the state. Soon, its wreckage lay before me through which I made my way to the friendly cottage on the hill.

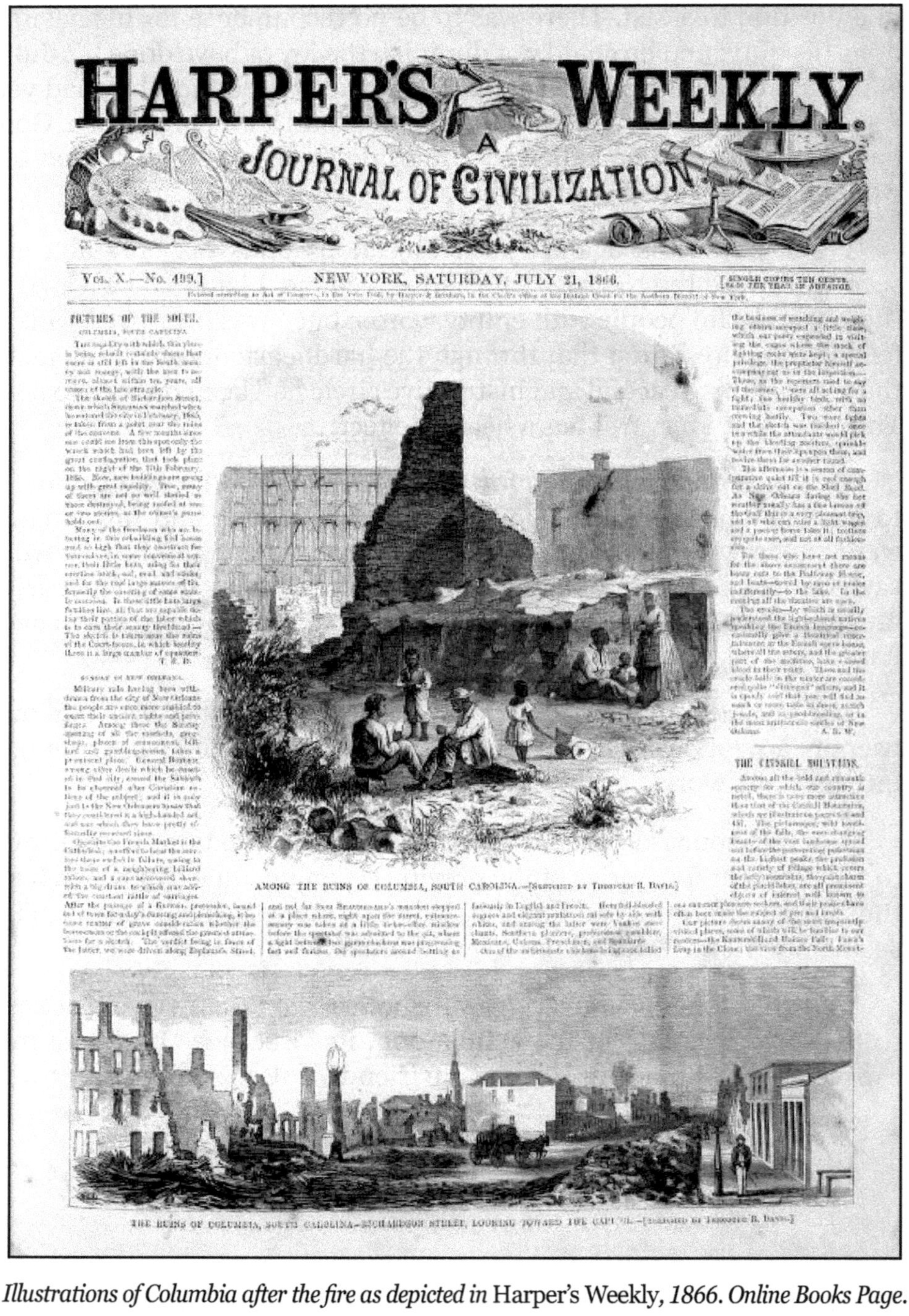

HARPER'S WEEKLY.
A JOURNAL OF CIVILIZATION.

Vol. X.—No. 499.] NEW YORK, SATURDAY, JULY 21, 1866. [SINGLE COPIES TEN CENTS. $4.00 PER YEAR IN ADVANCE.

PICTURES OF THE SOUTH.

COLUMBIA, SOUTH CAROLINA.

AMONG THE RUINS OF COLUMBIA, SOUTH CAROLINA.—[SKETCHED BY THEODORE R. DAVIS.]

THE CATSKILL MOUNTAINS.

THE RUINS OF COLUMBIA, SOUTH CAROLINA—RICHARDSON STREET, LOOKING TOWARD THE CAPITOL.—[SKETCHED BY THEODORE R. DAVIS.]

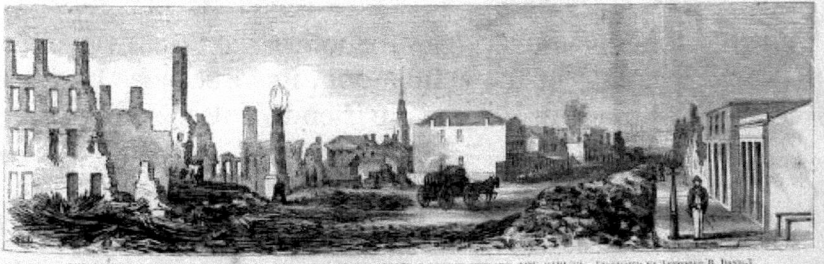

Illustrations of Columbia after the fire as depicted in Harper's Weekly, *1866. Online Books Page.*

Chapter 25

TRAVEL PLANS

The kind family Groning received me with a hearty welcome and did not know how they could make short my stay pleasant enough. Once more, I enjoyed the pleasant testimonies of friendship before I had to separate myself from these loyal people, likely for the rest of my life. The longing to again see my beloved homeland, my loving mother and my siblings was now admittedly greater than this other feeling. As soon as it was in any way possible, I wanted to satisfy the former.

The situation in Columbia had changed somewhat in the meantime. The lot of those suffering had likely improved somewhat with the arrival of food and preservatives against hunger. Some of the unfortunate ones had been picked up by members of their families or had taken it upon themselves to make the difficult trip by foot in order to free themselves from the worst of the privation and to find livable shelter. In general, however, the sad circumstances of deprivation and helplessness still dominated.

The people of this city of ruins created a state for themselves since up to that point there was no government to take care of them. The leaders of the city were keenly engaged in creating better conditions, among them the previous mayor who displayed a warm interest and active engagement. They passed ordinances which mandated that all available resources had to be temporarily made available for the welfare of everyone and which mandated that a corps be instituted consisting of men who were in anyway capable. This corps was to submit to the ordinances of the provisional government and execute all duties which appeared to be necessary and to carry out related tasks. No man could leave the city or, better put, the region of debris, without proof that he was doing so to get help and support for those left behind.

These ordinances did not affect me. I would have gladly made my services available for the hapless people, which I would be able to do to a small degree by means of a sum of money when I had recovered some wealth. In spite of all compassion, my purpose was more important, a purpose to which duty attached me, namely to get to England as quickly as possible.

I, therefore, prepared myself for the trip to Charleston which would claim three days. I wrote out a pass for myself as representative of a neutral foreign power by which I hope to be allowed into the territory occupied by Northern troops without difficulty.

In spite of that, I gave up this plan at the last moment. Some of the travelers coming from Charleston reported heinous incidents. They said that it would not be prudent to travel on the roads in that region because a band of robbers operated there, robbers which attacked and plundered those passing through. They themselves had been attacked and had saved themselves in the nick of time by fleeing; however, they had seen several naked bodies hanging in trees. Based on these reports which were quite credible, I did not wish to submit myself to this fate. After some consideration, I decided to make my way to Richmond and to attempt from there to take a truce boat which carried out the exchange of prisoners between the North and the South to Washington or to some other Northern harbor locale. The execution of this plan was difficult and laborious. It had to be followed, however. As much as I would have liked to visit Charleston one more time in order to see old acquaintances and to get to know the new conditions, I had to reject it because of the dangers associated with such a venture.

Against all expectation, the enemy had treated Charleston quite well after the capitulation. The most hated city, which had given impulse to the entire war, which had fired the first shot and which had resisted the enemy for years was neither plundered nor burned. [99] The

---

99 Conrad is incorrect that Charleston was not plundered. The pillaging of houses and other buildings began as soon as the besieging enemy forces moved in to occupy the city

peaceful citizens enjoyed the full protection of the newly established authorities and had no reason to complain about the behavior of those who had vanquished them. [100] In contrast, innocent Columbia fell in a horrible manner to the wrath of an inhuman enemy or to the anger of a band of robbers in the service of that enemy.

On the 20th of March 1865, I took leave of my wonderful friends, the Gronings and the McCullys, in order to begin my journey. At that time it was admittedly in the certain expectation of seeing them again soon; however, it must now be understood to have been a farewell for this life. Our hearts had been knitted together by a rich measure of proven, sacrificial love and by the common experiences of good fortune and suffering, making the separation mutually difficult. I was going toward a worthy goal and was thereby able to overcome the loss of such loyal people; however, those who remained behind, whose future lay so dark and hopeless before them, saw their old companion with double wistfulness departing, although they granted me the good fortune in which they could not participate. With a last handshake, we confirmed an eternal friendship, and we have been loyal to our mutual promise. In the frequent exchange of correspondence which keeps the relationship alive I receive the proof that the sentiments of love and gratitude the other side of the ocean find a pure echo.

One more time I took a final, long look at the people whom I had come to love, people who had given me escort to the little friendly house with the green venetian blinds and its enclosing veranda. To the right and below was the beautiful valley from which my old friends, the monuments of former good fortune and wealth jutted.

---

in mid-February 1865. Most of the residents had evacuated the city, and when many returned after the war's end they found their homes emptied of all or most valuables.

100 In occupied Charleston, only South Carolina residents who took the oath of allegiance to the United States were afforded any legal protections by the occupying military authorities. Those who did not take the oath were not allowed to travel, nor were they given any protection for their private property. Charlestonians were generally not happy living under military occupation and Yankee rule.

I then reined my horse in the direction which I had taken fourteen days earlier because I had to put the same distance behind me in order to reach Chester in order to use the railroad which was to take me northward.

Chapter 26

Homeward

Earlier, I had rejected with indignation the suspected kinship or resemblance of my horse to the well-known Rosinante. Still today, I hold to my assertion honoring the courageous, fine horse. A little less decisively am I unable to deny that the burden which he was carrying resembles, in a certain manner, the character of the genial Don Quixote. To the rank of "knight" I have not and had not in those days risen; I was merely a "rider" without spurs, without lance and without sword. My other equipment, however, would likely bring others to laughter. Under other circumstances, for a civilized region rather than the one through which I was traveling, I would not have made use of implements.

The things which I had saved from the possessions which I once had, what I had purchased as absolute necessities or which had been donated to me, I took with me. The good Lady Groning had provided me with wonderful baked goods, cold sausage and other small delicacies and had thereby executed her last duty in love. I had to carry along food for the horse since I could not count on acquiring it along the way. Many of the hapless people of Columbia had given me a great number of letters for their family members in Charleston, in the Northern states and in Europe. Since there was a major shortage of better paper, they were written on little snippets of paper. Not until Richmond or in reaching the North would I be able to put them in a form for postal transport, acquire stamps, and send them. These various things were contained in several sacks, pouches and bags of all possible forms and colors and were affixed to the saddle or the back of the horse in the best possible way. The unavoidable movement of the various forms of luggage must have embarrassed the horse and likely offered a laughable view rather than one of symmetry. A pair of containers which cannot be adequately described were pants, filled with corn and bound at the bottom, which hung from the saddle on both sides of the horse and served excellently as a fodder sack, this for lack of anything better. It contributed a lot to the comic effect. My attire, namely my hat and boots which had become quite wretched through the influence of time and weather and the notoriously evil grey coat which I could not bring myself to abandon for a more modern one when I later had the opportunity because of the loyal service which it had rendered to me in the past an on this trip, likely contributed in part to the representation me as "The Knight of the Sad Countenance." As it is written, "Necessity knows no law." I did not worry one bit about my otherwise peaceful appearance, particularly since the people with whom I would likely come in contact were little given to making mocking comments.

It was a wonderful morning on which I took the road which I knew so well. The sun shone warmly on resplendent nature clothed in a lush spring dress. The pear trees and the almond trees were lavished with pink blooms and rose charmingly contrasted themselves with the fresh green. The yellow jasmine, the honeysuckle and other plants which grew in the woods spread an exhilarating fragrance. Among these trees and plants, brightly feathered singers rejoiced and sang their spring and love songs.

Nature was in her festive garment and radiated peace. She divined and proclaimed the end of the "anxious and terrible time" and the return of a new and happy life. Who indeed could not take joy in her bounty, her admonitions and her words of solace?

From the sublime to the laughable is only one step. In the opposite direction, the distance may not be further. If my outward appearance on that morning by my own judgment and description which I just gave seems to be comical and laughable enough, I had nonetheless awarded myself a spirit of celebration whereby my inner Ego contrasted to my advantage with my outer self.

My sentiments were heavily influenced and my contemplation was deepened by the enchanting outbreak of spring which transformed an already wonderful area into a paradise; by successive farewells from people and places I had come to love, people and places to which I was bound by joyful and painful memories; by the fate of those which I had left in distress and worry; by the happy future, the worthy goal toward which I was now going; and by the difficulties which would yet place themselves in my way. Man busies himself far too little with himself. It is precisely such self-introspection which brings about a healing influence on his mind and which creates in him exhilaration or solace or an unerringly wise life. I was able to give myself completely over to my thoughts and sentiments as I rode through the peaceful countryside. When a certain wistfulness passed through me, it was advantageously of a joyous nature. Behind me lay a time of hard but interesting work for which God had richly blessed me and on which I could look back with complete satisfaction. Further back there are the recollections of a happy childhood which ended painfully with the loss of my loving and caring father. Then there was my steadfast home, my loyal and loving mother and all of the love which she always extended to me. Finally, there was my departure from them and my entry into the adversities of life, the hunt for happiness, and the many new impressions which I received and gathered. There was the acquaintance with new realities, lands and people, many of whom having earned my greatest respect. They became worthy examples and friends. In addition, there was the hazard-free military service, the war with its horrible episodes as well as the good fortune which the war brought me but the suffering which it brought the country and its people. Finally, there was the departure from these dear people and from a place that was once so uplifting but which was now transformed into a place of suffering. In the most recent years, not a little had gathered itself together which has now become alive in my thoughts. There are many uplifting images; but some dark shadows of the past appear as well.

In front of me was a new life of joy and hope of a happy reunion with my people. To be sure, there was yet much time and space with perhaps some intermittent discomfort, but this did not discourage me. After all that had come against me up to this point, I was determined to reach this worthy goal. In my mind, I drew for myself a beautiful scene which was tied to my arrival and my stay in my father's house.

The past filled me with appreciation to God for the few successes, for all of the joys and lessons, which He allowed me to have, for the fortunate escapes and overcoming of dangers to which my life, my minuscule wealth and likely also my honor were exposed. The future showed me only rich enjoyment, a happy and long family life without burden and a time of peace and restoration. These quickened in me all good intentions to be modest and to be thankful when I achieved the happy end, when the satisfaction of my longing would be fulfilled.

That day, on which I decided to cut out an important slice of life consisting of previous relationships, activities and lifestyles and on which, in the long run, I would set myself toward a new phase of life which the magnificent beauty of nature began to unfold and awakened in me as a sublime sensibility and admonition, deeply influenced my thoughts for all time and, although it was of itself devoid of any meaning, created an important moment in my life, one which would have a lasting effect.

I have already described my outer and inner reality and thought which were by far more pleasant that those of a few weeks before. Today's companion had a quicker gait and appeared to likewise be more satisfied with the world as compared to the bastard of the past. I could, therefore, allow more frequent and longer rests. The roads were dry and level. The rivers which crossed them had retreated into their normal beds and were easily crossed. Nevertheless, things in such places still looked dead and sad where life had once showed itself. The farm land which should have necessarily been tilled, still lay in a winter's sleep because the owners, who themselves were also likely not present because they had not returned from their exile, lacked the work animals. The restoration of the railroad had not begun at all. Even the rails which as old iron would have nevertheless had an appreciable value remained an unclaimed asset which was untouched by the owners and the thieves because there was no way to transport it. Some of the cadavers of horses, cows and pigs had been buried; but a large part lay out in the open, half eaten by buzzards and crows and emitting across a large area foul odors whose horrible effects on the organs of smell and breath I attempted to lessen by means of a quick gallop through the area of the pestilence.

My earlier hosts in Winnsboro willingly gave me quarters this time and obliged themselves to provide to me and to my horse the necessary provisions. They now had lots of food stuff when just fourteen days ago that had asserted that they were lacking. I had, however, already given myself the legitimacy that I was a good payer with "silver" and had proved that my coat did not cloak a vagabond or robber. For that reason, I could be welcomed.

Early the next morning, I again set out on my trip which was one more time blessed with beautiful weather, which passed with good fortune, which afforded me with the necessary breaks for restoration and for feeding the horse, and which ultimately brought me in the evening, in good order to Chester. I found once again a friendly reception from my colleague Barbot who would later go to Charleston and there, along with our director, close out the business of the firm. I spent the night with him and, since I no longer had need of my good horse, I left him with Barbot with the condition that upon the first opportunity that it be sent back to by friend Groning in Columbia by a dependable man.

From here on the train took me more quickly and more comfortably toward my destination, first to Richmond, which I, however, did not reach until several days later because the rail traffic had been reduced to the absolute minimum according to necessity. I was, therefore, obliged to spend and waste long periods of time at different stations.

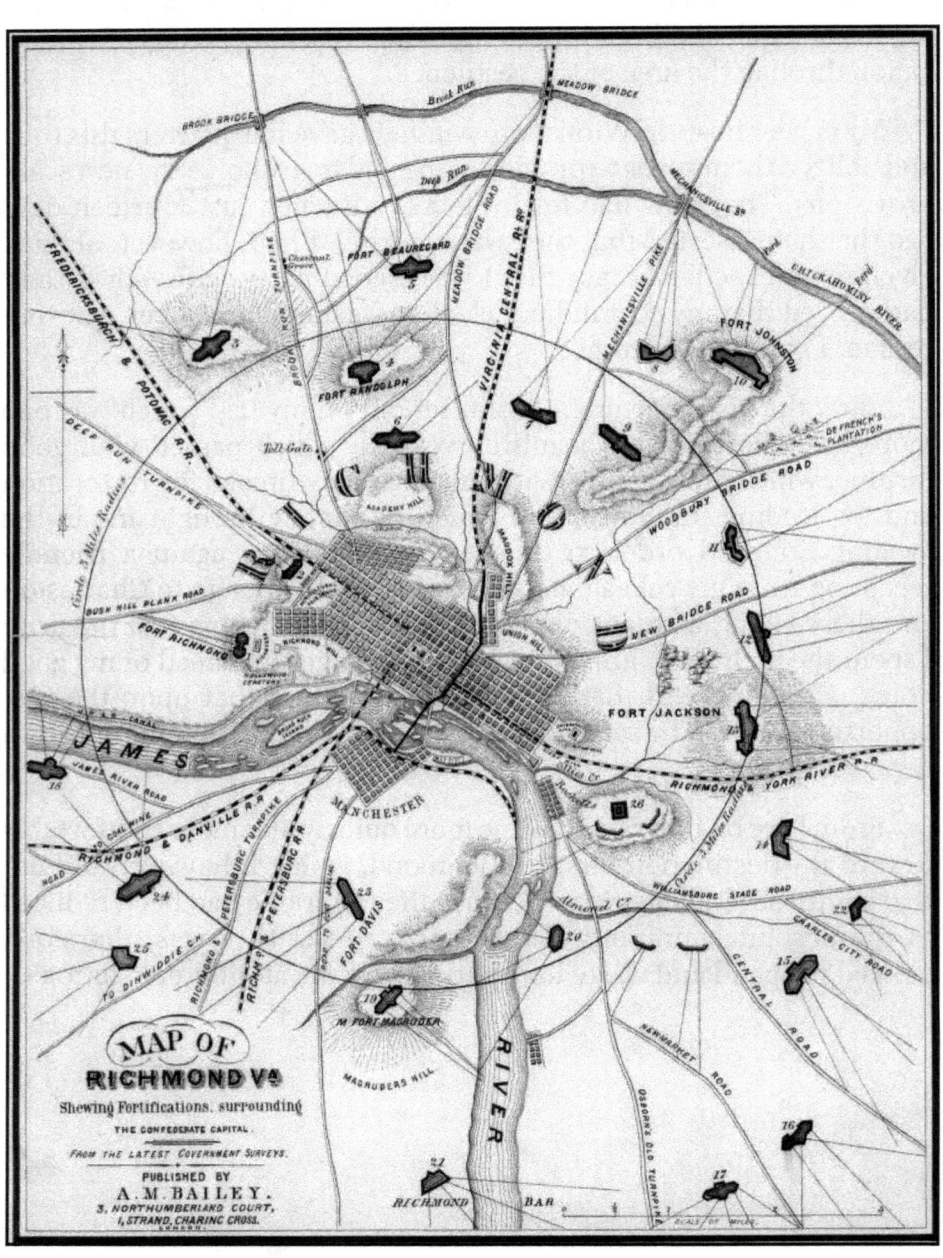

Map of Richmond, Virginia, 1860. Library of Congress.

Chapter 27

RICHMOND IN VIRGINIA

I had gotten to know Richmond earlier on a business trip. It was the capital of the State of Virginia and at the same time the capital of the Confederate States. This city was likely given this honor because it was held to be the most dignified and the most appropriate among her Southern sisters and through its choice as capital likewise the State of Virginia which had already enjoyed a certain respect in the former Union, noting that Washington and Lees as well as other great statesmen had been Virginians. Virginia was now the mainstay of the South and had provided the South with most of its most capable generals. It was also a recognition for its having joined the Confederacy.

The city with about 35,000 inhabitants was geographically located in a beautiful place. It was, in fact, compared to that of Rome. It was located on the James River about seventy miles from the river's mouth at the ocean. Only the first thirty miles thereof were, however, navigable. The city contained many beautiful buildings and churches as well as broad streets and squares. There was lively trade and activities in good times. Even now it was, relatively speaking, quite lively, likely because of the many projects which the various branches of the general government required and in spite of the many battles which took place nearby over the course of the years.

On a hill in the middle of a nice park with a fountain and a mounted statue of Washington which was of enormous proportions and finely crafted was enthroned the capitol in which the main office of the general administration was located. It was the same building which during a session of the state legislature had collapsed inside and buried a number of representatives and observers.

In one of the good hotels I found, after much wandering around and several privations, extremely genial board and quarters. There I managed to completely restore my withered stomach and my maltreated body. I paid homage with gusto to the sumptuous pleasures after a long, lean time without and after such had to again partake. These pleasures were, however, limited to a rich selection of food. To drink wine with meals is or was in those days not a custom in America, something which would be an affront to a German hotel owner. By contrast, the water of the James River was a favorite and well-known drink, this in spite of the fact that there were good wells and springs. Although its waters are murky throughout the year, it is drunk from colored glasses so as not to arouse aversion. Despite this objectionable quality, the water has an exquisite, fresh and aromatic taste.

Many of the stockholders of our company were in Richmond. Thanks to its successes and my position in the company by which I carried out the payment of the rich dividends, I enjoyed with all with whom I came in contact, with the authorities with whom I had to deal concerning the next phase of my trip, a certain respect which filled me not only with a certain pride but proved to work to my advantage. With these firms we had had lively business relationships. They gave me unequivocal support in my negotiations through letters of recommendation and introduction to Philadelphia, New York and Boston if I were to have need of such. These would afterward prove to be of great value. I was also accepted into the families of the owners.

I spent a very pleasant time during the six days for which I had to extend my stay. I met with many old acquaintances from Charleston and Columbia who in their civil service capacities had fled here with their offices as the enemy had encroached.

The authorities placed no difficulties at all in my way and officially recognized, based on my pass, my position as consul my right to leave the country, discreetly, however, because of my business mission. This would have otherwise not been permitted since all young men were to be conscripted. The last moves were being made, but the South made even then every effort to protect itself from the collapse. I received the necessary permits to pass the Confederate outposts. I was even given a general recommendation to the commander of the posts in question. The purpose was to ensure that I would get as far as possible with protection and transportation.

The original purpose of this circuitous trip, as I noted earlier, was to catch the prisoner-exchange steamer which came once a week to City Point, the point to which the James River was navigable, and from there to be transported to Northern territory. To my surprise and disappointment, however, I found out that this simply would not work offhand and created unexpected difficulties. The boat took only prisoners held by the South and with exception only those passengers who had a pass from the government of the United States. If these conditions were not met, then progress by this method was impossible. In order for me to meet these requirements, I had to first send my petition to the consul general in Washington and send it with the next boat. The consul general would have to forward my petition to the Union government and support it. My desire would then perhaps be fulfilled and I would receive the necessary permit.

In addition, the rare possibilities for transport had been terminated for weeks. That would be too long since I had already lost so much time and, in addition, since I could not reckon with the fulfillment of my desire. I therefore gave up that plan and followed a new one which was less comfortable and convenient but which could be executed immediately.

I had been given to understand that many had secretly left the country and had reached Northern territory at different points on the border formed by the Potomac River, a border which was closely guarded by the United States. On the Southern side, the Virginia side of the Potomac, there was considerable business pursuant to getting travelers across the river to the Northern or Maryland side. In Richmond, there were numerous people available who led such travelers by unprohibited or prohibited means to points in question where the crossing of the line between North and South would pose less difficulty. The railroads in this direction had long been destroyed, and the three-day trip was only possible by wagon, by horse or on foot.

Admittedly, this new travel plan was not to my liking; but what was I otherwise to do other than make use of this plan if I did not want to perhaps wait weeks in uncertainty for making use of the more comfortable plan. From the Confederate side, I had the necessary permit to pass through the line. I determined to legitimize myself with the Northern military posts or authorities if I fell into their hands. I had nothing to fear on this account. It was, however, likely the way through the territory of both sides was not secure from attacks by robbers. Here, however, I again trusted in my lucky star and was even more reassured by the guide which had been recommended to me that he had already brought numerous travelers to the Potomac without having suffered the slightest mishap.

The man in question whom I came to trust based on dependable recommendations did not make a good impression on me. The look from his blood-shot eyes and his pale face gave him an eerie thrall. This impression was, however, mitigated by the expressed confidence with which he presented himself, with the way he explained the travel plans and by the respect which he enjoyed from my acquaintances.

I negotiated that he would bring me to the Potomac in three days by means of a two-horse wagon. I paid him the amount for his service, fortunately or perhaps unfortunately, in advance.

I had purchased new clothes and had exchange my previous pieces of luggage with a new suitcase. The gold coins from Columbia which were left over from expenditures for the needy I complimented with 450 dollars through the sale of a draft. I long debated whether I should acquire a revolver for emergencies. I finally convinced myself, however, that the possession of such a weapon could be, under certain conditions, more of a liability than an asset for me.

Chapter 28

Desperate Situation

After I had settled affairs and had taken leave of my friends, I had my guide pick me up at the hotel early in the morning of 1 April 1865. The guide asked permission to allow a poor woman with two small children to come with us, wherebey my comfort with his manner should have been affected. I demanded and gladly informed him that I would at least have to request that a portion of the money which I had spent for my personal use of the wagon would have to be returned, a point on which I prevailed after much haggling. I liked his excessive uprightness; yet, I did not see the trap which his manner cloaked.

Our travel companions were picked up, and we pressed on to our destination. The conveyance consisted of two powerful brown horses hitched to a box wagon coved by a strong canvas which kept the effects of the weather out of the inside. As per my desire the poor, young woman made herself and her helpless children comfortable at the back of the wagon, while I preferred to take the forward seat, still well protected, behind the owner who was driving. I did this to be able to look out on the countryside and to have conversation with the driver. Stored in the middle of the wagon were my luggage, a trunk belonging to the woman, some sacks filled with horse fodder and the owner's provisions.

I had acquired a new valise with new articles of clothing and other items of comfort as well as a stock of food which, if necessary, would last several days. The letters which I had brought with me from Columbia as well as other important papers were in an old bag which

I had kept, in part because of respect for Mrs. Gronig who had given it to me and in part because there was no room for them in the valise.

My body was completely covered in new clothes except for the old coat. I carried the heavy gold hidden money belt around my waist. I had placed approximately thirty dollars in gold and silver coins in my change purse so that I would not have to disturb my secret cache until I had arrived in a more civilized region but also to distract a would-be plunderer from the greater treasure. In addition, the change purse held the refunded sum in Confederate money with which I had original paid the fare.

The drafts which had been given to me by the director, with three copies of each, I had carefully concealed in an old wallet which I had carried for years in my pocket. The wallet had been given to me by my dear mother at the hour of departure and was for that reason of extraordinary value. I had divided the drafts. I had shoved the drafts between the inner and outer sides, that is between the leather and the lining, and closed the former. This manipulation had succeeded very well so that the process as well as the hiding place of the documents could not be discovered.

In addition to the wallet and the coin purse, I was carrying the various items which I would normally have in my pockets: a watch and chain, smoking utensils, and other items.

Here it is necessary that I list these items in particular, the reason for which to be explained in a later description.

So we traveled away with our team in a northerly direction. The horses moved spryly along, and the driver employed no few admonitions. One milestone after the other informed us of the ever greater distance which separated us from Richmond. The road paved with highway stone made quick forward progress possible and contributed to a steady motion of the wagon so that the trip was without bodily discomfort and went smoothly.

The area had no appeal at all. It was an eternal sameness of flat terrain and woods and then some cultivated land just as I had likewise experience on my wanderings and on railcars in South Carolina. As there, here also one could everywhere catch sight of the signs of war with demolished or abandoned homes and farm buildings. It was only that here the ruins were older, and the devastation was more thorough because of the years' long movement of both armies on this territory. In more recent times no battles had taken place here because the land was so exhausted that neither of the two forces took possession of it in actuality. This area was already outside the line which the Confederate army maintained for the defense of Richmond and was up to the Potomac in a state of anarchy. The few people who still inhabited this region or who had returned to it attempted to gain their subsistence from the land but found themselves without protection and without authorities and were at all times subject to new attacks and new plundering. It is to be noted that these inhabitants were real Virginians and had their own particular patriotism for their "state" and were committed devotees of the South. Had Virginia in those days decided to cast its lot with the North, all of the people would have been likewise loyal to the Union. The weather honored the beginning of April. Intermittent warm sunshine gave way to showers which did not further bother us except that they overshadowed the already dismal countryside.

I had to dispense with the enjoyment of nature which I had hoped for. In contrast, the conversation with my companion, noting that the woman in the back of the wagon remained remarkably silent, was very interesting. He told me of his different contraband trips which he had always carried out without any incident. The trip in this case was not one on which an incident should be anticipated since we would not need to fear coming into contact with either of the armies. He clarified the details of the trip, its phases, the stations where we would overnight, the ways and means of further travel after he had brought us to our destination as well as the general conditions in the most detailed and most obliging manner. For my part, I was careful and reserved in my statements.

About ten miles from our starting point we passed the Confederate border post after we had encountered several detachments and patrols which had allowed us to pass without stop after proper identification. The driver was at my instigation my guide for whom I had necessity. I had, therefore, provided him with a pass as well. The woman did not have one and did not need one. At the aforementioned outpost, the inspection was more thorough. The wagon was searched, and we had to submit to questioning. After all suspicion had been thereby allayed, we were allowed to leave Confederate controlled territory; thus we then entered for the time being a no man's land.

After five further miles we came upon a small locale with the name Hanover Court House, in which, respective to its nearness, the progeny of Washington had their property and their house. [101] It was, however, abandoned by its inhabitants and lay dead on the way. Only a tavern along the road was open with rooms. It was also filled with some noisy fellows with whom I did not wish to have close contact. At my insistence, we traveled on without fortification, but a bit pent-up at missing a good opportunity.

A short stretch thereafter we crossed the Pamunky River by means of a ferry. Here my companion told me that he had to stop on the opposite bank in order to give rest to the horses and to feed and water them.

Court House is the main locale of a district, the seat of the court and other subordinate authorities and is therefore always of some importance.

We traveled for about another mile, following the river upstream, then further until we had reached the appropriate stopping place. I was likely about 1:00 p. m. We found ourselves in a place which remains clear in my mind's eye and which I will never forget for the rest of my life. The road opened into a large clearing and went for some distance straight through it to the forest which made a ring around the clearing. To the left of the road flowed the Pamunky, likewise separated from the road by woods. Just as the road came out of the forest, under the last tree, Jones, which I will call my companion, unhitched the horses. After he had given them fodder, he led them a piece back where they could be watered. With this, he left my field of vision.

---

101 Conrad added this footnote concerning Hanover Court House: "The State of Virginia has named some of its districts with the names of German countries such as Hanover, Brunswick, Luneburg, Mecklenburg and so on."

There was again a mighty downpour of rain. I had no desire to leave my dry seat, so I used the opportunity to prepare my stomach a little treat. After I had successfully done so with bread and cold roast, I spent the time reading and at the same time enjoying a cigar. It was virtually impossible to carry on a conversation with my female traveling companion who was a member of the working class. She sat silently in the dark corner and busied herself with the children. Their crying brought me to regret my willingness to bring this company along. There was, however, nothing which could be done about that. Besides I was in the mood to take such inconveniences with ease in order to be accommodating to my fellow men.

Well protected from the rain, comfortably stretched out on the forward seat, I was interrupted in my rest and activity by four riders who suddenly appeared before the wagon. They must have come out of the woods because had they come down the road, I would have seen them much earlier from my seat. I do not know how it came about, but on first sight of these people a fear enveloped me. It was probably warranted in the initial moment by their sudden arrival and their questionable appearance. It should have been heightened through their behavior afterward. In spite of that, I would not be able to resist any actions on their part.

The young men were dressed almost the same. I would say that they were in uniform. By their dress, which was neither that of the Northern or Southern military uniforms, I should have been able to recognize what country and what estate they belonged to. What they had on and around them were clothes out of a brown material which was sound and clean. Their horses were well fed and outfitted with good leather. There impression was that of the military and not of vagabonds. There was no visible sign of weapons about them.

One of the men rode up to me and asked about my destination. When I told him that it was the Potomac, he asked for a pass. I handed it to him. He read it and gave it immediately back to me, whereupon the cavalcade rode by me silently in the direction from which we had come.

After a quarter of an hour, during which I could not rid myself of my concerns, Jones finally returned with his horses and hitched them to the wagon. I recounted the incident for him with the question whether or not he had seen them. He gave me to believe that he had not seen them and could not make a comment, given my description, as to what kind of men they might be.

We set out on the trip and had gone about one-hundred steps where the road was still accompanied by the last trees on the left when I suddenly saw the head of a horse protrude at the edge of the wagon covering. This moment brought me to quaking, and a terrifying foreboding awakened in me which rose as the full appearance of one of the known riders was before us.

Then, all four of them were there. They overtook us and placed themselves in front of our vehicle and demanded and compelled us to stop.

The previous spokesman again took up the conversation and rode right up to me and said: "You are traveling into the land of the enemy and are carrying, without doubt, a lot of gold there. We request a toll of the amount." The highwayman was very polite and to a point even modest. It was now clear what I was dealing with.

I responded to him that I was but a poor refugee and that I had just enough in my possession to pay my crossing of the Potomac and the travel costs to Baltimore and that I would gladly pay him a tribute if I had more means. To the question how much I had with me, I gave the sum of thirty dollars and took out my change purse and poured the entire contents in my hand and counted out to him the few gold pieces, silver pieces and paper bills. As soon as these were back in the change purse, he ripped it out of my hand and took it for himself. As angry and fearful as I was at this behavior, I did not lose my composure. I presented myself as being quite unhappy at this loss. I professed my helplessness in that I did not know how I would get by without a cent and pled earnestly that I be refunded at least the half. The man went over to his companions who had behaved quite passively up to this point and whispered something which I could not understand but which pointed in my favor. I even believed to have won the game, or that I would at least not experience any further molestation. Then the conference ended and the results hit me with its full severity.

The spokesman and gang leader, instead of giving me the alms for which I had begged, began to again interrogate me with the utterance, "You have more money with you; out with it now!" In that moment, my fate was clear; however, in the moment of distress, a man grasps for a straw; and I began the quite superfluous, repeated denial of any further possessions. I thereby achieved nothing. The fellow jumped from his saddle, pulled me to his chest and jerked me from my seat and out of the wagon so that I felled crumpled before him. I was overcome with an impotent anger, given such treatment; and I had I that revolver with me I would have certainly shot the ruffian during this raw attack; but I would have immediately suffered the same fate; and my legs which would have been eaten by ravens and would now giving penance on Virginia soil. I at least managed to keep body and soul together.

The three accomplices likewise dismounted. One held the reins of their four horses, and the other two rushed to assist their comrade. I was pulled through the mud in front of the wagon which contributed to blocking the way where my trembling body was brought into the vertical position. Two of the rascals held me painfully tight, each with one of their hands, while in the other hand they held two drawn revolvers with the hammer cocked directly on my head and threatened to shoot me on the spot if I moved a muscle or made a noise. In this horrible situation, my life was of the utmost importance such that if possible I wanted to save it. In that frame of mind, I calmly indulged everything else.

The leader of the bandits took care of the plundering. First, my pockets were examined and emptied, and each item of clothing was thoroughly searched to determine whether there was anything between the surface and the lining. My boots and hat were likewise searched. The man seemed to take a liking to the latter. He set it on his head and threw his on hat high into the air so that it caught and remained hanging on a limb in a tall tree. With this thorough search, there was revealed a considerable swelling and hardness in the area of my stomach, and the reason for this would soon come to light.

Even today, I can see the sweet grimaces of the robbers and hear their cries of joy as the main hero held up the money belt and based on its weight determine the approximate value of the contents. His estimation was a bit larger that the gold therein contained was worth. That was a prize which they could not have expected even if they had been practicing this noble craft for a long time.

With this, however, they were not finished. One of the robbers jumped into the wagon and searched it. He came out only with my suitcase which they then took possession of.

I was spiritually and physically devastated. I was hardly able to gather my wits about me to determine my loss and to measure the effect that it would have on my future. Nevertheless, I made bitter pleading and called on the generosity of these rogues to at least leave me a part of their rich prize so that I could continue on my trip and not starve to death. They, however, earned me only sneers and taunts as well as the offer if my existence were so cumbersome to gladly "blow my brains out!"

Now they were also in possession of my wallet in which the drafts were hidden. I once again dared to attempt to at least get it back in order to save the valuable content. I hope to make later use of it if I kept my life and if I ever came to be among civilized people, the hope of which, given my current distress and broken condition, lay far away.

Once again I pled with these fiends to return the old wallet which was useless to them because it was a dear reminder of my mother whom I would perhaps never see again, a reminder which I would like to keep with me until the last moment of my life. If there were no sense of humanity about them, they might still fulfill this wish for the sake of their own mothers for whom they would certainly have a spark of affection.

That must have touched them a little. The one who had it, after he had emptied it and thoroughly looked at it, tossed it and my pass back to me, without having found the hiding place. Further compassion from them was, however, not to be had. To the contrary, they would have likely completely disrobed me and were in the process of taking off my boots when a wagon became visible on the other side of the clearing. This unforeseen occurrence caused them to quickly mount their horses and to hurry off in an easterly direction.

I stood like a stone in the pouring rain which had wet me to the bone during the entire drama and watched my treasures as they disappeared with their new owners into the forest.

And my travel companions? The woman cried and whined with the children as things unfolded. Jones sat on the front set and held the reins of the horses. He, however, appeared to have been befallen by a great fear; and he took no active part in the matter. He did not rise to my protection or to my defense. I could not hold it against him given that his support would have been unsuccessful against the superiority of the bandits. It did, however, appear quite suspicious to me that the robbers did not concern themselves with him or the others and that they did not unhitch the horses which could have been useful to them and that they did not disturb the rest of the contents of the wagon which did not belong to me.

I stood there bareheaded without any means of subsistence, however, at least still clothed, but otherwise, save for the wallet, completely rifled and robbed. No one said a word for a long time. It required a strain of my willpower to awaken me from the tumult of fear and to measure my misfortune and to be able to consider further necessary steps. Without money, I could not think of getting across the Potomac, even if I had free transfer to that point. After my arrival in the United States, I would have to hope to beg my way through until I received help from a second brother who was in the west; or in the best case, based on the letters of reference from friends in Richmond, I would be able to turn a draft into cash.

The shattering feelings, worries, distress and despair cannot be explained any further. No one who has not himself been in such a situation can empathize with it. It must be remembered that I did not have one penny of money or tradable item at my disposal; that I was in a wild, strange, uninhabited and desolate country; that I still had many days before me until I perhaps came into better circumstances; and that, without question, some means would be absolutely necessary.

There was no one to be found for a long time from whom I could expect to have an interest in me. In addition, there was the growing mistrust of the person who could have perhaps helped: my guide. From a comfortable room, a man cannot place himself in the condition of my helplessness and hopelessness which were brought on by the collective conditions of those days.

After I had to that point cleared my thoughts in order to come to a decision, I share it with Jones, namely that I wanted to return to Richmond. The inconveniences associated with a longer wait were now no longer a consideration; and although I did not gladly want to submit to this delay, it seemed to be the only solution.

The good man wanted no part of that. He would take care that I would successfully get over the river and would suffer no need through his acquaintance with the Potomac shippers and the people from whom we would get quarters for the night. If need be, he would support me with his meager means. Against a return to Richmond, he had all sorts of objections, namely that we would have to overnight somewhere and that there was no location which would guarantee an overnight. The cogent reason he, however, presented that he had undertaken to bring the woman away and that this verified the necessity to move on as quickly as possible. She had paid for that service; and he had to, for that reason, insist on continuing the trip.

With that, I was simply beaten. To go alone and by foot the long way back would be impossible for me to accomplish. I would have surely died on the way. I had to build my constructed hopes in the opposite direction and submit to this reality. How tame a man is when he is in distress and is suffering, and I was brittle enough.

We moved on, rather I walked along beside and behind the wagon in order to be alone with my excruciating sensibilities, to be able to consider my fate and at the same time, however, after the rain had ceased, to keep my wet body in motion and to somewhat thereby dry my clothes.

I was being hindered in raising my spirits. I came to doubt the possibility of reaching my goal which had previously hovered before me, namely to again see my folks. With calm wistfulness, I thought of them as they were just today celebrating the birthday of my sister in my father's house even as I had just barely escaped death and had to endure a sorrow of the soul. I considered that I had been called to face my doom in this large, strange world where I would starve to death or be assassinated.

With longer consideration, the conclusion that Jones had been in on the plot with the robbers gained the upper hand. I may be doing him an injustice; but I was unable to rid myself of this thought. I was, however, puzzling how he could have come to know of the large sum of money which I had. First there was the repayment of part of his fee which gave him total authority over the team. Then there was his refusal to return to Richmond in order to forefend that the matter would be filed as a complaint which might have brought an investigation of him and might have ruined his reputation. For those reasons, he gave promise to support me, a promise which he did not keep. Then there was the timing of the initial phase of the attack in his absence and the likelihood that he had met with the accomplices during that time. Finally, there was the main point that his belongings remained completely untouched and could have just as easily been taken as were mine.

All of these reasons for suspicion awakened in me a great mistrust of the man and moved me to fear. I therein recognized his interest in hindering the return to Richmond. He could have perhaps more easily had opportunity to get rid of me rather than simply having me for a burden for yet more days on the way to the Potomac. My agitated nerves sensed here the danger of death through murder and there the danger of death through starvation. The desire rose up often in me to find work on a farm and thereby gain my subsistence or to earn over time enough so that I could end and get away from these unsustainable conditions. Even such solace was, however, not to be shared with me; for there was no one far and wide who needed a farmhand, who could much less feed and pay him.

I again had to take my seat since, because of the longer break, we had to travel faster in order to reach the quarters which we had envisaged. Toward evening, we managed to arrive at a very humble house which at least initially gave the opportunity to dry out before a cheery open fire. As agitated and mistrustful as I was, this house, inhabited only by a woman, her boys and two Negro women, appeared to me to be a hostel for both robbers and their victims. Jones was right at home here and had spent the night here on his earlier trips. Likewise, other passersby had stopped off here, but whether they had left here alive I did not know. These people lived off those who passed by whom they charged for lodging and meals. Since I was not capable of reimbursing those services, I was very coolly received. I felt embarrassed to take my share of supper. Jones gave me a snack from the provisions which he had brought along, but he himself dished up a good meal. The other travel companions likewise partook of their own provisions.

I asked but one favor: to be able to spend the night on the floor at the fire, and would have preferred this location; however, the hostess was of the opinion that she had beds and that I should use one of them. Jones stepped in as protector and stated that he would take care of the matter and that I should accept the convenience. I slept in the same room as he; that is, I did not sleep, but was kept awake by troubling thoughts and by the fear of an attack by my bedfellow. When sleep did indeed attempt to deliver me from this terrible situation, I scared it off so that I could encounter the ghost of death which hovered over me in my fantasy.

Now, since the danger is long over and proved to be unwarranted, I must wonder myself about the boundless fear which filled me in those days; however, I had cause not to take my situation lightly; and the terrible incidents had massively shattered my nerves. Jones snored through the night without interrupting his sleep or his musical talents with no opportunity to murder me. One can be an insidious scoundrel without being a murderer.

The next morning, we continued on our journey after my companions had a good breakfast with me looking on. Although Jones again gave me a little from his provisions, it was not enough to still my raging hunger.

Heaven had closed her locks and laughed upon the woods and meadows which increased in appeal the farther we traveled into the region. The terrain became more and more hilly and offered a greater diversity; however, my mind, suppressed by an empty stomach as well as fear, distress and worry, only became more and more anxious.

The behavior of my guide, in whom alone I saw a support and a savior despite the active mistrust, became ever more worrisome and sinister. As helpful as he was at the beginning of our trip, the more withdrawn he now became. The questions which I posed to him about my future, about which I was anxious and with which I struggled, he answered very curtly that I would find this out later. Other conversations which I attempted to initiate he rejected in a brusque tone. My requests for food, for which I would have later paid him well, he reciprocated in the beginning a bit with reluctance. Later, however, he completely denied it to me with the worry that he hardly had enough for himself for the trip there and back and would perhaps not be able to see himself through to the return. When the wagon encountered an incline, he required me to leave the wagon, which was likely justified, although he himself remained seated. As irritated as I secretly was over this injustice, I would not and could not allow myself to irritate him; besides a walk from time to time was pleasant.

It, however, repeatedly happened, when the terrain allowed it, that Jones would set the horses in a quick trot so that I had to remain behind and was only able to get back to the wagon with a steady run which completely exhausted me.

On the second evening we made our quarters in a humble house. My travel companions took their places at the table, but I was denied participation. I have always had the suspicion that it was done at the behest of my tormenter on whom the people were likely dependent and could not afford to spoil that relationship; otherwise, the friendly innkeepers would have undoubtedly had compassion on me and extended the healing balm of food to me. They thus commiserated with me in their own destitute state which did not allow them to hand out such gifts without payment.

What this man had in mind with his hardheartedness remains to this day a puzzle for me. The only possible explanation is that he wanted to get away from me by hindering me from getting to an inhabited area where I could make known the suspicions which I fostered against him. He perhaps hoped that I would waste away in the wilderness or die of hunger. He appeared himself not to be of one mind. Would it be better to get me out of the country, or would it be better to escort me from life? In any case, he was not evil enough or feared the consequence if he had taken the last way out.

Despite my desperation, I was determined, as far as my strength allowed, to hold out to the last moment and to be on my guard. As meek and broken as I was which the nightmarish incident had brought upon me, I was yet defiant toward the man who, in my opinion, was determined to bring my ruin. I no longer addressed him for any support or communicated a word with him. I hoped to endure until that moment which through the arrival at our destination freed me from him, a moment which would come the next day.

I did not want to enjoy the grace of the compassion of people. I came to disdain people who became aware of my suffering, which perhaps they did not directly apprehend, but did nothing. That is how I felt. I rejected the bivouac which was offered to me and used instead the hovel in the wagon instead. I did this in part for spite but also because I did not want to get separated from him because, based on the previous incidents, it was not impossible for me to think that Jones would secretly steal off with the wagon and the other travelers.

The containers with the provisions had been taken out of the wagon and brought into the house; otherwise, I would have likely forgotten myself and misappropriated some of the contents. I was, however, spared this temptation.

If this uncomfortable lair only inadequately satisfied my desire for sleep and the forgetting of suffering during its duration, I nevertheless had peace concerning attempted murder and being left behind. I also had the hope of that things would soon change and that my situation would better itself. All of that likely relieved the terrible conditions of the present. While the rest of them strengthened themselves for the rest of the trip with breakfast, I quickened myself with at a spring with fresh water, both inwardly and outwardly. I refreshed my spirit for the future worries and burdens which lay before me.

The trip began in silence. I asserted my place in the wagon so that he could not slip away from me and compelled myself to be patient so that I could bear the pangs of hunger which were more and more gaining the upper hand.

*A sketch of the Rappahannock River made by Edwin Forbes in 1864.
Library of Congress.*

Chapter 29

HELP IN DISTRESS

My expectations did not fail me. By two in the afternoon, after we had crossed the approximately two-mile wide Rappahannock River by ferry, we came to a friendly, inhabited village: Westmoreland Court House. This was the final destination of the wagon trip.

I did not know what difficulties would place themselves in my way or how I should get further without any means. At this moment, however, I thought less about that. I was initially unburdened from the uneasy feeling of being fettered to a man whom I had to view as my enemy but from whom I had earlier been unable to free myself, and I was quickened by the hope of attaining food and by the coming final separation.

The hotel where we alighted was positively alive with inhabitants of the village and the region as well as with travelers who had just arrived. They had the same purpose as I did I. In spite of the immediate nearness of the border with the enemy and of the illegal business which these people here carried on through their lucrative blockade business, life was relatively good and peaceful.

The first thing, which my distress demanded after I had cut the tie with my tormentor, was that I solicit some food for myself. After I had told the story of my misfortune, precisely that was granted me by the innkeepers in great quantity. I was allowed to take part in a noon meal which had just been set out. That I made unlimited use of such grace follows from the condition of my stomach.

I saw Jones shortly after our arrival driving away. The female travel companion and the two children disappeared without a trace, whereby I came to the suspicion that she was also part of the robbers' plot or was at least a tool used to hinder my return to Richmond.

The support and recommendations which were promised to me by Jones for the continuation of the trip did not, of course, come about; and based on his previous behavior, I did not count on them. I held it to be beneath my dignity to even address him about it. It was a relief to get the man who appeared to be dangerous out of my presence, hoping, that my further travel would be made possible with the help of the community of the inhabitants of the village and the travelers.

Under other circumstances, I would not have let the man off so easily and would have requested an investigation of him. I was, however, in my situation not so minded to for revenge and prosecution. Although my suspicion that he was a participant in the robbery was almost a certainty, it would have been difficult to prove and a complaint on my part would have probably been useless. In addition, an investigation of such would have taken a long time and made it necessary for me to remain there longer, whereby I would have likely been even more annoyed. In my own interest, I allowed him to move on.

The sumptuous meal and enlivened me and strengthened me. With that, the most immediate privation was alleviated. Now it was a matter of acquiring the funds to travel on. To receive the travelers, there was in the hotel a representative of the people who provided the transport across the Potomac. I requested from this representative free transport which, despite all sympathy for my plight, he asserted not to be able to provide because the association of contrabandists consisted of many members which ran the business at different points along the river and did so for an agreed-upon price. Their agreement to such a sacrifice would be necessary but could not be acquired in such short order. At first, the denial seemed unjust and hard; but after I had later observed the conditions in which the people toiled and faced dangers, and how every little space in their small boats was carefully used and paid for, I was unable to fault the denial of my attempt. If they made exceptions, there would have been many under the cover of poverty who would have demanded the same consideration.

I could therefore not reckon on free passage and had to myself acquire the money for the necessary cost which was twenty-six dollars in gold. Necessity knows no rules, so I was compelled to beg for the amount. With begging, I had no luck at all with men, in spite of the fact that I agreed to pay them the full amount of the advance when I arrived in New York. Perhaps they were not in the position to grant such that might have helped me out of my distress, and that was probably the case with many. Small donations did not help at all since it was thereby impossible to raise the considerable passage money. My appearance and the stories which I told probably did not instill confidence. I could not reasonably hold it against anyone that they did not wish to give an advance based on my pleas. In contrast, two ladies who were wanting to make the trip to the North came to my aid when they had learned of my distress: Mrs. Waters from New York with her small son and Miss Worrel from Baltimore. This they did, although I definitely knew that neither were of substantial means and that the consequence of their sacrifice to me would result in even less means. I received fifteen dollars from them. The way and manner with which these two ladies freely shared their limited holdings without having proof that my story was rooted in truth or that they would be recompensed for the loan by a completely strange person was touching and filled me, in addition to the happiness which came from being in possession of this sum of money, with inner gratitude toward God and toward these benefactresses as well as an inner adoration of the later. I was completely drawn to them; and until our ways parted, I remained their loyal and appreciative travel companion.

From Westmoreland Courthouse we still had to make the two miles to the Potomac and to the point where the crossing was to take place. We walked this road, being led by the previously mentioned representative of the contraband company. After dinner, he loaded the luggage of the other travelers on a small wagon.

I felt happy again; and the horrors of the last days faded more and more into the background after I had found charitable people, after a substantial meal, and because I had so much money that I would at least be able to enter the United States. Once I had crossed the "Rubicon," I would no longer be afraid of closing in on my longed-for goal. If the bitter losses were not so easy to get over and if the enduring torment of my nerves was still present, my doubts had diminished such that I could face the future with inner peace and hope. I no longer had to fear a robbery with the small amount of cash I had, nor did I have to fear starving to death.

A person has to have gone through bad times before he can rightly value the blessing of health, bodily subsistence, and benevolence. With this, he can recognize how unreliable earthly possessions are when other means of assistance, namely the blessings from God, are not present. He is thereby humbled, thankful and truly knows himself, namely that his fate lies in the hands of the Most High. On the one hand, he is to struggle with attaining his life's goal and with retaining it; but one the other hand, he is obliged to assist his fellow man who is in real distress or to help him with all means available.

I came away from all of this blessed. The lesson which deeply formed me through this opportunity had not been too expensive since I had greater means, which I at the time simply did not know how to value and which meant nothing to me without the help of the experience.

My body had new strength. My mind was quickened with new hope. I felt myself to be a different person and found interest and pleasure in my surroundings.

The region through which our little troop wandered was charming and showed no evidence of fiendish plundering and destruction. It was puzzling that the Northerners had entirely ignored and spared this unprotected territory which lay so close to their own, especially since its inhabitants took full advantage of the flourishing blockade and contraband business. The reason for this consideration likely lay in the fact that this little piece of land was to Americans a classical and holy terrain. Here, along our way to the Potomac, stood the charming holdings of the great general Robert E. Lee, who, although he was a

Confederate general, had earned, even among the Unionists, through his capabilities and noble character a high degree of honor. [102] Just a few miles away was the birthplace of Washington, a place which no American would have dared touch or desecrate. [103] It is here that the foundational stones for the building of the great and powerful republic had been cut; and here arose the first capable men who founded the republic, who brought it to power and who governed it. It is here that they gained many victories in their War for Independence, and it was here that the existence of the republic was made possible.

The fact that this territory was spared by the enemy was likely grounded in these considerations and was why the region enjoyed a calm peace. Given the character of Americans, this should come as no surprise. Did not General Grant himself give the express order to his troops that by the subjugation of the enemy and the suppression of the rebellion, the greatest forbearance was to be exercised toward the Confederates because they were "Americans" and were their brothers and should be treated as such?[104]

---

[102] Arlington, the plantation home of Robert E. Lee and his wife Mary Custis Lee (a descendant of Martha Washington), was seized by Federal forces early in the war. Soldiers quickly began looting the house, which was filled with many items which had belonged to George and Martha Washington, including portraits, china, Washington's bed, and other things from Mount Vernon. Those relics not carried away or destroyed by soldiers were taken to Washington, D.C., and placed in the Patent Office, where they were exhibited with the label "Captured from Arlington." In the early days of the war, Arlington was first seized by Federal troops to prevent its use as an artillery emplacement by the Confederates. What happened there later on, however, was not a matter of military necessity, but hatred and vengeance. A military cemetery was created at Arlington in 1864, when U. S. soldiers were buried next to the house. By the end of the war, thousands of soldiers were buried around it.

[103] It was largely due to the efforts of Ann Pamela Cunningham, a lady from South Carolina, that Mount Vernon was held as neutral territory during the war. In the 1850s, she founded the Mount Vernon Ladies Association for the purpose of raising funds to purchase Mount Vernon from its owner John Augustine Washington, Jr. (the great grand-nephew of George Washington) and to preserve and restore it. John A. Washington, Jr. served as an aide de camp to General Robert E. Lee with the rank of lieutenant colonel and was killed in battle in September 1861.

[104] Conrad is possibly referring to General Grant's courtesy toward General Lee and his army when they surrendered at Appomattox in April 1865. Grant reportedly disallowed a victory celebration by his men, stating, "The war is over. The rebels are our countrymen again."

Had Sherman only harbored such sentiments or had he been able to carry them out, then Columbia, the beautiful city, would not have had to experience such horrible suffering.

Chapter 30

On the Potomac and through the Blockade

After a one-hour march, we reached the much-promising Potomac, and a fantastic picture unfolded in front of my eyes.

The Virginia bank on this side of the river rose up to a height of forty to sixty feet above the surface of the water and was covered with a beautiful high forest. The river which was here at least ten miles wide was actually a bay of the ocean and spread mirror flat out before us, adorned by a small island.

Several sail boats lay in the water awaiting the whims of the wind. Steamers went up and down the river, and in the spaces between lay the gunboats of the United States for the purpose of guarding the country and to tax and control the blockade and contraband business. The surface of the water extended infinitely to the left and to the right, and beyond this surface was the coast of Maryland which rose somewhat farther inland. In spite of the distance, it was clearly visible because of the clear air. The afternoon sun was reflected in the houses which lay across from us and lit up the meadows which resembled gardens. Directly and abruptly below us the waves rippled and splashed against the stones. A deep peace lay over the magnificent scene which so pleasantly surprised and mesmerized my companions and me.

Over there, therefore, I caught sight of the promised land for which I was filled with great longing and from which I was separated by a water trip of only a few hours. I hoped to set foot on its territory and thereby end my odyssey.

A few hundred steps from the point where we had enjoyed our first view of the Potomac, there lay a house in a gully which was at the same level as the water of the river. The house was the headquarters of the contrabandists who gathered and met there only after darkness fell so that they did not fall into the hands of either Northern or Southern patrols since their business was forbidden by both sides. The Confederates likely gladly tolerated the import of the goods smuggled from the other side; however, they had to suppress the leakage of potential conscripts in this area. Union authorities were less concerned about refugees or even deserters as long as there were no spies among them for whom they diligently searched. They also did not want to be adversely affected by the smuggling of Northern products which would undermine their cause, even if it gave only a meager advantage. For this reason, the smugglers were always, particularly on their long water trips, subject to pursuit and, therefore, had to observe the strictest of precautions.

From our guide came the less than comforting news that the crossing would likely not take place that night because the waters were becalmed with the consequence that the strokes of the oars made sounds which could not completely be avoided and which could be heard on board the gunboats which were stationed on the river. This would result in their pursuit of our expedition.

For me personally, it would not have been in the least problematic had we fallen into the hands of the enemy, namely into the hands of the Unionists. I would have thereby come more quickly to my destination since I had already determined, compelled by my impecuniosity, to reach out to the next military or civilian authority as soon as I arrived on Northern territory and acquire from them a travel pass and other support. The entrepreneurs of this expedition had, however, their reasons for avoiding the Northern border patrols; and I had to submit myself to those reasons along with the others.

We then together walked toward the quite poor hostel of the smugglers which, however, given the purpose which it had served for a long time, namely profit from the travelers, was well outfitted with physical comforts, so that one, without having to make too much fuss, could find food, drink and sleeping quarters. It was a very ordinary but respectable fisher family to whom the house belonged and who took responsibility for the guests. None of us, I least of all, gave any importance to the taste or the amount of food or the quality of the sleeping quarters. We were quite satisfied with what was offered to us.

The wind regrettably remained calm and actually prevented our crossing on this night. We gave ourselves over to our fate and spent the time as best we could. In addition to me, there were both of my patronesses and the boy of the one. Both were well educated and lovely ladies to whom I felt myself drawn in appreciation as well as in recognition of their social standing and their lack of a masculine guardian. It was a pleasure to converse with them. In addition, our little band consisted of two Englishmen of the working class who had refused every attempt at conversation. They were, however, quiet and modest and in so far as the opportunity allowed, very amiable to deal with.

With one of these two Englishmen I had to share a bed for the night. For the other one, there was only a straw bed available. The latter would have been sufficient for me, but the small amount which we all had to pay for the stay was the same; and I had need of a normal place to sleep after my long privations. I had nothing to fear from my bedfellow as I reflected on his innocent and open character and on the fact that I had an utter lack of valuable objects. I, therefore, went to sleep in the knowledge that I had overcome the greatest dangers and that the events which still lay before me would have a fortunate course. The next morning, I awakened newly strengthened and enlivened.

Our hostess took good care of us. Afterward, I wanted to pay my bill from the little which remained after having paid my passage and openly handed the lady money in the presences of the others; however, she secretly returned it to me with the comment that "over there" I would have great need of it. She naturally knew of my experiences and condition, and I was moved to accept this valuable gift.

As the day began, an absolute calm still held; and we were thereby brought to great unease, even more so because we were told that if we did not get across during the upcoming night, we might have to wait weeks because of the coming moonlight. An experienced skipper, however, announced a rising "breeze" for the evening; and his prophecy came true.

After the concern was uttered, I fell into real worry how I was to sustain my life for so long since even the ladies were likely not in the situation to pay the considerable costs and that I would be morally obligated to pay back the advance which they might give. The skipper to whom I had expressed my situation, responded, however, that they had enough provisions of bread and meat; and if we were content with that, they would share it with us before they would show us the door. That was again a piece of American generosity.

Fortunately, we did not have to become a burden on the good people. In the afternoon, there really rose a fresh and playful wind. The ships which lay in the river spread their sails and moved forth to their points of destination. The flat surface of the water began to ripple, and the waves began in concert with the wind to surge more mightily against the shore. For that reason, we were all chipper and filled with hope.

As twilight broke, the preparation for an interesting trip had been undertaken. A large boat was brought out from some hiding place after yet more men were engaged in the work for the water trip by night.

We stood ready with our luggage. Mine consisted only of the remaining wallet with the letters. I had not yet been able to come up with headgear. We paid for the passage which left me with only five dollars to spare. With longing, we waited for the departure. The number of passengers had suddenly multiplied appreciably. The newcomers were primarily purely young people who had apparently hidden during the day and who were just now coming out to desert their fatherland. That they were of age for military service, their shy appearance, and their anxious impatience with which they awaited the departure justified the suspicion that they were wandering a forbidden path and that they had the worst to fear if they had been surprised by a Confederate patrol.

After the night had completely enveloped us and after we had all taken our assigned seats in the boat, the leader of the expedition who had given us our last quarters gave us the warning that we must maintain absolute silence since the least noise could possibly be heard by the alert enemy and deliver us into his hands. Quite obviously, such an eventuality could have serious consequences for him and his men. We, however, gladly followed the warning which was given, for his sake and that of his men.

There were four men who constituted the crew of the boat. They would take turns between the oars and the rudder. With the crew, there were approximately sixteen people on board. Along with these people, the boat was completely filled with baggage as well as bundles and sacks to fill with wares to be brought back. The oars were in place. Where they touched the boat, they were thickly covered so that they would not make any noise.

We then found ourselves traveling silently through the night into the broad river toward the destination for which all of us were longing. The man at the ruder coursed himself by the stars with consideration for the tide and the current which meant that our boat had to make a long arc in order to arrive at the point which our leader had determined. The oarsmen were so practiced that the in-and-out movement of the oars made no noise whatsoever, and the unavoidable sound which they did make disappeared in the distance with the wind. The secretive, silent trip; the bearing, consequently expertly executed; the absolute silence of so many people; the darkness and the stillness of the night; the large body of water over which we glided; and the monotone atmosphere brought about a certain allure. I took sight of the breaking day with great hope but not without concern for the near future. I thought about the possibilities which could positively or negatively affect my plans. I would need a lot of luck, given the little cash which I had and given my ignorance of the location of these completely strange localities, if I wanted to get to New York safe and sound.

Perhaps in this very night or in the next moment there was an adventure which I would have to endure if we were picked up. It was not even clear to me whether or not I desired such an instance or should wish that we would get across. It seemed that I was predestined by fate to be the cue ball and that I had to submit to its whims. We could not sleep, nor were we permitted to sleep. Only the little Waters boy was unable to resist the sandman. He had slumbered into sleep out of boredom sitting at the feet of his mother, a position which ensured that he was not in danger of falling overboard. It required a great effort to remain awake; and for me there was an even greater unpleasantness that the increasing coolness of the night affected my exposed head. One of the ladies lent me a handkerchief which I did not possess. It mitigated the effects of the cool air.

The trip took approximately eight hours which offered but little variation, save for the exchange of oarsmen and the frequent full stops to listen for a sound from any direction which might indicate danger. Everything remained deadly still. The trip suffered no further interruptions; and at the break of day, we saw quite close to us the coast of Maryland which we all greeted with joy and which we would soon reach. The crew had navigated so well that the boot landed almost exactly on the planned landing spot. A place had been selected for this which offered the best opportunity for a hiding place to house the passengers and to store the valuable cargo for the return trip. The bank was overgrown with reeds and bushes. Hidden among these was a canal the navigation of which was quite difficult. It was covered with almost impassible vegetation and widened into a pond which belonged to a farm which reached down to the Potomac. We put into this canal overarched with a dark canopy of leaves and landed at a spot at which the passage through the vegetation was possible but nevertheless difficult.

We found ourselves safe and sound on Northern soil on a well-tended farm. All of my fellow travelers were free and happy. I had made an essential step forward, but I was not yet freed from my plight. Even if I did not doubt further progress, it was nevertheless quite unpleasant to have to depend on the help and the support of authorities and private persons on whom I would yet have to depend for some time.

Some distance away was the stately house of the landowner who was contracted with the Virginia smugglers. Here he provided them a place to hide. He also acquired the wares which they would transport. Along with the services which he offered to refugees, he thereby made a significant profit.

We directed our steps to the house. There we found, in spite of the early morning hour, a cheery and well-warmed room in which we could enliven our limbs which was for starters a great act of charity for us. Soon thereafter, we were served for our benefit an excellent warm breakfast. Despite a lack of cash, I was not able to resist taking part in it and gave a dollar for the pleasure.

The crew disappeared after they had brought us to the house. They had to remain hidden for the rest of the day in order to escape the possible inquiries which their accomplices already had to face. By the next evening, they wanted to have the boat loaded again and set out on the return trip the next night. They had fulfilled their obligations to us which had been well earned even if the price was high. I wished them further good luck with their enterprise which would, however, with the coming events find its own end.

We were indeed well taken care of in our accommodations, but we had to be thinking about quickly getting on. This had its own difficulties. The place where we now found ourselves was quite isolated and far from a railroad or a larger transport hub. Our host recommended that we take the way that previous travelers who had stayed with him had taken. He would provide us with a sail boat to travel to the next town, Leonardstown which lay about ten miles downstream on a bay of the Potomac. From there, we could take one of the steamships put in port there to either Washington or Baltimore. The majority of our party took this offer which, of course, brought more costs. Some of the young Confederate deserters chose to walk inland. I opted to go with the former party since I considered that it brought me a quick and cheap arrival at a place which had direct connections with a larger city.

In this way, we took up the continuation of our trip again by a boat trip on the Potomac. It was by far more comfortable than that of the previous night because we did not sit so tightly; we could talk freely; and we could observe the scenery which was illuminated by the warm sun. The boat hurried toward its destination, driven forward by a good wind. It held close to the Maryland bank and allowed us a full view of the imposing farms, of the fruit trees which were in full bloom, of the friendly houses and of the fresh, green meadows as we quickly passed by them. Over on the other side, the forested bank of Virginia, which we had left yesterday, rose up. It was now a foreign land for us but never an enemy land for me. The feared gunboats, which we had so fortunately been able to avoid the previous night, were stationed on and maneuvered in the middle of the river along with a large number of sailing vessels which pursued their peaceful business.

Chapter 31

Imprisonment

In the first hours of the afternoon, as we were but a few miles from our destination and had even reached the bay on which Leonardstown was located, we caught sight of a skiff which was headed directly for us. [105] Among its occupants I soon recognized several armed soldiers of the United States. Although I had nothing to fear from them, these uniforms, having imposed on me an abhorrence because of the events in Columbia, nevertheless caused me horror and worry. The non-commissioned officer in charge, as the both boats met, commanded us to lower the sail. When that took place, he entered the boat and asked for our passes as well as the purpose of our trip. I had only my pass to legitimize me; the others had nothing. The commander of the patrol did not appear to have the authority to hear the long-lasting contentions of each individual; nor did he have the authority to judge them. He obliged us in a very friendly manner to follow him to the military post from which he had been sent. Two of his people seated themselves in our boat to oversee the execution of the order. Our boat was rowed away by his men next to the other boat. We had thusly been arrested, but in a proper manner. Although our travel plans had suffered a disturbance by the arrest, we did not fear any trouble or a longer stay.

The destination for which we had not volunteered was a little island which was located hardly two miles away. It was outfitted with a

---

105 Leonardtown, Maryland.

lighthouse and some buildings which now served as a military outpost. The garrison which consisted of a company had the duty to oversee the immediate area on the water and along the coast for the purpose of searching for spies and smugglers. We had fallen into the hands of a patrol with this duty. Upon our arrival, we were very politely interrogated by the captain in command; we were however detained because he appeared not to have enough information and because of the lack of proper authority, with the comment from the captain that he could not give us passengers our freedom but would have to deliver us to higher authorities in Leonardstown. This could not take place until the morrow because this day was too far spent to make the trip.

The leader of our boat, who was able to identify himself as a good citizen of Maryland, was allowed to return; but had to listen to some hard words relating to the support of enemy interests on the part of his principals.

Based on my consular pass and on my report in which I avoided all mention of my earlier active connection with the blockade business and the Confederate army, I was declared to be legitimate. Since we had to spend the night there, I was quartered with the officers and was well taken care of. My travel companions were also treated very fairly. A special room was arranged for the two ladies. The other men who did not rise to our rank were quartered with the enlisted men.

Although it was not good to have lost yet another day, our imprisonment, which is how our stay must be described, did not make itself tangible. The officers were noble men who were quite interested in my story. They condemned the behavior of Sherman's troops in Columbia as abominable and as beneath the dignity of the Union in spirit, purpose and reputation. They likewise sympathized with my misfortune on the Pamunky. One of them gave me a hat which was well worn but still useable, from which the military insignias were removed. I now at least had a head cover even if it did not go well with the rest of my clothes. To the contrary, it furthered my appearance as a vagabond.

Though this encounter, I had completely reconciled with the Union soldiers and experienced a pleasant evening with my prison wardens. I was able to get plenty of food and drink without depleting my funds much at all. My worry about the future was reduced considerably when my host stated that if there were further privations, I could assuredly reckon with the assistance of American authorities.

The next morning, we were again placed in a sail boat under the command of a lieutenant. We were to be delivered to Leonardstown for further investigation. The trip there did not go as well as had the previous ones. At the start, a strong wind rose and became so strong as to be a real hurricane which drove the sails before it and threatened to capsize the boat. The Potomac became angry and created high waves which alternately tossed us high above the surface and then drove us into the deep. Often, the craft bored through a mountain of water or cut with its angular design through the flood, again and again rising up but not without being filled almost to the rim with the wet element which we all took to bailing with all available containers which were more or less suitable for such, including hats and caps.

It was a terrifying trip across the water, definitely the most dangerous which I had ever made. Mortal fear showed itself on everyone's faces and was vented through the cries of the women and the child. It was difficult after I had overcome the dangers of murderous bands and the threat of starvation to yet again have the same fate before my eyes. It was only through the manly and prudent behavior of the lieutenant who was guiding the boat that we were somewhat reassured. In the end, we had his competency to thank for our lives being saved. Afterward, he himself admitted that he harbored little hope of getting through the storm and had foreseen a watery grave for us all; this, however, with the full horror of it, had driven him to energetically persevere.

Dripping with water and with all of our luggage completely wet, we overcame the adversarial power of storm and flood; however, immediately after having overcome this danger, a new one again broke over me. After we had with good fortune made landing, we were immediately led, in our wet condition, to the commander in Leonardstown. Each one of us was interrogated by a major. The stuff which we had brought with us was searched. All of my travel companions passed this test and were, without further investigation, released. I, however, was confronted by the decision that I was suspected of being a spy and that I was provisionally under arrest. I saw myself robbed of my freedom with the possibility of being executed in short order, this now after I had believed that I had fortunately survived everything. To me, it was as if heaven had removed its hand from me; but I nevertheless reckoned with God's protection in this my new calamity since He had guided me through things up to now.

The reason for this suspicion was the large number of letters which were found in my possession, the only thing which the thieves had left behind. Without thinking of the possible consequences, I had agreed to ensure their delivery as a favor for my companions in suffering in Columbia. These letters were now seen as war contraband. It was quite possible that there were treasonous statements among the letters. In which case, I would have to pay the penalty under the rules of war for transmitting them. My consulate pass and my report were, to be sure recognized as truthful. It was obvious that it was uncomfortable for the investigating officer that I had the "misfortune" to be carrying these letters. He himself wished along with me that I would have been robbed of these letters; but given that I had them, there was nothing else to be done. Everything depended on the content of the letters which were to be read and analyzed. I would either be set free, or I would suffer the punishment of a spy.

By the way, I enjoyed every possible consideration and a very proper treatment on the part of those in authority. My fellow travelers went into the city and got themselves on the way to their different destinations, save for the two ladies who wanted to go by steamer to Baltimore. Since the steamer would not arrive until some days hence, they found it necessary to remain here until the arrival. The financial sacrifice which they had made for me meant that they were not able to afford a stay in a hotel; so the commander, at his on costs, provided them with quarters as they were bestowed on me.

I was led a little distance away from the city where there was posted a garrison consisting of a company of cavalry with the men housed in tents and the horses in wooden sheds. The officers lived in town. The ladies got a tent to themselves which was outfitted with the necessary accoutrements. I was to share one with several people, which was not in the least pleasant for me, but which, given my worrisome situation, did not bother me. I was very fortunate with my lodging. The occupants of the tent consisted of a German sergeant, born in Baden, and a trumpeter who likewise spoke German. Both were well-behaved young men, as it was in the entire company which was part of a Pennsylvania regiment which consisted of men which were all good and solid if not exactly the most educated. Strict bearing and order set the tone such that the ladies were in no wise harassed. They were handled with all courtesy and attention. My quarters had enough room and comfort so that my stay there was tolerable. In addition, I was given the amenity of taking my meals with the ladies in their tent. The meals served there were quite satisfactory.

I had given my word of honor that I would not leave the compound. For that reason, I did not have a special guard. I had no reason at all to complain about my fate as a prisoner, save for that fact itself, which filled me with ever-growing dread as to how my innocent misdeed would play out and how it would perhaps be avenged.

I carried on quite pleasant conversations with the two ladies who were upstanding and sympathetic as well as with the soldiers. To my regret, the ladies departed on the third day but not without conveying to me all courage and hope. In return, they received from me the promise of everlasting appreciation and of the intent to pay them back for all of the support which they had given me, if I were not shot as a spy and finally extricated myself from the labyrinth of tests which I was undergoing.

The extreme amount of free time which I had, namely when my tent mates were on duty, I used for writing home, to my friends in the South and to my second brother who was in Rock Island in the state of Illinois. I was preparing him to send me money so that I could continue my trip, noting that I could not visit him because of the great distance between us. I was, of course, not able to send these letters while I was in investigative custody. I could do that when I was free, were I ever to be free!

The soldiers were very interested in all that I was able to tell them about my experiences and about conditions in the South. They were upset about the incidents in Columbia and could not comprehend how such behavior could be possible from those who served under the glorious banner of stars. It was also incomprehensible to me because I had not met a man on Northern soil, who wore the same uniform, who had the least resemblance with that large band of scoundrels.

My fellow countryman took a special interest in my fate and increased my capital by five dollars in paper, which he wanted to be nothing but a gift for which I could not give even the smallest guarantee for the reimbursement which I promised. He was, in spite of his class and rank, a man of no little means. He had come over as a boy from his German homeland and had worked for a long time on a farm in Pennsylvania. He had gained the trust of his employer as well as the heart of the farmer's only young and beautiful daughter, as the photo which he had attested. He was also very happy with her inheritance which had transferred to him. It was not until recently that he had entered active service after several substitutes, whom he had purchased, had fallen. He now had to carry out his duty because the pending end of the war had made it even more difficult to engage a substitute.

My second tent mate was an amusing patron, uncommonly good-natured but, at the same time, the clown of the company. He was the only signal trumpeter and presented his talent with variations which could not be misunderstood. He placed a lot of emphasis on his ability to speak German as it was spoken or more to the point "misspoken" in the districts of the Pennsylvania Dutch. With this usage, he brought to light comical expressions which were supposed to represent pure German but which were clearly expressed with a weak mix of English. Some of his more curious sentences remain in my memory. For example:

Likest Du Milk? – (Liebst du Milch?)

Die Bell hat zu Dinner gerungen. – (Die Glocke hat zu Mittag geläutet.)

Die Kau hat über die Fence gejumpt. – (Die Kuh ist über die Hecke gesprungen.)

All of his discussions in German consisted of this mishmash. When he spoke English, it was fluent without error and was for me more understandable; nevertheless, I preferred to converse with him in my mother tongue which, however, could only be understood by those who were well versed in English.

I was not informed as to how long this dreadful situation of imprisonment and the uncertainty concerning my fate would last. The officers from whom I had asked an explanation when they first arrived in the compound avoided my questions and expressed their regrets at the danger which I was facing and hoped that it could be favorably dealt with.

I therefore spent several days in anxious doubt and half-way came to terms with death if the dice were to fall to my doom. I trembled at the verdict which was pending over my case. But then, I was still alive. Although my condition at the time was not very enlivening, it offered me more comfort than the image which hovered over me of a scary position on a pole with a half-dozen loaded guns pointed at me. The full knowledge of my innocence again gave me hope. It could not be possible that I was to suffer such an undeserved penalty. I was disposed to do the utmost to overturn this verdict, were it to come to pass, by appealing to the consul general and even to President Lincoln. Surely I would be given the time and the opportunity for that. After I had made it through five days of anxiety and hope, it was disclosed to me on the morning of the 11th of April that my letters and my pass had been sent to the commanding general in Point Lookout and that I now had to go there to receive my verdict. I would finally have certainty. I took leave of the friendly men from Pennsylvania and boarded a small transport steamer which was ready to depart with a small detachment of guards. The steamer would take me to aforementioned place where a decision would be make about my life or my death.

A bird's eye view of Point Lookout Prison Camp, Maryland, 1864. Wikimedia Commons.

Chapter 32

Point Lookout

One charitable feature of the World Government is that the mirthless and painful moments which come into the life of every man, more or less bitter and numerous, are eased and blurred as soon as joy moves into the heart of a man. The experiences and the despair which pervaded me in the last weeks would have otherwise embittered and destroyed the rest of my life. Things in those days were really bleak for me; and if those sensibilities continued to have an effect on my nerves and my spirit for a long time thereafter, they were perhaps not without benefit for my principles and my later behavior. The terrors are now indeed gone and live on without arousal in my memory.

The little steamer quickly put the twenty-mile long distance on the ever-widening Potomac behind us. The people who were on board with me did not know the distress in which I found myself. The closer I came to my destination the more anxious my heart began to feel. That it was no small matter, namely the decision of life and death and weight placed on the matter, was demonstrated by the fact that the judgment would be made by the highest authority.

After the arrival at Point Lookout, about which I will have more to say later, I was brought before the military court after a wait of several hours. A brigadier general was the presiding officer. My first glance fell upon the corpus delicti, the derelict wallet with its ominous contents. It had been forwarded here for the purpose of thorough investigation. It appeared that my guilt or innocence had already been decided; however, I was again thoroughly questioned. I had to observe the greatest of care not to betray myself by my earlier activities in the Confederate States of America. My neutrality, which had already been proved, likely was the main reason that I was spared worse inconveniences. The pass had already been sent to Washington and its authenticity confirmed; otherwise, things might have indeed gone bad for me. The letters were not found to be without concern, and several of them were retained because they had messages which could be construed as treasonous. It is quite possible that the correspondence had harmful consequences for the sender as well as the receiver; however, it was recognized that the content of these letters was unknown to me and that I, therefore, could not be made responsible for it.

The court was therefore content to address my imprudence with an addressed laced with reproaches which I, with great joy, allowed to wash over me. I found myself freed after I had sworn a oath of neutrality. The pass as well as the greater part of the opened letters was returned to me.

The good fortune which I felt at this fully compensated for the fear which I had suffered and, initially at least, allowed me to forget the worries which were still before me. I no longer wanted to appeal to the military command for pecuniary support. I hoped to get such as an advance from the nearest consulate. Until I reached Washington or Baltimore, my limited cash would probably suffice. On the other hand, the commander offered me free passage on the first steamer which would depart for Baltimore on the same evening. I took the offer with gratitude. With my papers, my passport and my ticket in hand, I was released from detention. Since there were several hours still available to me before the departure of the ship, I used my reclaimed freedom to take a look at this very interesting place.

Point Lookout is the outer point of the southeast-most tongue of land of the state of Maryland where the Potomac meets Chesapeake Bay. The sandy, unfertile soil of this peninsula, which produced only some scraggly pines, had been, until just a little time ago, unimproved and unused except for the lighthouse located here which had been erected to warn of the many dangerous sandbanks on this riven coast. It was the only indication far and wide of human existence.

Over several years, however, an astounding change had taken place here. Many thousand men were breathing the fresh sea air, most of them, to be sure, without their consent. An entire city had suddenly arisen, and numerous steamers and sail boats gave life to the newly built harbor built on the very spot which ships in the past had avoided with trepidation.

This magical metamorphosis had been conjured up by the hapless war. Since the beginning of the war, it had been a prisoner of war camp for the Confederate soldiers, or as they were called "Rebels" who had fallen into the hands of the Union army. On the farthest point of land, bordered on three sides by ocean, men, counted in the thousands, had been housed. The sides surrounded by water protected against escape and was only guarded by a few sentries and the gunboats stationed on the Chesapeake and the Potomac. On the narrow landward side, the prison barracks were sealed off by an earthen wall which had passages that were usually secured and which could be climbed from the outside. I was permitted to climb the earthworks and thereby had an overview of the entire region.

The prison camp gave the impression of a small city. The structures were none the less simple and monotone wood houses which stretched out in long rows in length and breadth over the entire area, creating wide streets and squares. In the middle of the compound, there rose up individual but excellent buildings such as a church, a hospital and a commissary which were necessary for the most immediate needs as well as other structures. The entire complex was systematically governed by the greatest order and cleanliness. The occupants, dressed in their uniforms, camped and played games in the streets and appeared to feel at least physically well in their situation, save for the fact that they had been robbed of their freedom, the pressure of which I had just felt under an ever greater danger. [106]

---

[106] This large prison was actually considered one of the worst of the Union prisoner of war camps. Rations and sanitation measures were chronically inadequate, even though the U. S. government had the resources to provide better conditions for the Confederate prisoners. Before the war, Point Lookout, a sandy peninsula at the junction of the Chesapeake Bay and the Potomac River, was the location of a resort with a hotel, cottages, boarding houses, and commercial establishments. When the resort was converted into a

From my lofty standpoint, which also gave the sentinels an overview for watching the entire camp, the view engendered in me a great interest in the facilities and the residents as well as in the endless flatness of the masses of water made up of the Potomac, Chesapeake Bay and the Atlantic Ocean bordered these facilities and residents but which also drew the distant bank of Virginia into the panorama.

On the other side of the earthen wall there had awakened new life. As a result of the prisoner of war camp, a new and extensive settlement had been founded. Large homes, hotels, churches, warehouses and the like had been conjured up by necessity and by speculation, for which I, in vain, attempted to find a purpose once the war had reached its end. Perhaps these palaces would become the living quarters of poor fishermen or water birds if they had not succumbed to decay of found other use or had not fallen victim to a particularly powerful storm.

The feeding and watching of so many prisoners demanded, after all, numerous personnel and the appropriate living and supply structures, which were put up with American swiftness. Many families, craftsmen and merchants had settled here so that there was a continuous increase in population and an expansion of the town. The large bakeries, slaughterhouses, the numerous storehouses and depots, the workshops, the department stores and the smoking smokestacks made a magnificent impression and contrasted to the good with the structures of the prisoner of war camp which in its uniqueness was actually worth seeing and which brought many strangers which made the hotels quite popular.

---

prison in 1863, Union officers used some of these buildings as their quarters.

Chapter 33

GLIMPSES OF THE SUN

In the meantime, the moment of departure had arrived, and I boarded the steamer "Kent" which was docked there ready for departure. It was to bring me gratis to Baltimore. The ship was in the service of the government. For that reason, the commander of Point Lookout could give me free passage and guarantee it. The ship also carried freight and passengers and was supplied with all of the amenities for the latter who were on board in great numbers.

It was a beautiful evening. The air was warm. The Chesapeake, on which the ship calmly steamed ahead in order to cover the distance of seventy-five miles to our destination, this without subjecting the passengers to seasickness, lay flat before us. The sun had just set, and the crescent moon cast its magic light over the peaceful scene. The two banks lay outside the field of vision; anyway, they were removed from sight by the dimming twilight.

The signal for the evening meal rang out, and all of the passengers hurried to the dining hall in order to enjoy a sumptuous meal by means of the commensurate fee. I would have loved to take part, but I did not know what necessary expenditures were still before me; nor did I know how soon I would be able to increase my limited supply of cash. I therefore found it advisable to abstain from this luxury, given that I could forego this meal even though my abstinence imposed by necessity panged my heart.

All was still on the forward deck which was devoid of passengers and crew. Only the helmsman turned his wheel, and the officer of the watch silently paced up and down the bridge.

I stood at the railing, looking into the clear tide waters in which the moon was mirrored and through which the ship plowed its course, and daydreamed through my thoughts. With horror, the images and feelings of the past rose up before me, and I was hardly able to suppress them with the awareness of security which I henceforth had. Those events had, however, been overcome; and I was happy and filled with thanks that my life and my freedom had been saved and that I was going into a better future; nevertheless, this future brought with it new worries. As long as I was destitute in the world, I could find no peace or satisfaction. Many a sigh wrested themselves from my breast and echoed through the still night. The smells which were coming up from the kitchen likely also contributed to this state. As the restaurateur C. in Hannover said as he canceled his contract with an unpopular guest, "Don't let the smoke of the kitchen get to you!"

The thoughts in which I was engrossed were suddenly interrupted by a voice behind me: "Now, sir, the bell for supper has rung, and you are still standing here? You are not seasick, are you?" I turned myself to face this molester and saw a blacked and sweat-drenched fireman who had come up out of the boiler room to catch a breath of fresh air on the empty deck, something which he had had to forego below.

The friendly tone of his address with which he spoke his astonishment at my separation from the table guests brought me to enter the conversation and answer his question with the comment that I was not in the least disinclined and the condition of my stomach even allowed me to order myself to the dining hall but that my kitty did not sanction the dollar necessary for this purpose.

The compassion and the sympathy which this reason and the associated stories of my experiences raised in this man were sufficient to substantiate my worth with this common worker under whose filthy shell a noble heart beat. I was filled with yet greater amazement and with the feeling of emotion and veneration as the man reached into his pocket and imposed a paper dollar on me with the comment that he had he had satisfied himself with a meal and if I wanted to ensure that he would work in peace down below, then I would reciprocate and take this small offer which he was regrettably not in the situation to increase. No man may suffer from hunger in America!

What was I to do? If I declined the offer, I would do injury to this fair and noble man, even if my sentiments were against the transaction. For that reason, I took the gift. Never in my life had such a worthy gift provided me with such joy. Surprised and overcome with joy, I was not able to express my gratitude with words. Even less, I neither could nor did I want to reduce the sublimity of this sacrifice through promises of recompense. Struck dumb, I shook his rough and sweaty hand; and from the look in his eyes, I knew that he understood what I was feeling. His free time was over, and he went back down into the narrow space to his strenuous work. As his head disappeared into the opening, he let it be known with a quiet smile that he had carried out a normal duty of helping a fellow man in distress.

I, however, thanked God that He had allowed me to come to know a man with such generosity. Although I could have indeed foregone the meal, I went down with a happy heart in order to use the gift for the purpose for which it was intended. I nourished myself at a sumptuous table for which I had the simple worker to thank. He had to content himself with a simple mean; but he gave his hard earned wage for the pleasures of a man whom he did not know, pleasures which he had likely not experienced himself. The name of this honorable man was Harrison Phoebus who remains in my thoughts of gratitude. [107] His actions teach that the character of a man are not determined by his class or estate or his outward appearance and that it is often easier to receive help and support from a poor man than from those whom fate has placed in the position to guarantee the same.

I was later able to demonstrate to this man that he had not given his assistance to a man with no gratitude.

---

107 There was a Harrison Phoebus (1840-1886), a native of Maryland, who became a notable entrepreneur and hotelier after the war.

That was again a glimpse of the sun in my life which had moved my troubling memories and future worries, but the shadows disappeared little by little. The further I went, the brighter it became for me.

After I had taken supper, I enjoyed yet more time on deck the beautiful evening. The satisfaction of the stomach gives the mind more energy to overcome unpleasant emotions and creates ease. For the interim, I had nothing which brought discomfort. It was now possible to enjoy the present, the calm and the nice trip while my virtuous friend down in the boiler room had to earn his charitable gift of money by twenty-four hours of hard work.

I thought about all of this for a long time and how, after all of the misfortunes, I had fully experienced the grace of Heaven. I then followed the other passengers and went to the cabin which had been designated to me based on my free-passage ticket and found repose. There, in expectation of the events which a new day would bring, I fell asleep.

When I came up on deck the next day after an invigorating sleep, a new picture appeared before me. The Chesapeake had narrowed itself from a sea to a mighty river which abounded with larger and smaller vessels. The bank to our left, close to which we held, was built up with beautiful cottages, factories and well-kept farms of which the early morning sun gave a stunning view. In front of us rose the city of Baltimore which sat somewhat higher with its numerous steeples and countless masts.

We soon arrived at the appointed dock. After I had again, one more time, taken leave of my charitable friend, I left the ship and attempted to seek my good fortune and my way in a strange world.

A crowd of people full of curiosity had gathered on the wharf so that they could gather news from the new arrivals who in part came from the South and in part from the border regions. I, too, was encircled and questioned. Turnabout is fair play. After I had quickly spoken of the most important things, I asked about the residence of the Hannover consulate. Several of the residents of Baltimore offered to take me there. I took one of the gentlemen up on the offer. Along the way, I was compelled to tell him more of the original story while he gave me all of the information which I asked for. The city was decorated with flags as a result of the big victory of Union troops in the last few days. It was said that the Confederate army under Lee had been completely defeated and that the capital city of Richmond had been taken. The existence of the Confederacy was then over. It was not only an end of their hope of the independence of the Sothern states but also of their suffering. I had expected this fate, sooner or later. It hardly surprised me when I got the news, but it was painful for me that all of the sacrifice and energy, all of the patriotism of my Southern friends, and all of the fighting and the stubborn resistance, and all of the sanguineous hopes had been in vain. They now lay, humiliated, at the feet of their enemy. It was, however, fortunate that this brothers' war had come to an end. Had the closing catastrophe occurred just twelve days earlier, then I could have immediately allowed myself to be annexed into the United States there. I could have gotten away from there in a more comfortable manner and would not have to have suffered so much adversity and so great a loss.

The active business and trade life and the hustle and bustle on the streets which my companion and I passed made a big impression on me. I had not experienced such so extensively even in my years in Charleston at the time of peace. In the last four years, the South had been in a sleep of death. It was just then the morning hour; and everyone was rushing to his job; and for that reason, everything was twice as lively.

I was received in the office of the consul. Regrettably, I was given to understand that he was away and would return on the following day. The staff was not authorized to provide me with the support which I had requested. I wanted to consider whether or not I would await the return of the consul on whose help I had hoped for, or whether I should use the remaining cash money to get to Philadelphia and to seek my security there, for which my means would probably suffice. My friendly companion had waited for me in front of the house. After he had learned of the failure of this visit, he gave me advice which proved to be valuable. I should turn to the owner of a large German trading house, Schumacher & Co., who, because of his liberality and charity, was highly esteemed. Given my situation, I could not be embarrassed at requesting assistance from a stranger. For that reason, I gladly made use of the opportunity offered to enrich my holdings.

My companion accompanied me to the place. I presented Mr. Schumacher with my plight. [108] I gave him the description of the circumstances through which I had come to this bad situation to cash the bills of exchange of others with which I had been entrusted and my own in Liverpool which the funds were available. My requests were, however, not compatible with his principles of business. It was not possible for me to hold against him the fact that he had denied my request against him. As a counter measure, he gave me ten dollars which would have been a considerable sum for a beggar. This gift immediately brought me out of my financial distress. With it, I would be able to get to New York comfortably; and if I nourished other sources of help, I could count on the support of my brother and calmly await the arrival of his cash advance.

Such a gift as the one which I received from this dear old man, a type of loan, as I saw it, I had certainly not been expected; and my joyous surprise was large. I thanked him with the assurance that would send him the sum in a few days, whereupon he responded that if I could afford it in the future, I should make use of it for assisting someone else in need and that he viewed the sum as a gift.

About a year ago, I read in a German newspaper that death had taken the warm heart and the beneficial acts of this noble man. Among all of the charitable deeds which were publically mentioned in his obituary, which gained him the honor of his fellow Americans and his German countrymen, which had minimized and eliminated so much suffering, the assistance and the relief which he had given me became a evergreen leaf in his laurel wreath which has been woven by the appreciative recipients of his charity.

After I had acquired plenty of travel money, I did not stay in Baltimore any longer. I certainly regretted it later as well as not having

---

108 This was likely Albert Schumacher (1802-1871), a German immigrant and a prominent Baltimore businessman.

seen the nearby capital Washington; however the excitement and restlessness of those days drove me hurriedly on. This was, to me, completely necessary, given the interests of my previous business, to get to England as soon as possible.

For this reason, I used a train for the rest of the trip to New York. Although the region had nothing in particular which drew one to it, it did provide me with things of interest in that they were completely different from those of the South. In the South, the train chiefly passed through primeval forest and by cotton and rice plantations, or, more often in the last years, with the collapse of the rail system and its supplies, by places which had earned the name of a town or city but where the train seldom stopped. Here in the North, the train roared through fields of grain with larger and smaller places. The Northern style of structure and landscape had a completely different character from that of the South. The industry which the South lacked was all the more prevalent here as evidenced by the numerous smokestacks of the factories. For a short time, the train stopped at the upper Chesapeake Bay and provided a view of the water surface which was becoming ever-more narrow. The train moved quickly through Maryland and Delaware and passed through the lively city of Wilmington, Pennsylvania, before arriving in the afternoon in Philadelphia. [109] In Philadelphia, the passengers traveling on to New York had to change stations. The other station was at the opposite end of the city. At the cost of the railroad company, we were transported there by a horse-drawn tram. The long transfer gave me an idea of the expansiveness of this city which was the second largest city in North America after New York. Since a longer stay was not advisable, I was at least glad to get a quick look at the city. It was friendly and clean and had luxurious houses. Streets which seemed to have no end crisscrossed the city at right angles, and there were numerous boulevards; nevertheless, Philadelphia seemed to be dead in comparison to Baltimore. Whatever might have been the case, this deadness was particularly present in the parts we passed through. It may have been influenced by the time of day.

---

109 Conrad misplaced Wilmington, Delaware, in Pennsylvania.

*A bird's eye view of New York City
created by R. Kupfer in 1867. Library of Congress.*

The new train, which we boarded, passed through the state of New Jersey and through its capital Newark without stopping. After a few hours, we arrived at the terminal station of the railway: Jersey City, separated from New York only by the Hudson. We crossed the Hudson by means of a steam ferry. From the vantage point of the crossing, we were provided a view of the American metropolis in its expansive form, along with lights beyond counting and a veritable forest of masts going up and down the Hudson. Along with them, smaller steamers were crisscrossing the water. It was a wonderful sight.

Chapter 34

NEW YORK

So it was the evening of the 12th of April 1865 that I entered the world city of New York. I had finally reached the goal of my long and difficult trip which had been accompanied by so many dangers, burdens and terrifying impressions. I hoped to finally find peace and that the embarrassing excitement and worry would be lifted, this, even though the violence of the most recent events still burdened me greatly and made me incapable of really enjoying the interesting sights.

How long and how much had I longed for this moment! It had finally arrived. At the landing place, omnibuses were available to take passengers to their homes or to their hotels. I had decided to look for the recommended Astor House, a hotel of the first class and had myself taken there. As I entered the building, built of white marble, outfitted in great grandeur and luxury, I had a peculiar feeling in my heart. Aside from the fact that I had never known a place like that, I sensed immediately how little my clothes matched the elegance of the place. Still halfway broken in spirit, I considered myself a vagabond who was quiet cheeky and carefree to desire quarters here.

I was, therefore, not in the least surprised that the clerk posted in the vestibule behind a marble desk examined me from head to toe and rejected my inquiry of a room with a derisive smile, saying that no room was available. I did not feel myself to be in anyway aggrieved at his dismissal. I certainly realized the reason for it and was, to the contrary, relieved as I put the hotel behind me and began to contemplate on the sidewalk of Broadway where my steps might take me.

My personal appearance did not measure up to New York. Think of the coat produced in the South (homespun) with a dubious color and as a result of the trials suffered shaded various hues. Add to that the cap of a soldier with a dirty, cotton bag with letters under my arm. If the good reader were to ever encounter a man so dressed that he was too good for a beggar but not fitting for a gentleman, along with a hardened face, one could not hold it against a person if he showed me the door even if a person such as the clerk claimed to have before him a racketeer of the most terrible kind. My case simply showed that there are exceptions and that the innocent must suffer with the guilty. In spite of that, many good people have assisted me and have given me their trust. It would have been even worse for me had I not been in North America.

I first had to find a place to stay. I however did not wish to be seen as a newcomer and ask about a place to stay. On the way from the river to this point I had taken note of a number of smaller hotels which, I had concluded, might accept me as a guest. It was, however, the same story in the Merchants Hotel and the National Hotel as it had been in the Astor House, although in each case the quality was a step lower. I had come to believe that I had fallen so far as to have to settle for a dive. I then found lodging in the Courtland Street Hotel, a less pretentious but yet still decent house. My modest demands were satisfied to the fullest. I got an excellent meal and a comfortable bed and likely felt much better than I would have in the marble palace on Broadway.

The hotel was located on Courtland Street which was very lively and which lay just off Broadway. It was at the center of business traffic. The next morning, I immediately began with my important day's work. It was the search for mammon without which I could not begin the sea voyage and without which I could not afford to remain here for very long. For this quest, I put in play all of the means at my disposal. The first step was to telegraph my brother in the west that I had arrived in New York and that he should transfer to the address given enough money sufficient to get me to England. I next went to a friend of my brother, a particular countryman. I knew that he had business connections with my brother and that he was likely somewhat beholden to my brother.

I was quite certain that I would at least get momentary relief from him or at least an appropriation for me in this quite alien place.

This man lived several miles away in the upper part of the city. I went by foot in order to take the opportunity to take in the grandeur and the life of this world city. The recent victory was understandably manifest here as well with great fanfare. The Stars and Stripes waved over the roofs and out of windows. This display was multiplied by banners of all possible shapes and patterns. A large crowd of people had assembled in the city park, which was on Broadway with gardens and trees across from the Astor House. In the middle of the park was the stately city hall. Numerous streets radiated out from the park. Here a large crowd had gathered. The voices drowned out the noise of the traffic. Upon closer inspection, I determined that men were being recruited for military service. The method being used was quite strange for me and piqued my interest. Men stood or sat on raised stands and challenged those standing around to join the army, much in the manner of our show booth managers or red-capped junk dealers at our amusement parks. In full-throated speeches they raised up the sacredness of the purpose as well as the amenities and advantages which those who joined would be offered. In addition to a high wage, the recruit would receive a bonus, payable immediately, which was raised or lowered at the whim of the recruiter. When a new recruit stepped forward, he was brought up on the platform, adorned with honors, and immediately at that time and place sworn by placing his name on a list and given the promised bonus. The crier continued during this process. This continued without interruption throughout the day. As often as I passed this point, I was a witness to the spectacle. Broadway, up which I was walking, is definitely unique in the world, given its length, the endless rows of stately buildings which almost exclusively serve as retail shops with huge department stores and elegant showcases, and the enormous amount of traffic. The broadness of the street, after all quite grand, is not sufficient for the traffic. It is quite often jammed, and crossing it is quite difficult. An entire corps of policemen is dedicated to keeping the traffic moving by clearing interruptions in the flow and by getting pedestrians to the other side. One cannot imagine the numerous cabs, private carriages, omnibuses, horse riders, and the various transport vehicles which animate the street during the day. All of this undulates and surges in long rows the entire day.

While I made it through the ball of humans on my way to visit the gentleman, I was able to observe the area, which was quite interesting, as far as that was possible. I then found the abode of my countryman and was immediately able to meet him. After I had proved my identity, I placed my request before him.

This request, which was to be booked to my brother's account, was for an advance necessary to pay for sea travel and to cover various little loans which I had incurred since I could not know whether or not my brother was home or if the transfer of money from him would necessitate an a stay of undesired length, which I wished to avoid. The good man regretted that he was not in the position to assist me because he was in the process of renovating his business locale and was subject to large expenditures; otherwise, he would have gladly assisted me. That was all possible. I then asked, however, would he help me utilize a bill of exchange through the identification of my person or through his bank account. The good friend also rejected this request with "I regret" because he had no bank connections and did not do business with those who "did such business." All that he could do for me was to give me a loan of ten dollars.

That was little help to me I would have preferred to reject the offer of my countryman with his strong sense of charity because I knew that he had means based on his special relationship with my family and had a reasonable expectation of such. I did not know, however, whether or not I would need the money and took it for such a case, this without accepting his demand.

I was disappointed as well as filled with indignation concerning the cool, detached behavior of the man on whose material and indirect support I had reckoned. I had proved to him beyond a doubt that I was not a swindler. He had known my situation and could not have possibly believed that the advanced sum would not be paid back. He could have at least given me some advice or invited me to meet his family. So I left my good friend S and prepared myself to have to wait several days until the anticipated support from Rock Island arrived.

I had the address of a New York firm, David & Turner, which I had received with a letter of recommendation written by business partners in Richmond. I ascertained the address and headed that way. I did this less in the hope that I would acquire something and more because of the sense of duty to carry out my obligation to my business partners which was to inform those at the firm about them and the conditions in the South. Perhaps here I would meet people of good will who would stand by my side with counsel and deed.

After I had been well introduced by the letter, I was then received in a quite friendly manner by the director of the house. My plight was revealed without direct request based on my descriptions, on the bills of exchange sewn into the wallet, and on the fact that that I had means in Liverpool on which I could draw if I could find a buyer, given that I knew nothing of New York and that it was impossible to prove my ownership and the authenticity of the bills of exchange. The trust which I had not hoped for I received in that Mr. Turner, without hesitation, agreed to discount a bill of exchange from Liverpool.

Who could have been happier than I in that moment when I received the stack of United States notes (Greenbacks) in the sum of approximately four-hundred dollars? With one strike I was relieved of my worries. The possession of such a large sum of money was strange to me, and it took some time for me to get used to the fact. The trust which I had thereby acquired filled me with genuine gratitude toward the gentleman whom I did not know. He assisted me in every other way possible by giving his support and offering his help. He told me that above all I need to acquire a good hat; and he himself accompanied me to a department store in order to procure the necessary improvement to my rough appearance. The he gave me the name of the first steamer to be departing to Liverpool and guided me to the company in question where I reserved a place on the steamer "Etna" which was to depart the next Wednesday.

Yet again I had found a loyal ally who freed me from my wont. The friendly American had dignified me with his trust and had kindly supported me while the German who was known to me left me to my fate although he had the means to assist me.

No longer influenced by worry, I arrived at the hotel for the purpose of once again enjoying a good meal and found, waiting for me, a telegram from my brother. In it, he directed me to his previously mentioned friend who would pay out the necessary funds.

I took great pleasure in visiting Mr. S that afternoon and producing the dispatch after I had made him aware of my good fortune and that I had found assistance. Without this, under the prevailing circumstances, namely that I was dependent on him, my embarrassment would not have been relieved. I took pleasure in his embarrassment, and his assurance based on the telegram that he would in any case had given me counsel and would have been at my service had I needed any means or appropriation left me completely indifferent. I paid him the loan which I had guaranteed with an unaccommodating expression of appreciation and took leave of him as quickly as he had taken me in and then dismissed me when I first came to him.

If one of the dear readers ever has the good fortune to try his luck in America and comes to plight, I give him counsel to seek pecuniary and active support from an American and not from a German countryman. Charity and philanthropy are much more at home with the former than with the latter. It is in the character and in the faith of the American to help his fellow man how and where he can. He does it gladly without making a spectacle of it. He sees it as a duty and not as a sacrifice. There are, of course, exceptions on both sides as proved by Mr. Schumacher in Baltimore who had American sensibilities. As time goes by, many Germans in American are filled with the spirit of America to be kind and willing to sacrifice.

There was little time left for me to take in the sights of New York since my departure was fixed and I had to forego seeing and visiting many of the art works, the public buildings, the entertainment centers and the general area, although I did make the best possible use of my limited time of stay.

New York is not only the most important and tone-setting city in America and the third largest city in Christendom, it is also a very beautiful place as it relates to its location and architectural style. [110]

---

[110] At this point in his narrative, Conrad begins to describe New York in the present tense for several pages.

The view of the city is one of the most beautiful in the world, with the different small islands and forts, surrounded by the hilly villa island called Staten Island on the one side and long Island with the populous "church city" of Brooklyn on the other. In the distance, there is the mountain range of the Hudson. Then there are the waterways of the Hudson River and the East River which are swarming with the ships of all nations between which Manhattan Island on which the world city is built, is located.

The Hudson, on which trade takes place with the interior of the state, is often compare with the Rhine as it relates to the beauty of its banks. It may well be that the scenery deserves such praise, but because of the lack of romantic fortresses and castles as well as vineyards, the Hudson can hardly be compared with the Rhine.

On the far side of the Hudson in the State of New Jersey appear Jersey City and Hoboken. On the other side of the East River is Brooklyn. It is one with the metropolis, separated only by the waterway.

The lower city is almost completely dedicated to business. The magnificent buildings were made necessary by the ever-expanding trade, including warehouses, a customs house, banks, the stock exchange, a post office and the like. There were sixty-three such buildings at the time. There was a never-ending life here during the day; however, during the evening and on Sunday, the silence was absolute. From here, the main artery, Broadway, took the strength of life into the city with widely branching streets and out of these, back again the next day. To the right and left of Broadway run the tree-lined avenues from north to south. Here one finds the huge estates of millionaires and of those who are not quite millionaires, while those of less financial means live in more modest homes and villas on the cross streets which bisect the avenues at right angles and cut through clear spaces of equal size. Horse-drawn trams and omnibuses crisscross the city. There are in fact very few streets which they do not serve.

In those days, New York had no less than two-hundred fifty-seven churches or houses of worship. There are likely many more than that now since the necessity for such in America is quite obvious. Among these churches, many stand above the sea of houses with their stately steeples. Trinity Church, erected in Gothic style at enormous costs, stands out above all of them. In addition, this church possesses a wealth in the millions because the congregation was constituted when the city was founded and the expansive property on this original spot had a massive appreciation of value. One of the pastors of this church was the famous and notorious Pastor "Beecher" whose name is known worldwide because of the various scandals and trials associated with him. [111]

The city has retained pleasantness and fresh air because of the parks and open squares early on constructed in the middle of the city. Standing out as such is Central Park which in its inception was placed at the edge of the city but which is now surrounded by structures. It is spread out over a large area and has everything which nature and art can create. It is the gathering place for those who need fun and relaxation, from the highest class to the lowest.

On the southern edge of the wedge-shaped city, on the most beautiful spot, is the incomparable Battery located on the most expensive property. It is a wide-ranging promenade which serves as the terminus of all of the important business streets. It offers to residents, tired from mental and physical work, a close-by retreat, a beautiful view, summer shade and places to rest. The full overview of the entire harbor is breathtaking in its diversity, which has already been mentioned, and its grandeur. Surrounded by water and linked to the battery by a bridge is a place which was originally a fort but which is now the facility for processing immigrants through which all immigrants before entering the United States must pass and must provide evidence concerning their sanitary, pecuniary and other conditions, so that those aliens who might lack means or work do not fall into the hands of hustlers or do not immediately succumb in the large, strange city.

---

111 Henry Ward Beecher (1813-1887) was a prominent New York Congregationalist clergyman and abolitionist. In the 1870s his friend Theodore Tilton accused him of having an affair with his wife, and a sensational trial resulted. Mrs. Tilton had confessed her inappropriate relationship with Beecher to her husband, but she did not testify at the trial, which ended in a hung jury. Even before this scandal, Beecher had a reputation for inappropriate flirtatiousness with women. He was not the pastor of Trinity, an Episcopal church, but of the Plymouth Congregational Church in Brooklyn.

New York is overabundant with institutions of charity of all kinds. Many were founded and are supported by private individuals; others, by the city; and yet, others, by the state. They are for the poor, the invalids, the orphans, the deaf and dumb, the blind, the mentally ill, and the dying. They are all seemingly well managed and, pursuant to their purpose, excellently furnished and administered.

It is not even remotely possible to name, much less describe, all of the facilities in New York. In New York the most diverse interests will be completely satisfied, but it would have taken more time to see them than I had available.

From among the many places with art treasures and other amusements, I was only able to visit the world-renowned Barnum Museum which has a rich collection of living human beings and animals with anomalies. [112] There were people from distant parts of the world, giants, dwarves, armless and legless men as well as other curiosities of creation. There were those who could use their lips to quickly and legibly write. There were those who had abilities which could not be explained. I recall a man who could immediately remember the exact chapter and verse in the Bible or in Shakespeare which corresponded to the sentence given to him. Were it reversed, he could quote the words for the chapter and verse in these works. I was further astounded by a mathematical wizard who could, for example, solve in a few seconds a problem given to him which consisted of ten or more numbers in a multiplication problem. He could write down the answer after just a quick glance at the numbers.

I had to use the evening hours to place the ominous letters which had been entrusted to me into envelopes to send them elsewhere since they had been opened. I also had to put stamps on them. I also had to send the letters which I had written in Leonardstown with some addenda. In addition, I attested my gratitude to those people who had graced me with their charity and their trust and who had likely faced ruin by sending back to them in full the loans and gifts which

---

112 Barnum's American Museum was established by the famous showman P. T. Barnum (1810-1891) in 1841. Located in Lower Manhattan, this building was destroyed by a great fire in July 1865.

they had made available to me. I demonstrated to Mrs. Waters, Miss Worrel, Sergeant Schmidt, Harrison Phoebus and Schumacher, all of them, that they had not graced an unworthy man with their trust and compassion. I was very glad to be able to convince them and to remove the last suspicion which they were possibly harboring concerning my honesty and my recognition of their service to me.

I was absolved of my obligations to these people, but my sense of gratitude and my honor for these good people has not lapsed and remains so. Such acts of charity, such sacrifice and such kindness can never be forgotten. This attributes did not apply to me but to other fellow men who were also suffering and who, in part, themselves had their own burdens which they gladly bore. Only a few day or minutes were sufficient to create perpetual and unselfish friends whose memory I will hold warmly in my heart forever. They build up on the bright side of my life important and salient points which time and new impressions cannot erase. Among these, the poor boiler tender takes his place along with the rich trade merchant.

When I entered the hall of the hotel the next morning for the purpose of taking breakfast, I was surprised by a general stir among the hotel staff and the guests gathered there. The reason for the tumult was the news which the newspapers had reported that President Lincoln had been treacherously shot with a revolver by the actor Booth while seated in a theater loge. The murderer had escaped, but he had barricaded himself and was brought out dead after an aggressive shootout. The news brought about the greatest sadness and disgust which was to be seen, without exception, on every face in the excited crowd. Businesses were for the most part closed. The decorations of the victory celebration had been taken down, and black flags and staffs were put up in their place. Most ladies came out in black. The sincere love and honor which the man enjoyed could be seen by the behavior of the populace. Given my sympathy for the South, I had a certain aversion toward the man from his election to his position concerning the grim war and the suffering of my Confederate friends, although this sentiment had substantially changed since my presence in the North and by the descriptions of his good character traits. Given the heinous nature of this crime, even the most sanguineous of Southerners would not have counseled it. I, however, had heartfelt sympathy for this noble man, his family and for the country as it anticipated his loss.

Lincoln was still alive, and crowds gathered at newspaper offices and at other points where within minutes new information about the condition of the President came in. The reports ranged from hopeless, to doubtful and then to favorable. In general, however, the worst was soon to be expected. The murder came exactly four years later when the first shots between Union and Confederate troops were fired in Charleston, shots which actually inaugurated the war. [113] This happened just when goal of the Union, so expensively won, had been reached, when the South had been suppressed and when the war had been viewed as won and over.

After I had acquired for myself some dress clothing, some underwear and other necessities for the ocean trip, I boarded Etna at the time appointed for departure. Instead of leaving at 1:00 p. m. as planned, the departure was put off from hour to hour. The captain was awaiting the announcement of Lincoln's death for the honor of bringing the news thereof to Europe. The telegraph across the sea did not exist then, and the news was worthy for the entire world. [114]

About 6:00 p. m., the telegraph brought the news out of Washington that Lincoln was dead. The machine was set in motion, and the important trip got underway.

For a long time, I enjoyed the unforgettable view of the region until darkness hindered it. I watched as the huge steamer rushed through the green flood, passing ships going in and out, passing ships anchored, going by huge forts and finally into the endless ocean.

Very quickly the large numbers of houses in New York, in Brooklyn and in Jersey City disappeared in the distance. At the next horizon in front of us was Staten Island with its imposing hills, woods, green

---

113 The bombardment of Fort Sumter began on April 12, 1861. Abraham Lincoln was shot on the evening of April 14, 1865.

114 The first transatlantic telegram was sent in 1858, but the cable failed soon afterwards, and the telegraphic service did not resume until 1866.

lawns and villas of the greatest beauty. What after that? In the far, far distance was my longed-for goal: my home with the loyal hearts which beat for me. With them I was to find the love and peace which I so desperately needed, if God grants me the good fortune to see them again after such a long separation!

From night to light!

Behind me, the huge city disappeared as well as the powerful country which I regrettably came to know in its darkest days but which I learned to treasure very much, a country which still bled from its war of brothers and which, in the greater part, was mourning its leader. Behind me were sorrow and hardship which I had had the opportunity to observe and in which I had a part. A piece of my life was herewith closed, full of work, fear and distress as well as blessings and joys.

In front of me the moon rose out of the immeasurable deep. I was being brought toward him, the light. As he drove away the darkness of night, so the glimmer of hope gifted me a happy future side by side with the gloomy sentiments which burdened my mind.

Everything which had brought suffering to me—the dismal and painful, and ill will of the past, the country and men—I cast into the sea of forgetfulness at this important turning point. I, however, held fast to the gratitude, to all of the beautiful memories, to the people and places I had come to love, to the pleasant impressions of men and places, to the joys which the country had proved me, and to the lesson and successes. These I took with me into a life of new beginnings and full of hope.

Free of all bitterness, that moment shone bright and unforgettable into both the present and the future. All of the wonderful moments, the scenes and experiences as well as my noble friends and benefactors have not lost their value despite time and distance.

With unmitigated gratitude, I remember them, and the blessed country which I came to love, which gave me such invaluable service and in which peace and union have now returned. In addition to my reverence and appreciation of this county, I am drawn to it by a powerful longing as it inexorably rises again to an incomparable flourishing, be it ever so difficult, after the consequences of a long war and failed policies and politics.

If the dear reader has given his attention to this description which depicts a person who is in essence a stranger and a person of little consequence has read it to the end and has attained some interest in the matter, then the purpose of this grateful author is completely fulfilled.

Bibliography

Published Primary and Secondary Sources:

Alden, Henry Mills. "Four Years Under Fire at Charleston." *Harper's New Monthly Magazine,* vol. 31, 1865.

Chichester, Jane E. *A Lady's Experience inside the Forts in Charleston during the War.* Charleston, S.C. : privately published, 1895.

Davis, Jefferson. *The Papers of Jefferson Davis, Volume 12, June 1865-December 1870.* Baton Rouge: Louisiana State University Press, 2008.

DiLorenzo, Thomas J. *The Real Lincoln: A New Look at Abraham Lincoln, His Agenda, and an Unnecessary War.* New York: Three Rivers Press, 2003.

Emerson, W. Eric, and Karen Stokes, eds. *Days of Destruction: Augustine Thomas Smythe and the Civil War Siege of Charleston.* Columbia: University of South Carolina Press, 2017.

Emerson, W. Eric. *Sons of Privilege: The Charleston Light Dragoons in the Civil War.* Columbia: University of South Carolina, 2011.

Gibbes, James G. Who Burnt Columbia? Newberry, SC: E. H. Aull Company, 1902.

Historic Rock Island County. Rock Island, IL: Kramer & Company, 1908.

Ingraham, Joseph Holt. *The Sunny South; or, The Southerner at Home.* Philadelphia: Evans, 1860.

Marshall, John A. *American Bastille: A History.* Philadelphia: Thomas W. Hartley & Co., 1883.

Mehrlander, Andrea. *The Germans of Charleston, Richmond and New Orleans during the Civil War Period, 1850-1870.* Boston: Walter de Gruyter, 2011.

O'Neall, John Belton. *The Negro Law of South Carolina*. Columbia, SC: John G. Bowman, 1848.

Owsley, Frank Lawrence. *King Cotton Diplomacy: Foreign Relations of the Confederate States of America*. Chicago: University of Chicago Press, 1959.

Pepper, George W. *Personal Recollections of Sherman's Campaigns in Georgia and the Carolinas*. Zanesville, OH: Hugh Dunne, 1866.

Porcher, Frederick A. "A Newly Discovered Chapter of Frederick A. Porcher's 'Upper Beat of St. John's Berkeley.'" *South Carolina Historical Magazine*, 117 (July 2016): 205-255.

Porter, Anthony Toomer. *Led On! Step by Step*. New York: G. P. Putnam's Sons, 1898.

Ramsay, Jack C. *Photographer Under Fire: The Story of George S. Cook*. Green Bay, WI: Historical Resources Press, 1994.

Reid, Whitelaw. *Ohio in the War: Her Statesmen, Generals and Soldiers*. Columbus, OH: Eclectic Publishing Co., 1893.

Roos, Rosalie. *Travels in America, 1851-1855*. Carbondale: Southern Illinois University Press, 1982.

Salley, A. S. "The Jervey Family of South Carolina." *South Carolina Historical Magazine*, 7 (1906): 31-46.

Sandler, Christoph. *Handbuch der Leistrungsfahigkeit der Gesammten Industrie: Deutschlands, Oesterreichs, Elasass-Lothingens und der Schweitz*. Leipzig, Germany: Herman Wolfert, 1873.

Seigler, Robert S. *South Carolina's Military Organizations during the War Between the States: Statewide Units, Militia and Reserves*. Charleston, SC: The History Press, 2008.

Simms, William Gilmore. *A City Laid Waste: The Capture, Sack, and Destruction of the City of Columbia*. Edited by David Aiken. Columbia: University of South Carolina Press, 2005.

Skelton, Linda Worley. "The Importing and Exporting Company of South Carolina." *South Carolina Historical Magazine,* 75 (1974): 24-32.

Stokes, Karen. *Incidents in the Life of Cecilia Lawton.* Macon, GA: Mercer University Press, 2020.

Tagg, Larry. *The Unpopular Mr. Lincoln: The Story of America's Most Reviled President.* New York: Savas Beatie, 2009.

Thomson, David Kelley. "Bonds of War: The Evolution of World Financial Markets in the Civil War Era." PhD diss., University of Georgia, 2016.

Trowbridge, John T. *The South: A Tour of its Battlefields and Ruined Cities, a Journey through the Desolated States, and Talks with the People.* Hartford, CT: L. Stebbins, 1866.

Ural, Susannah J., ed. *Civil War Citizens: Race, Ethnicity, and Identity in America's Bloodiest Conflict.* New York: New York University Press, 2010.

Young, Rogers W. "Castle Pinckney, Silent Sentinel of Charleston Harbor." *South Carolina Historical and Genealogical Magazine,* 39 (January/April 1938): 1-14, 51-67.

Manuscripts:

Anthony W. Riecke Scrapbook. South Carolina Historical Society (SCHS)

Bee-Chisholm Family Papers. SCHS

Orders pertaining to courts and freedmen, 1865-1866. SCHS

Vertical File on Bee Family. SCHS

W. C. Bee and Company Records. SCHS

Latest Releases & Best Sellers

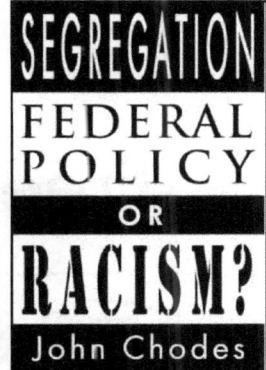

Over 70 Unapologetically Southern
Titles for You to Enjoy

SHOTWELLPUBLISHING.COM

Free Book Offer

DON'T GET LEFT OUT, Y'ALL.
Sign-up and be the first to know about new releases, sales, and other goodies
—plus we'll send you TWO FREE EBOOKS!

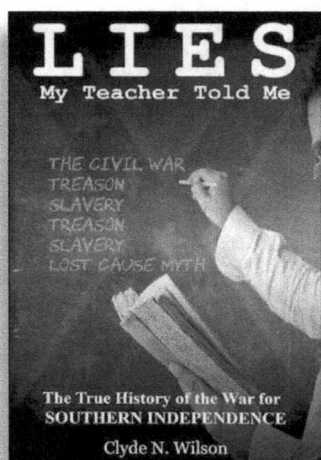

Lies My Teacher Told Me:
The True History of the War for Southern Independence
by Dr. Clyde N. Wilson

Confederaphobia:
An American Epidemic
by Paul C. Graham

FreeLiesBook.com

Southern Books. No Apologies.
We love the South — its history, traditions, and culture — and are proud of our inheritance as Southerners. Our books are a reflection of this love.

www.ingramcontent.com/pod-product-compliance
Lightning Source LLC
Chambersburg PA
CBHW050242170426
43202CB00015B/2881